ALBUQUERQUE
PORTRAIT OF A WESTERN CITY

ALBUQUERQUE

PORTRAIT OF A WESTERN CITY
Many Cultures & Opportunities

Edited by
MARY KAY CLINE

With Contributions by
Tomás Atencio, Jayne Aubele, Tim Aydelott,
Cynthia L. Chavez, Larry Crumpler, Jerry Geist,
Tazbah McCullah, Tom Miles, Jim Moore,
Sherry Robinson, Tom Rutherford, Joe S. Sando,
Carlos Vasquez and Jim Walther

CLEAR LIGHT PUBLISHING
SANTA FE, NEW MEXICO

First Edition
10 9 8 7 6 5 4 3 2 1

Library of Congress Cataloging-in-Publication Data

Albuquerque : portrait of a western city—many cultures & opportunities / edited by Mary Kay Cline.— 1st ed.
    p. cm.
Includes bibliographical references and index.
ISBN 1-57416-087-7
1. Albuquerque (N.M.)—Description and travel. 2. Albuquerque (N.M.)—Guidebooks. 3. Albuquerque (N.M.)—History. I. Cline, Mary Kay.
F804.A3A55 2006
917.8'610454—dc22

                                                    2006002978

Front and back cover photos © MarbleStreetStudio.com
Cover design: Marcia Keegan and Carol O'Shea
Interior design & typography: Carol O'Shea
Timeline elements © Tom Miles

Special thanks to the following:
Contributors: Tomás Atencio, Jayne Aubele, Tim Aydelott, Cynthia L. Chavez, Larry Crumpler, Jerry Geist, Tazbah McCullah, Tom Miles, Jim Moore, Sherry Robinson, Tom Rutherford, Joe S. Sando, Carlos Vazquez, Jim Walther
City of Albuquerque: Ed Boles, Joe Sabatini, Deb Slamey and Dave Mathews and Ruth Hazelhurst
Albuquerque Tricentennial Committee
John Yost at MarbleStreetStudio.com and other photographers as noted
Special thanks to Daniel Todesco
Special thanks to the Albuquerque Convention & Visitors Bureau, Tania Armenta and Maresa Thompson. The Albuquerque Convention & Visitors Bureau has provided content but is not responsible for errors or omissions.

WELCOME TO ALBUQUERQUE

"I can trace my own ancestry back over 300 years in this community and very much appreciate our rich history and culture. And it is no coincidence that our city is now the backdrop for so much economic and cultural dynamism, as we find ourselves recently rated so highly by Forbes, American Style, USA Today *and* Kiplinger's.

This book celebrates our rich tapestry and captures so much of what Albuquerque has to offer."

Mayor Martin Chávez

TABLE OF CONTENTS

"We are unique among all cities in the nation. To find the greatness of a community, you look within. That's what's going on here. We are telling the world who we are." —Mayor Martin Chávez

FOREWORD
The Albuquerque Tricentennial

By Jerry Geist, Tricentennial Jéfe

What's wonderful about Albuquerque is the light we enjoy here—sunrises, sunsets, sunlight, luminarias. This is how we arrived at the theme of our city's Tricentennial celebration: "An illuminating experience." During the celebration year, everyone who attended a flamenco performance, enjoyed a lecture or put out luminarias for the first time caught a bit of the magic.

How did it all come about? Planning began in early 2003 with Millie Santillanes, then director of cultural services for the City of Albuquerque. Dr. Joseph Sanchez, of the National Park Service, led the Strategic Planning Task Force. At the time, they envisioned a year-long event, to begin April 23, 2005 and end April 23, 2006, which is the city's official birthday.

Five additional task forces took charge of special events, merchandising, protocol, education and history. Each of those task forces had multiple subcommittees. The Tricentennial's executive committee coordinated the task forces, with the goal of commemorating the city's 300 years while being mindful of cultural differences and renewing citizens' pride in Albuquerque.

It became apparent that for the event to be successful, it would need broad support in the community as well as financial sponsors in the private sector. During a meeting in October 2004, Mayor Martin Chávez and Millie Santillanes asked me to become Tricentennial "Jefe" or Leader. I thought the Tricentennial was important to Albuquerque, and I was willing to do it, but I asked for sixty days to talk to various people in the city to get some feedback. I found little awareness of the event and little support.

I agreed to chair the event, provided that we create a tax-exempt organizing group, move the organizing out of City Hall and become more autonomous, with the understanding that Mayor Chavez would continue to support us and the city would provide staff support. The Mayor agreed and became an even more enthusiastic supporter of the Tricentennial.

The maiden flight of the Tricentennial Balloon, April 16th 2005. Photo by Anthony Segura.

FACTOIDS

Fun Facts about Albuquerque

© Albuquerque300.org

Four flags have flown over New Mexico. The flags of Spain, the Republic of Mexico, the Confederate States of America, and the United States of America have all flown over the state.

Albuquerque is called the Duke City. In 1464, King Henry IV created the Dukedom of Alburquerque, which continues to this day. The Spanish governor named the Villa de Alburquerque de San Xavier del Bosque in 1706 to honor the tenth Duke of Alburquerque, who was then Viceroy to New Spain.

The name Alburquerque (with an r) dates from the time of Romans in Spain.

Albaquercus, from the Latin *albaquercus* (white oak), was the name of a town. This is why the Alburquerque coat of arms displays a single white oak on a crimson background

Founders' Day parade in front of San Felipe Neri Church in Old Town. Photo © Gene Peach. Courtesy of the Albuquerque Tricentennial.

Ultimately, we enjoyed the support of all levels of government—city, county, state and federal.

A conversation with the Albuquerque Convention and Visitors Bureau revealed that they needed more time to promote the event. At that point, we decided to extend the celebration to fall 2006, for an 18-month run.

From the outset, we saw this as a World's Fair type of celebration, with grand events that could put Albuquerque on the map and have a lasting impact for the city. We also wanted a theme, or brand, for the city that would not only embrace all the events but go forward—not just "Albuquerque Tricentennial: An Illuminating Experience" but also "Albuquerque: City of Illumination."

In no time at all, we had 80 pages of activities. The first twelve months had a different theme each month: Heritage Month in April, Visual Arts Month in May, Dance Month in June, Music Month in July, Agriculture and Cuisine Month in August, Architecture Month in September, Sports Month in

descendants of founders carrying family crests. Photo © Gene Peach.

The Roadrunner is the State Bird of New Mexico. The bird, which can race along at nearly 20 miles an hour and is also known as the chaparral, is a species of cuckoo.

The state animal is the black bear, chosen in 1963 because of New Mexicans' fond memories of a cub found in the Lincoln National Forest after a forest fire. The cub was later named Smokey Bear.

The Zia design, created Dr. Harry Mera of Santa Fe, is a modern interpretation of an ancient symbol of a sun design inspired by Zia Pueblo pottery. Red and gold were the colors of Queen Isabel of Castilla, which the Spanish Conquistadores brought to the New World. The design was adopted as the state flag in 1925.

The state motto is "Crescit Eundo" which translates to "It Grows As It Goes." It was used on the first Great Seal of 1851.

October, Science and Technology Month in November, Festival of Illumination Month in December, National History Museum Month in January, Authors Month in February, Theatre Arts Month in March, and History and Education Month in April.

If you look at the first twelve months, all the committees have performed well and gotten the community involved. We're proud of the offerings. There really was something for everyone, and many of the events were free.

For example, during Cuisine and Agriculture Month, we had cook-offs on Civic Plaza that included the most creative 300th anniversary birthday cake, the best green chile stew, the best pecan, apple or sweet potato pie, the best turnover, and the best Mexican wedding cookie. During Architecture Month, members of the public brought their ideas, sketches and photos for a discussion with architects, planners and educators at the Architecture Road Show.

Science and Technology Month had a wonderful variety of events for every age group and activities nearly every day. The

Albuquerque has the same latitude as Tokyo and Kashmir, and its terrain resembles parts of Spain, Greece and Israel.

The Sandia (means "watermelon" in Spanish) Mountains are the first mountains to be encountered west from the Mississippi River.

The Sandias, and especially the small Ortiz Mountains northeast of the Sandias, contain a large amount of gold ore, attracting many weekend prospectors. Lack of water has been the main obstacle to mining the gold—even Thomas Edison tried, using electricity, but failed.

Sandia Student Science Symposium linked high school students with lab scientists and engineers to discuss selected world problems. Intel, then celebrating its own 25th anniversary, held an Innovative Technology Demo to showcase some of the innovative high points during its time in New Mexico. Science Crawl brought more than 500 middle school students to spend the day at the city's four science museums.

Authors Month featured talks by local authors in city libraries as well as such special events as a memoir-writing workshop with Mari Luci Jaramillo, a science fiction authors panel, and a mystery-writing workshop with Tony Hillerman.

As public awareness grew, more individuals and groups came forward with plans and ideas. To coordinate all the activities, we formed the Tricentennial General Committee, which served as an umbrella group for volunteers, sponsors, vendors, city employees and others. In monthly meetings, each group could keep the others informed, and new ideas could be heard. We found over time that each effort fed other efforts, and they all merged in an exciting whole.

On April 23, 2005, we kicked off the Tricentennial celebration with a day of activities.

The day began with a bang—literally—as 452 runners competed in the Albuquerque Tricentennial Half Marathon,

Spanish dancers in Founders' Day Parade. Photo © Marcia Keegan.

Pueblo Indian dancers in the Parade of Eras. Photo © Marcia Keegan.

which began at 6:30 a.m. They ran 13 miles from Coronado State Park in Bernalillo to Balloon Fiesta Park. Just as the runners were arriving, 100 balloons rose in the Tricentennial Mass Ascension. High schools got involved with band concerts by the newest and oldest bands, plus performances by cheer and dance groups at mid-morning.

In one of the most spectacular performances in city history, we had the Parade of Eras, which was, in fact, "parade theater," with a cast of hundreds. Performers represented each era of the city's history—Native American, Spanish, Mexican, Territorial and Statehood.

For the Native American Era, we saw Pueblo and Navajo tribes represented, with participants wearing traditional dress. The Spanish Era featured performers representing Albuquerque's founder, Don Francisco Cuervo y Valdés, as well as the first mayor, Captain Martín Hurtado, and first priest, Padre Minges. Seventy-six settlers dressed in period clothing carried the coats of arms of the founding families. There were also flamenco dancers and *Matachines* (Pueblo Christmas Dance of Spanish/Moorish origin) dancers. The Mexican Era included Aztec dancers, Ballet Folklorico and *mariachis*. The Territorial

Agriculture in the Rio Grande Valley goes back to 2,000 B.C., making it one of the oldest continually cultivated areas in the world.

When the Spanish first arrived in the Albuquerque area under Coronado, there were 12 to 16 pueblos in the Middle Rio Grande Valley. Today there are four: Isleta, Sandia, Santa Ana and San Felipe.

Duke and Duchess de Alburquerque, Ioannes Osorio y Beltran de Lis and Blanca Suelves Figueroa, entering the Royal Ball celebrating the Tricentennial at the Albuquerque Convention Center. Photo © Glen Morimoto. Courtesy of the Albuquerque Tricentennial.

The Rio Grande Rift is a huge depression that sank so low that portions of the same limestone that appear as the "rind" on top of the Sandias are now 15,000 ft. (4,572 m.) below sea level under Albuquerque. The only other such formation known in the world is the Great Rift Valley of Kenya on the African continent.

Some 400 species of resident and migratory birds inhabit the bosque along the Rio Grande.

Era was represented by a sizable contingent of the New Mexico Carriage Association, Buffalo Soldiers, Union and Confederate soldiers, and the New Mexico Gunfighters Association.

Children of all ages were thrilled to see Los Gigantes, 15-foot-tall puppets representing a variety of the city's 72 cultures.

As festive as it was, it was really a dress rehearsal for the main event on April 22 and 23, 2006.

The day began with the Fiesta de Albuquerque Marathon and Half Marathon, from Balloon Fiesta Park to Old Town, as well as a Mass Ascension with 300 balloons. At mid-day we had a Founder's Day parade with costumed participants.

For our distinguished guests, the Duke and Duchess de Alburquerque of Spain, Ioannes Osorio y Beltran de Lis and Blanca Suelves Figueroa, and the Marquis and Marquise of Caridad, Gonzalo Ulloa Suelves and Mercedes Llanza Figueroa, we held an elegant, black-tie Royal Ball and Banquet. The original opera *Time and Again Barelas* was performed.

The two-day pageant of La Entrada, a re-enactment of the arrival of the first Spanish settlers, began Saturday and ended on Sunday. This unique effort involved 150 participants and

Conquistadores in the Founders' Day Parade. Photo © Marcia Keegan.

hundreds of animals traveling from Bernalillo to Albuquerque. They spent the night at Sandia Lakes, remaining in costume, in an encampment faithful to that era. When they arrived in Old Town on Sunday, they re-enacted the founding of Albuquerque, with Mayor Martin Chávez playing the first alcalde mayor, Captain Martín Hurtado.

On Sunday, there was also an all-faiths service at the UNM basketball arena, to celebrate our history and our many cultures growing and living together. On both days, the Tricentennial Fiestas at newly renamed and reconstructed Tricentennial Tiguex Park provided children's activities, entertainment, food and an arts and crafts market.

Sunday afternoon, the Old Town Merchants Association held an old-fashioned Fandango. The day ended with the lighting of special, 18-inch candles of wood and stained glass designed by internationally known artist Simone di Amico, who lives in Albuquerque and in Italy. Each candle bore the name of the sponsor who purchased that candle. And the city dedicated Tricentennial Tiguex Park.

Also on Birthday Weekend, the Indian Pueblo Cultural Center launched its first annual Indian Market.

In some ways our birthday celebration reprised the *Enchantorama*, a two and one-half hour, 16-act portrayal of the

Five small dormant volcanoes are the chief landmarks of Albuquerque's west side. They were formed about 190,000 years ago, but are considered to still be in the cooling stage.

The Atchison, Topeka, and Santa Fe Railroad (AT & SF) arrived in Albuquerque in 1880.

The state slogan is "Everybody is somebody in New Mexico."

The yucca, a member of the lily family, is the state flower, and the piñon is the official state tree.

Two vegetables share the honor of representing New Mexico—chile and beans (*frijoles*), both staples in New Mexican food specialties.

city's history during the 250th anniversary celebration in 1956. Titled "Tom Toms to Atoms," it had nearly 2,000 performers and was held outdoors at Zimmerman Field, the former UNM football stadium. The stage was a block long and had seven levels. Every night it drew an audience of 4,000.

Among the high points of the year was an art exhibit of the Spanish masters at the Albuquerque Museum. In three shows, the exhibition of nearly 100 paintings and sculptures represented the best of Spanish art from the late sixteenth to the early twentieth centuries, including the works of Ribera, Murillo, Zurbaran, Dali, Picasso and Miró. It was a spectacular, year-long effort and a once-in-a-lifetime opportunity for visitors.

Guillermo Figueroa, Music Director of the New Mexico Symphony, and composer Miguel del Aguila presented the world premier of the original opera, *Time and Again Barelas*, which deals with the history and people of Barelas neighborhood. The opera, which includes the children's choir from Manzano Day School, conveys some of the sights and sounds that contribute to the Albuquerque's cultural diversity.

The six-part colloquium "All Roads Lead to Albuquerque" series focused on transportation through the years, from trails to rail to aviation. These three-hour talks were well attended, and even the experts learned something new.

Spectators were in awe of Los Gigantes, 15-foot-tall puppets in the Parade of Eras. Photo © Marcia Keegan.

World premier of opera *Time and Again Barelas* performed at the National Hispanic Cultural Center. Photo © MarbleStreetStudio.com, courtesy of the New Mexico Symphony Orchestra.

The Festival of Illumination turned into quite an adventure. We asked Albuquerqueans to make pledges of luminarias or lights on Christmas Eve, hoping for 3 million lights. The question arose: How would we count? We decided on pledge forms, both written and submissions on the Web, as well as spot counts that night.

Ultimately, the pledges totaled more than 8.2 million. Many of the youth groups sold out. The Youth Symphony, for example, filled orders for 13,000 dozen luminarias. Not a candle could be found in the city by the afternoon of December 24.

The Tricentennial didn't end in October 2006 with its official closing. Twin 65-foot-tall monuments to the city's history—the Tricentennial Towers—were erected at Rio Grande boulevard and I-40 in memory of this great celebration. And during August and September we held a series of community conversations about what values are important. We expect the results to inform future planning decisions.

We expect the memories to carry forward in education, the networks of people we formed, and in the spirit of the community. The Tricentennial has been an illuminating experience for us all.

Turquoise, a phosphate considered a precious stone, is the state gem.

And the state even has an official cookie! It is the Biscochito, a small anise-flavored cookie brought to New Mexico by the early Spaniards.

Albuquerque is a mecca of urban sophistication and nightlife. Photo © Ron Behrmann.

On July 4, 1882, Park Van Tassel, owner of the Elite Saloon, made the first balloon ascension in Albuquerque. The gas balloon, named "City of Albuquerque," launched from a vacant lot near Second and Gold. It landed in a cornfield near Old Town

INTRODUCTION

From the beginning, Albuquerque was a multicultural city. Indian, Hispanic, Anglo and various immigrant groups came together, creating a rich and vibrant metropolis. The young city attracted dreamers, adventurers, entrepreneurs and others who would gamble on success at the expense of personal security. Some came to establish farms and ranches. Others sought their fortunes in the boom following the coming of the railroad. Tuberculosis patients looked for the clear, clean skies to renew their health. Artists came, enchanted by the light. Today people are still coming, drawn by the open spaces and the still seemingly limitless opportunities available, especially with the expansion of the high tech and aerospace industries and the vast supply of vacant land surrounding the city. Now as then, newcomers are searching for a better life than what they had left behind. Perhaps more than any other city in the country, Albuquerque brings the pioneer spirit into the modern age.

One purpose of this book is to chronicle the historical and cultural threads that bind the city and its neighborhoods together, creating a dynamic modern urban center. The other purpose is to help visitors and residents alike become aware of what makes the city and its attractions unique.

Part I of the book begins with a historical/cultural retrospective, including illuminating contributions from representatives of museums and cultural centers, a fascinating short history of Old Town drawn largely from old documents and original sources, historical and economic summaries, and an introduction to the city's various neighborhoods. Photographs and other illustrations show the city as it was. This human history covers who came and why, and how each group influenced the whole, making Albuquerque unique. Rapid growth in recent years is part of the story of a city that is constantly evolving and recreating itself, based on the needs of its diverse citizens, coming together to create a rapidly growing modern city. This section also contains a sidebar of factoids collected for the Albuquerque Tricentennial and historical events drawn from the Tricentennial Timeline by Tom Miles.

Part II provides a travel guide to the various destinations that make Albuquerque a special place. Visitors will find plenty to do for the whole family, including a wide variety of museums, cultural centers, outdoor recreation sites, nature and wildlife centers, sporting events, and several Indian Pueblos featuring their own activities, arts and crafts events and casinos. Accommodations are listed by area, but restaurants, galleries and shopping areas are listed by category for ease of use. Another chapter summarizes nearby areas of interest, including Santa Fe and Taos. The book concludes with a calendar of annual special events, including the Albuquerque International Balloon Fiesta. The listing for each attraction includes its address, local and toll-free phone numbers and website (if any), so the visitor can find the most recent information online. A corresponding interactive link is available online at **www.clearlightbooks.com/albuquerque.**

In November 1897, J.L. Dodson bought a "Locomobile" in Denver and drove it to Albuquerque. It was the first car in the city.

The Albuquerque Municipal Council set a speed limit for automobiles of 8 miles an hour in 1908.

Albuquerque's famous racing family, the Unsers, got started in the 1940s when the Unsers operated a wrecking service called Unser Garage on 7700 Central SW.

PART I

ALBUQUERQUE
A Historical &
Cultural Retrospective

More than 20,000 ancient images are etched into the volcanic rock on the city's western edge in Petroglyph National Monument. Judy Keegan is admiring a petroglyph. Photo © Marcia Keegan.

FROM PREHISTORY TO THE PRESENT—Historical Overview

Prehistory

Paleoindian Period (9500–5500 BC)

The Albuquerque area has been populated since prehistoric times. Most archaeologists believe the earliest people probably came from northern Asia. Native mythology shows the people emerging from other worlds below this one.

Most of the archeological sites visible today are between the Rio Grande and Rio Puerco Rivers southwest of Albuquerque and north of Belen. The area's climate then was likely cooler and wetter than it is today. The ancient peoples of this time were hunters and gatherers who wandered across grassy plains searching for food. Spear points are the main surviving artifacts from this period.

Archaic Period (5500–400 AD)

The people during the Archaic Period people were more widely scattered than before. Some sites have been found farther to the west and some southeast of present-day Albuquerque.

During this period, people invented new tools and wandered less. They began cultivating wild corn and other wild plants. Enough moisture was still available that they did not need to be near the river to grow food, and they probably grew food to supplement their foraging. By the end of this period, people were building pithouses, cultivating maize (as opposed to wild corn) and starting to make and use pottery.

Ancestral Pueblo Period (400–1540 AD)

The term "Anasazi" has been used for the people living in the Albuquerque area during this period; however, "Ancestral Pueblo" is more accurate and less offensive, since they actually were the ancestors of today's Pueblo people, and *anasazi* is a Navajo word meaning "ancient enemy." By this time the climate was similar to that of today and subject to prolonged periods of drought. Quite a few more dwelling sites remain, about half of them around the river. In general, the sites near the river were larger and more permanent; those away from the rivers were more temporary. Exceptions to this were Tijeras Pueblo and other East Mountain sites.

During the early part of this period, people adopted a much more settled lifestyle, cultivating corn, beans and squash and beginning to build

ALBUQUERQUE TIMELINE

© Tom Miles

1400s
Some 40,000 Pueblo Indians live in the Nuevo México area, with first apartment structures, complex irrigation systems and trading with tribes in northern México. Indian Pueblos in Central Rio Grande Valley include: Acoma, Santo Domingo, San Felipe, Santa Ana, Zia, Isleta, Sandia, Cochiti and Jemez.

1500s
Aztecs dominate central and southern México from their capitol in Tenochtitlán. Draft animals do not exist so there is no need for a wheel. This lack of a wheel also places limits on empire building, commerce and war fighting. Nomadic plains tribes, later known as Navajo and Apache, begin raiding Pueblos.

larger pithouses. For food storage they used pottery, largely grey and black-on-white varieties (the paint was derived from minerals). Gradually, they began to build dwellings above ground and likely used pithouses more for ceremonial purposes. Artifacts from this period include pottery made from lead-glaze paint, which was widely traded throughout the Southwest. By the 1300s, some groups built large, multi-storied pueblos in areas rich with wild plants and game animals. They also may have traded with the Plains tribes to the east. By the 1500s, many of these areas were abandoned, however, perhaps because of long-term drought.

To learn more, visit Petroglyph National Monument, Airport Hamlet Site and the Tijeras Pueblo Site.

Period of Exploration and Early Spanish Settlement (1540–1706)

Pueblo communities could be distinguished by their languages: Tiwa, Tewa, Towa, Keresan, Zuni and Hopi. During this period, the Rio Grande Pueblos in the Albuquerque area were members of the Southern Tiwa language group, and some of them were included among the twelve described by the Spanish as in the Tiguex Province. Some uncertainty of identification exists due to discrepancies between the archaeological sites and early descriptions of Pueblos written by Europeans; the Pueblos, of course, did not keep written records.

In the summer of 1540, an expedition from Spain led by Francisco Vásquez de Coronado reached the area just west of Albuquerque. The local Pueblo people received the explorers graciously, feeding them and supplying them with needed goods, and the Spaniards made their winter camp at Alcanfor Pueblo, located near present-day Bernalillo and south of Kuana Pueblo, now in Coronado State Monument. Tensions soon developed, however, and many Pueblo people were killed before the Spanish left to explore the southern Great Plains. The following years saw various incursions of Spanish soldiers and priests, often with violent results. During these years, however, the Pueblo population was reduced more dramatically by European diseases such as smallpox, measles and influenza than they were by battle.

In 1598, Don Juan de Oñate brought soldiers and two hundred settlers up from Mexico. Between 1610 and 1630, Spanish missions, farms and ranches were established. The *Camino*

Real (Royal Road) was opened during this period, following the Rio Grande to Mexico.

This was a period of turmoil largely caused by the newcomers' lack of respect for the Natives, as shown by the systems of *encomienda* (requiring Indian people to "donate" a large portion of their crops to the occupiers) and *repartimiento* (forcing Indian people to work in Spanish households and fields without pay). In addition, the Spanish forced Catholicism on the Indian people, forbidding Native religion.

The turmoil, which resulted in skirmishes with bloodshed on both sides, including burning and destruction of entire pueblos, culminated in the Pueblo Revolt of 1680 under the leadership of Po'pay from Ohkay Owingeh (San Juan Pueblo). At this point the Spanish fled to what is now El Paso, Texas.

After the reconquest by Don Diego de Vargas in 1692, changes took place that greatly affect life in New Mexico today. The systems of *encomienda* and *repartimiento* were abolished, and the Indian people were no longer persecuted for their religious activities. Partly as a result of the Pueblo Revolt, the Pueblo Indian people have been able to keep their languages, religions and customs alive on their ancestral homelands. Although a few small skirmishes still took place, the Spanish and Pueblo populations became more co-operative with each other, working together to survive in a sometimes unforgiving landscape and against such common enemies as the Apaches and the Navajos. This cooperation was the origin of New Mexico's unique multicultural society.

Today you can see various sites from this period. You can drive the *Camino Real* (Royal Road) that ran from Ohkay Owingeh to El Paso, Texas. A probable segment ran along today's Edith Boulevard, north of Osuna Road.

Sites to visit include Piedras Marcadas Pueblo Site (located within Petroglyph National Monument) and Kuaua Pueblo Site (located within Coronado State Monument)

The Spanish Colonial Period (1706–1821)

Spanish settlements grew as people returned to their isolated farms and villages following the Pueblo Revolt. As families expanded through marriage and birth, the settlements gradually enlarged. From time to time new families joined on communal land grants and honored the village's founder by adapting his or her family name for their cluster of houses. By

1519
Hernán Cortez's Conquistadores launch conquest of México. They introduce the wheel, the horse, cows, sheep and many new crops to the New World; the New World introduces Spaniards to chocolate, new textile dyes, corn, and more

1519–1521
Hernán Cortez conquers Aztec's Tenochtitlán and renames it México City.

1530s
Esteban (Estevanico) the Moor is first African to arrive in Nuevo México as a slave with Cabeza de Vaca.

1539
Esteban guides Franciscan priest Marcos de Niza in search for fabled Seven Cities of Cibola; The first white man the Pueblos saw was a black man. Estevan reaches the Zuni village of Hawikuh where he is killed.

1540
Spanish explorer
Coronado arrives
seeking the fabled
Seven Cities of Cibola.

1573
The Spanish Pope
Paul III proclaims
American Indians are
men, and thus entitled
to property and liberty.
King Philip issues Royal
Ordinance outlawing
use of violence dealing
with colonized Indians.

1580
Spain is the greatest,
wealthiest power in
Europe with empire
spreading from Italy to
the Philippines.

1587
Sir Walter Raleigh
founds first English
Colony in North
Carolina and badly
mistreats Indians,
wiping out several
tribes by 1643. At this
same time, Spanish
Jesuits were creating
missions in Nueva
España's northern
frontier, including what
will become Arizona.

the mid-nineteenth century there were at least sixteen settlements and plazas in the area of the *plaza principal* of Albuquerque.

In 1706, after the Spanish reconquest, Francisco Cuervo y Valdés founded the city of Albuquerque (then spelled Alburquerque after the Duke of Alburquerque) as a *villa* (settlement) of New Spain. Cuervo chose the location because of its good farm and grazing land and the availability of wood. What is now Old Town was the heart of this settlement.

Other villages, all centered on plazas, were settled along the Rio Grande north and south of Albuquerque. They included Alameda, Los Garcias, Los Ranchos, Los Poblanos, Los Gallegos, Los Griegos, Los Candelarias, Los Duranes, Atrisco, Los Sanchez, Pajarito, Barelas and Los Padillas.

Over the years, these separate communities have grown into the Albuquerque of today, creating its distinctive narrow shape along the river and forming the nucleus of various neighborhoods. Farming and ranching were the major activities. The Spanish colonial people raised tobacco, grapes, corn, wheat, chile, cotton, sheep and cattle. The floodplain of the Rio Grande, where water could be diverted for irrigation, was the center of the farming activities. Livestock grazing covered the East Mesa (*la bajada*). Using local cotton and wool, weavers added to the economy. Mining for copper, silver, turquoise and lead was carried on in the hills around the town. Outlying buffer communities such as Carnuel, near Tijeras, were established to protect the area from Apaches and later Comanches and Utes. During this period, some families became quite wealthy.

In 1776 the Spanish government put the northern provinces of New Spain, including New Mexico, under the control of a military official based in Chihuahua. This had little effect on Albuquerque, since it was isolated from the rest of Mexico and was allowed no contact with other nations in Europe or the United States.

Sites to visit from this time period include the Plaza de Señor San Jose de Los Ranchos and San Felipe de Neri, on the plaza in Old Town.

The Mexican Republic (1821–1846)

Mexico won independence from Spain in 1821, and New Mexico became a province of the new republic. Contrary to previous practice, some New Mexicans were now able to become administrators. Another important change was the legalization of foreign trade, which led to the opening of the Santa Fe Trail, established in 1821 for commercial trade between the United States and Mexico.

The Territorial Period (1846–1912)

Prosperity 1846–67; Depression 1867–79

Several events took place during this period that affected the growth of Albuquerque. Following the end of the Méxican War, the Treaty of Guadalupe Hidalgo ceded the Mexican territory (including New Mexico) to the United States. Albuquerque saw the beginning of main roads and stagecoach lines, including a route from Albuquerque to California.

In 1846, at the end of the war, Brigadier General Stephen Watts Kearny set up a temporary quartermaster supply depot in Albuquerque. A year later this depot was made permanent and operated, with a few interruptions, until 1867. As could be expected, Army influence dramatically changed the ethnic and economic characteristics of the area. More than four hundred officers and enlisted men were stationed at the post, including recent immigrants from Ireland and Germany who had joined the frontier army to learn a trade. Other enlistees were from such countries as Switzerland, Poland, Denmark and Turkey. Because the quartermaster spent large amounts monthly for the post's food and forage, and soldiers spent money at local saloons and stores, the local economy flourished.

During the Civil War, Albuquerque was briefly occupied by Confederate troops from Texas on their way north to Fort Union. In April 1862, after the victory of Union troops at the Battle of Glorieta Pass, east of Santa Fe, these troops took Albuquerque without a casualty.

At this time, buildings in Albuquerque used adobes or *terrones* (sod bricks) for construction materials and featured simple floor plans. Milled lumber, bricks and window glass were rare. The village was arranged in classic Spanish pattern around a central plaza, with San Felipe de Neri Church and its rectory occupying the north side. Major businesses included Franz Huning's Molina de Glorieta flour mill on the outskirts of town and an assortment of general stores, saloons, markets and professional offices. The Army post was on the west side of the plaza across Main Street (now Rio Grande Blvd.). The 1860 census listed 1,608 persons.

1588
The English defeat the Spanish Armada.

1598–1599
Juan de Oñate creates first permanent Spanish settlement of Nuevo México, introducing the wheel, wheat, horses, sheep and much more. Franciscans begin establishing early missions. Conflict among Indians, Spanish colonists, military, administration and the Church plus extended drought will lead to the Pueblo Revolt in 1680.

1607
English Colonial Era begins with Jamestown Settlement.

1608
King of Spain makes Nuevo México a Spanish Royal Province and gives Franciscans permission to create missions here.

Molina de Glorieta Mill, 1900. Photo courtesy of the Albuquerque Museum, Image # 1978.050.671.

1609
Oñate is relieved as
governor and sent to
México City to be tried
for mistreatment of
Indians; a regular
mission supply system
has been established
between Nuevo México
and México City.

Depression took hold of the town when the Army left in
1867. The economy reverted to agriculture, and more business
was done once again by barter than with currency. The 1870
census showed a population drop of 289 persons and total foreign born at 52. Finally, in the winter of 1878–79, railroad
rumors reached the area.

Coming of the Railroad, 1880

Rumors of a railroad connecting the east and west coasts
through Albuquerque had persisted for several years. Finally, in
the winter of 1878–79, the Territorial Assembly in Santa Fe
passed a railroad incorporation act, allowing companies to
apply for and begin construction of branch lines through the
territory. The Atchison, Topeka and Santa Fe Railroad soon
organized the New Mexico and Southern Pacific Railroad company and began building south. Anticipating the railroad,
many businesses and branch houses began to be established
around the plaza.

1610
Spanish Governor
Don Pedro de Peralta
inaugurates
construction of Villa
of Santa Fe.

The railroad had already bypassed Santa Fe and Bernalillo
when railroad representatives approached Albuquerque. Local
businessmen Franz Huning and Elias Stover, along with attorney William Hazeldine, made a quiet deal with the railroad.
They began buying land in the proposed railroad right of way.
This land in turn they deeded to a railroad subsidary for a
dollar and a share of profits from sale of leftover land the rail-

NW corner of Gold Ave. and Second St, ca. 1890. Cobb Studio, UNM Library. Photo courtesy of the Albuquerque Museum, Image # 1978.050.116.

road didn't need. This deal for cheap land clinched the railroad for Albuquerque and, in the end, enriched the three promoters as well.

The railroad located not by the plaza but instead about one and one-half miles to the east. This was the most efficient straight-line path through the area; detouring to Albuquerque would have taken the track more than a mile off its direct line and passed through an area that was frequently flooded.

Creation of "New Town"

Photographers on the scene between 1875 and 1885 captured a town in transition. In the beginning, some businesses planned to remain where they were, while some planned to move closer to the tracks. By 1880 it was clear that the last option would be the most lucrative, and all attention was focused on New Albuquerque (New Town).

Albuquerque officially welcomed the railroad on April 22, 1880. At this time New Town was little more than a collection of wooden tinderboxes and false-front adobe sheds extending along the tracks up Railroad Avenue (Central) to Second Street and about a block and a half on either side. The town immediately began to grow rapidly, and more permanent buildings were constructed.

Two new hotels, the Armijo House on Railroad Avenue and the San Felipe on Gold Avenue, were reputed to be the

1620
Spanish Crown formally recognizes Pueblo sovereignty with "Canes of Authority."

Pilgrims land at Plymouth Rock.

1665–1676
Severe droughts hit southwest.

1680
Spanish demands and Indian resentments climax in the Pueblo Revolt which expels Spaniards for over a decade—the most successful Indian revolt in North America; priests and colonists are killed. Survivors flee to El Paso in the southern Nuevo México territory.

1680–1692
Without the help of Spanish deterrence, raiding of Pueblos by nomadic tribes increases.

1692
General Diego de
Vargas declares
peaceful reconquest of
Nuevo México and
Spanish recolonization
begins.

✓

1698
Governor de Vargas
makes land grants in
Albuquerque area
between Alameda and
the swamps of Mejia—
today's Barelas
neighborhood.

✓

1700
Many northern Nuevo
México Pueblos have
been sacked and burned
by returning Spanish
and most of the Pueblo
Indians have fled.

✓

1702–1711
Tenth Duke of
Alburquerque is sent to
be Viceroy of Nueva
España. (Note:
Alburquerque, Spain,
lies in the rugged
"Extremadura" region,
an area that produced a
great number of
conquistadores who
came to the New World
in search of land and
economic
opportunities.)

finest south of Denver and east of San Francisco. The Cromwell Building and the Central Bank Building were constructed on "Bankers' Corner," the northeast and northwest corners of Gold Avenue and Second Street. These handsome structures were not fully occupied until well after 1900.

Between 1880 and 1900 the city grew to become a compact, industrialized city of about 7,000 centered around the railroad with a few outlying residential districts. Air pollution from coal smoke was heavy, but street traffic was usually light. There was little construction east of Arno Street or west of Sixth Street, although by 1889 land had been platted west to Old Town.

Mail, supplies and people began arriving by train rather than by stagecoach. The population grew, and new ethnic groups— Irish, Italian, German, African-American and Chinese—arrived, bringing new traditions and starting new businesses.

Photographs document the change in New Town from its birth as a collection of tents, adobe sheds and frame shacks to its permanent establishment as a thriving, growing community. This photographic record is invaluable, since many of the landmark businesses constructed to last a century or more were destroyed by fires or urban renewal projects. Social customs, costumes and even the identities of the citizens of the period survive only by means of artifacts, antiques and photographs.

The warm dry climate was ideal for people with breathing problems, and tuberculosis sanitoria were established, bringing not only patients but medical personnel from all over the country.

Old Town Just After the Railroad

During the railroad boom era, people entered Old Town either from the west across a wooden bridge or from the east by Railroad Avenue (now Central), perhaps on a horse-drawn streetcar that connected Old Town and New Town. The plaza did not change much in appearance, except for a few touches like a picket fence and fresh plaster. The main street in town, James (now South Plaza), was lined with saloons, wool and hide dealers, and restaurants. Many establishments such as Central Bank had relocated to New Town and were replaced with saloons. Reminders of the past, such as the home of Mexican Governor Manuel Armijo and the Huning Flour Mill, were renovated in styles brought by the newcomers via the railroad. New structures included the Bernalillo County Courthouse and Jail. Herman Blueher developed his market

Hodgin Hall, University of New Mexico, 1905. Photo courtesy of the Albuquerque Museum, Image # 1980.159.004.

garden, or truck farm, on the east side of the plaza, and other truck farms soon followed.

Today few buildings in Old Town look as they did before 1891 due to subsequent restorations and alterations.

For more historical photos, see www.sgha.net/nmgt/history.html.

Incorporation

Albuquerque incorporated as a city in 1891. A public library, schools, an opera house, and other improvements soon developed. The University of New Mexico was established at its present location in 1892. Old Town remained a separate political unit along with the North and South Valleys. Residential areas of New Town spread east.

Meanwhile, Hispanic culture and Catholicism remained strong, and the Pueblo people maintained their traditional ways. Residents and visitors began to notice that what existed here was unique. Tourism began, with travelers coming long distances to see the cultural attractions of the area as well as the often dramatically beautiful scenery.

As was the case in most railroad boomtowns, family housing was at a premium in New Town. Many workers still lived in adobe homes in Old Town and commuted. Railroad workers and single men and women usually lived in small boarding houses before marrying.

The first public transportation was the Albuquerque Street Railroad, a horse-drawn trolley line that operated between 1881 and 1904 between Old Town and New Town along Railroad

1703
Farming village of Atrisco founded on west bank of Rio Grande

1706
Established April 23, 1706, as a Spanish colonial outpost, the Villa de Alburquerque was named by the a Spanish Provincial Governor Don Francisco Cuervo y Valdes in honor of the Duke of Alburquerque, Viceroy of New Spain. The first "r" was later dropped.

Second St., looking southwest, 1918. Photo courtesy of the Albuquerque Museum, Image # 1978.128.001.

1706
San Felipe De Neri
Church is constructed
on West side of plaza.
"Alburquerque" comes
from the Latin "albus
querqus," signifying
"white oak" on the
city's coat of arms
today.

Alliance formed
between Spanish and
Pueblo Indians to
defend both from
nomadic Indian raiding.

✓

✓

Ave. These horse-drawn cars were eventually replaced by electric trolleys, which operated between 1904 and 1927.

Even before New Town was fully developed, the first suburbs were being planned. The first residential districts to be developed were Franz Huning's Highland Addition in 1880, between Copper and Iron Avenues and High Street and the railroad tracks, and the 1881 Perea Addition in what is now called the Downtown Neighborhood District, between 11th and 15th Streets and between Central and Lomas Avenues. In accordance with the city's desire to be modern, these new developments showcased frame and brick homes in Gothic, Queen Anne and Italianate styles with creative gingerbread woodwork and elaborate brickwork. While these new homes were attractive, the old adobe houses with their thick walls were cooler in summer and warmer in winter.

By 1885, Albuquerque residents had all the modern conveniences found in most eastern cities. The public library was founded in 1891. Entrepreneurs gained rights to build electric, gas, water and telephone franchises. By 1885, one could have all the desirable services found in most eastern cities.

The six-day workweeks left little time for recreation, but people still managed to have some fun, and the weather almost always cooperated. Sometimes they took part in outings in such conveyances as twenty-passenger "tallyhos." They also

Relaxing on the UNM Campus, 1900. Photo courtesy of the Albuquerque Museum, Image # 1978.098.002.

1710
Alameda Land Grant made to Captain Francisco Montes Vigil.

1712
Land Grant of 70,000 acres made to Elena Gallegos and Ranchos de Alburquerque started.

1716
Isleta Pueblo people return from Hopi country.

San Clemente Land Grant founded which encompasses the present village of Los Lunas.

1732
Albuquerque established as annual meeting place for Camino Real trade highway (Northern Nuevo México to Chihuahua and Durango in Nueva España).

1742
Sandia Pueblo Indians return to Sandia land from Hopi country.

enjoyed parades, clubs, dances, theater productions, bicycling, baseball games, musicals and plays. Holidays were celebrated with public entertainment.

Territorial Fairs and Expositions

Almost as soon as New Town began, city leaders organized fairs and expositions for recreational and promotional purposes. The first Territorial Fair was held on October 3, 1881, at newly designed fairgrounds just north and west of present-day Central and Rio Grande boulevards. The Territorial Fairs reached their peak of popularity right after turn of century. Visitors came from Arizona, Colorado, Texas and the East to see the mineral, agricultural, mechanical, industrial and art exhibits as well as to enjoy sulky races, baseball games, Native American dances and U.S. Cavalry drills.

Several important events took place during these fairs. Tragedy was narrowly averted in 1903 during a Navajo vs. Cavalry re-enactment, when Indians emerged with their own pistols, not the blank filled ones supplied by promoters. They hastily changed the re-enactment to take place without firearms. One of the most important exhibits in 1908 was an

Entrance to the Sixteenth National Territorial Fair, 1908. Photo courtesy of the Albuquerque Museum, Image # 1978.050.451.

1748
Sandia Land Grant re-established to resettle Sandia Tiwa Indians. Corrales settlement begins. Sheep are used as medium of exchange.

imitation Pueblo, designed by University of New Mexico President William George Tight, who wanted to remodel the campus in that style. Other displays included a fake mine and various industrial displays. The first successful long distance balloon flight was undertaken in 1909 by Joseph Blondin and Roy Stamm. The 1911 Territorial Fair saw the first airplane flight in New Mexico.

Fairs were not held during World War I. Although attempts were made to bring the fair back at several sites about town, it was never successful again until Depression-period programs provided workmen and materials to build a new State Fair complex at its present location.

1750
Albuquerque satellite communities include Corrales, Los Griegos, Los Montoyas, Los Poblanos and Los Gallegos. Cemetery established in front of plaza church.

The Commercial Club

Area businessmen founded the Commercial Club, a precursor to the Chamber of Commerce, on May 21, 1890, to promote Albuquerque's climate, cultural assets and business potential. The club grew to more than 200 members and erected an impressive $70,000 building at Gold Avenue and Fourth Street in 1891–92. The building had meeting rooms, billiard rooms, bachelor quarters, a dance hall, parlors and business offices.

The Commercial Club was largely for men; women seldom went except for official functions. Most of its income was spent on advertising, especially the "booster booklets." These brochures, which painted an idealized portrait of the area's climate and investment opportunities, were sent to many newspapers to lure tourists to Albuquerque. After World War I it became the Albuquerque Chamber of Commerce.

The Railroad Brings Prosperity and Industry

Because Albuquerque had been designated as the site for the railroad's central division point between Kansas and California, it became the location of the Santa Fe's largest locomotive repair facilities west of Topeka. In 1882 the annual receipts of the railroad totaled $1,068,511.63. By 1900 it employed 575 men, sixty engineers and sixty firemen for an annual payroll of $376,000.

At the turn of the century, Albuquerque had 6,335 inhabitants. Only 15% of the population was Spanish, but the city was surrounded by Spanish settlements, including Old Town, Atrisco, Los Candelarias and Los Griegos. For a generation, the newcomers tried to reproduce the economic patterns, architectural styles and cultural institutions familiar to Eastern Victorian society. The railroad offices, repair shops and daily trains introduced wage labor, a twelve-hour industrial workday and six-day industrial workweek into a largely non-cash, traditional agricultural society. The quiet, slow pace of agricultural life was replaced by the time clock, the scream of the locomotives and the blast of shop whistles.

The railroad also led to the rise of commercial and industrial activity, including processing raw materials to ship east: sheep, cattle, wool, hides, railroad ties and lumber. Large wool warehouses and woolen mills, including Albuquerque Wool Scouring Mills and the allied Rio Grande Woolen Mills, took more than three million pounds of raw wool each year from New Mexico growers and either custom-cleaned it for shipment to the East or purchased it for production of rugs, cloth and clothing.

In 1882, the Albuquerque Foundry and Machine Works began casting rolling stock for the railroad and repairing mining and manufacturing equipment. They also made heating stoves for the local market.

Southwestern Brewery and Ice Company began in the 1880s, producing beer and ice cream for local homes and

1757
Governor Marín del Valle's map and census of Nuevo México shows 5,170 Spaniards with 2,543 horses, 7,832 cattle and 47,621 sheep and goats; Pueblo and Hopi Indians number 9,000 and own 4,831 horses, 8,325 cattle and 64,561 sheep and goats.

1760
The acequia (irrigation ditches) system becomes the lifeblood of Albuquerque settlements; Mayordomos are elected to supervise water disputes and supervise the annual cleaning of the acequias.

The Industrial Revolution begins in England.

1762
French cede Louisiana Territory to Spain to keep it out of English hands.

saloons. By 1899 the plant was enlarged and modernized, and shipments of beer were distributed to much of the Southwest.

Lumber was another major industry, and large sawmills began operation to the north of Old Town. Between 1903 and 1905, the American Lumber Company, which rivaled the railroad as an employer, was built on North Twelfth Street. This company produced milled lumber, doors, shingles and other building materials in quantity for the regional market. Its factory was one of the largest such firms in the West. The railroad foundry, wool-scouring mill and lumber company together employed more than half the city's male heads of families as late as World War I.

Despite industrialization, agriculture remained the most important source of livelihood for many in the area. Farming continued in the areas around Old Town, the North Valley and the South Valley. Sheep ranches, vineyards, market gardens and cattle feedlots were scattered around the outskirts of town. The area also produced large quantities of fine Southwestern wines. These enterprises shipped via the railroads, and by 1912 Albuquerque merchants and factories dominated trade in an area of 196,000 square miles.

Wholesale businesses thrived because of Albuquerque's central location and its railroad shipping facilities. Carloads of goods arrived daily from the East and were stockpiled for wholesale and retail sale throughout New Mexico, southern Colorado, eastern Arizona and west Texas. Major institutions like the Charles Ilfeld Company, the Stamm Fruit Company and L.B. Putney Grocery were heavily involved in the wholesale trade. In this era before chain stores, local grocery and hardware merchants imported vast inventories by rail. As late as 1925, Albuquerque was the only wholesale grocery distribution center in New Mexico, serving a trade population of 163,059 people through 677 retail stores in twelve central and western New Mexico counties.

Cultural as well as economic life was enhanced by the railroad. As the primary east-west route, the railroad offered a relatively cheap and rapid avenue to Albuquerque, particularly from older states of the Middle West. The 1930 census showed that 89 percent of the city's residents were American born, unlike those in urban centers in the East. Almost half the foreign-born came from northern Europe or Canada (Great Britain, Germany, Canada and Scandinavia, in that order).

The first generation of New Town residents built fifteen new churches and had over four dozen fraternal, social and labor organizations, a public library, a university and a public school system. The city had telegraph lines, two daily newspapers, four weeklies produced locally and magazines and books shipped in by rail. The railroad also brought culture. In those days before movies, pop culture included major dramatic and musical companies traveling the western circuit between Chicago and Los Angeles, from opera to vaudeville to melodrama to burlesque. The Elks Opera House (1902) and the Crystal Palace (1911) showcased these traveling performances.

The railroad also constructed the most important social center of town, the Alvarado Hotel, completed in 1902 at a cost of $200,000. The hotel and the adjacent Indian Crafts Building were the focus of an aggressive promotional campaign designed to stimulate Eastern tourist traffic to the Southwest via the railroad. The railroad also cooperated with town business leaders to promote Albuquerque as a location for conventions. These efforts brought tourist dollars and progressive urban settlers who decided to move to the city because of its many opportunities and progressive values.

Early Retail and Wholesale Businesses

It was reported that the first business in New Town was a saloon—a board over two kegs inside a tent, where whiskey and beer cost 5 cents a shot. From there, business architecture went through three phases: tent and shack to adobe and frame to masonry. The early tents and shacks were hastily erected to serve the rapidly arriving railroad employees. These temporary shelters were replaced as quickly as possible with adobe buildings, often with elaborate false fronts, or multi-story frame structures. Because so many buildings were lost to fire, after 1885 all major structures in the business district were required to be of masonry construction.

The heart of the business district grew up along Railroad and Gold Avenues up and down First and Second Streets. Gold Avenue became Albuquerque's "Wall Street," the location of most of the banks, real estate and insurance offices, utility headquarters, the Commercial Club, newspapers and professional offices. Railroad Avenue became the mercantile and entertainment district with clothing stores, restaurants, hotels, theaters, general stores and an abundance of saloons.

1792-93
Neglected San Felipe de Neri church collapses over the winter.

1793
Governor Fernando de la Concha orders every family to donate labor or money to rebuilding the church on north side of plaza.

1799
Census figures show 23,648 Hispanics and 10,557 Indians in Nuevo México.

1810
Bernardo Abeyta discovers a shining crucifix, which becomes the Santuario de Chimayó Shrine in 1813.

México claims independence from Spain; on September 16th, the "liberal" Miguel Hidalgo pronounces "El Grito de Dolores" (Cry of Sorrow from Dolores) igniting a strong, but divided, popular insurrection. Nueva España territory extends from Guatemala to Oregon.

The Portorico Saloon and Grocery, 1898. Photo courtesy of the Albuquerque Museum, Image # 1975.063.499.

1812
Don Pedro Bautista Pino publishes a census showing 40,000 in Nuevo México in 3 villas, 102 plazas and 26 Indian towns; Pino also speaks for Nuevo México before Spanish Parliament in Cadiz, Spain.

1812–1815
U.S. and Britain fight War of 1812; three soldiers later became presidents: Harrison, Jackson and Zachary Taylor.

Although some larger firms such as the Spiegelberg Brothers and the Ilfeld Brothers operated branch stores throughout New Mexico, most businesses were locally owned. Some investors came to start businesses, made their money, then left to go back East, but many were so entranced with the city that they stayed.

City boosters also promoted the climate for those suffering from tuberculosis and similar ailments. In 1910 Albuquerque had three major hospitals: St. Joseph (100 beds), Santa Fe Railroad Hospital (30 beds) and Southwestern Presbyterian Hospital (50 beds for tuberculosis patients only). By end of World War I, five additional private sanitoria had been established. The patients brought their families, and many stayed on after they healed.

Some newcomers also came as a result of the Federal Homestead Act, passed in the 1880s. This law allowed individuals to acquire ownership of tracts of land if they lived on them and improved them by farming and ranching. The turn of the century saw many homesteaders trying to find a new life in New Mexico, including the area around Coyote Springs, now part of Kirtland Air Force Base. Homesteaders grew crops, mainly pinto beans. Besides providing a day outing for Albuquerque residents, Coyote Springs offered fresh spring water, which was bottled and sold, as well as a saloon, small

Sheep in the Manzano Mountains, 1895. Van Daren Coke Collection. Photo courtesy of the Albuquerque Museum, Image # 1981.002.057. Share/History/Rio Grande Weaving Exhibits/Sandia Sheep.

hotel and one-room schoolhouse. Most of the homesteaders came later, in the 1920s and 1930s, especially during the Depression. Although the creation of Kirtland after World War II ended the homesteading there, remains are still visible on the grounds of the base.

1814
Albuquerque holds first election creating an ayuntamiento or municipal council.

Statehood Period

From Boom to Bust: Albuquerque in the Twenties

At the close of World War I, Albuquerque appeared to be another Western boom town on the edge of economic calamity. Between 1880 and 1910 the city's population had grown more than 80%. With 13,000 residents in 1910, Albuquerque was the only city in the territory with a population over 10,000; however, between 1910 and 1920, economic growth faltered dramatically, and the population rose only 16% to 15,175. The end of war brought a drastic drop in wool and livestock prices, causing a local depression made worse by a severe drought. One of the three local banks, the State National Bank, failed, while the others struggled to survive.

New Mexico became a state in 1912, but this had little immediate effect on Albuquerque's economy. When prosperity slowly returned to the area, the economy was no longer strictly tied to the railroad. The automobile began to transform the

1815
King of Spain dissolves Albuquerque's municipal council.

1819
Replaceable cast-iron
tip plow invented
revolutionizing farming.

1820
Méxican liberals,
centralists and,
conservatives debate
becoming a monarchy
or a republic.

Spain reaffirms Pueblo
Indian citizenship
status.

1821
Mexico declares
independence from
Spain and Albuquerque
becomes part of
Mexico.

Mexican Republic allows
trade with U.S.; Vial's
1792 trail to St. Louis is
opened to American
traders and named the
Santa Fe Trail, and
William Becknell arrives
from Missouri with a
pack train of goods and
gains the title of "The
Father of the Santa Fe
Trail."

physical and psychological landscape of Albuquerque, although less than twenty miles of downtown streets had been surfaced by 1920. City commissioners were happy to hold off further civic improvements "not necessary for the winning of the war." Prohibition, beginning October 1, 1918, led to a loss of substantial city retail liquor-licensing fees from three dozen saloons and took away a source of free labor for street maintenance (those who could not pay fines for drunkenness would be forced to work on the streets).

By 1921, the economic situation had improved and paving resumed. By 1930, the total paved mileage was double that of 1920 and covered downtown. Automobiles and paved streets became symbols of modernity and progress. Albuquerque became one of the first cities of its size to convert from trolleys to motorized busses.

Increased mobility facilitated a dramatic expansion of the city's boundaries just prior to the Great Depression. Because of the automobile, people could move out of the immediate downtown area into the vast surrounding open spaces. New Town itself had been founded in 1880 as a land-promotion venture. Even before the substantial development of the original town site, visionary promoters began platting new suburbs.

The city itself embarked on a building boom, much of it now using Southwestern-style architecture. Many years after President William George Tight adopted Pueblo Revival architecture for the University of New Mexico, Albuquerque business leaders began to see the wisdom in using picturesque Southwestern imagery to attract tourist dollars and commercial profits.

Erected in 1923 on West Central for a cost of $500,000, the Hotel Franciscan was one of the first major locally financed downtown buildings to capitalize on Southwestern motifs to appeal to tourists and convention visitors. It also housed the first studio of radio station KGGM. The KiMo Theatre, built in 1927 just down the street from the Franciscan, also showcased the downtown fascination with regional architectural and decorative styles. It made a flashy, almost make-believe presence, much like the new talking films projected on its modern screen.

Even the automobile dealerships featured Pueblo style architecture. The Galles Motor Company showroom, built toward end of twenties, modified the style with six-foot-high plate glass display windows running the length of its Central Avenue façade.

City leaders have always wanted Albuquerque to appear modern and up-to-date, and as a result, few of the original buildings still stand, at least with their original appearance. Two skyscrapers were built between 1922 and 1924: the nine-story First National Bank (housing the financial institution and various professional offices) and the six-story Sunshine Building (theater and office building). They gave evidence of new and growing middle-class wealth, more leisure time and the important role played by Hollywood in this leisure time.

In a move that would have significance to Old Town's status, the forty-year-old courthouse in Old Town was sold and a new one built at 5th north of Tijeras in 1926.

Middle Rio Grande Conservancy District (MRGCD)

In 1880, 120,000 acres of valley land were irrigated and under cultivation. The next forty years saw increasing human population pressure, land erosion farther north, and devastating spring flooding. This brought about an agricultural crisis, as large quantities of silt had caused the riverbed to rise and the banks to widen and shift. Adjacent lands began soaking up water, turning once fertile fields to alkali swamps and salt marshes. By 1920 local authorities estimated only about 40,000 acres in the valley were under cultivation.

To address the problems of flood control, drainage and irrigation, property owners formed the Middle Rio Grande Conservancy District, or MRGCD. This organization, with the powers of a municipal corporation including fiscal authority and eminent domain, extended its influence across four counties and six pueblos, from Cochiti in the north to San Marcial at the upper end of Elephant Butte Reservoir in the south, including some 277,760 acres of potential farmland.

Not everyone was in favor of the MRGCD. It usurped scores of traditional community ditches and assessed new taxes to pay for administrative costs. After final approval in 1925, the MRGCD devoted three years to a plan for an extensive network of dams, levees, drains, canals and laterals. Sales of bonds financing the project had just begun when they were dealt a near-devastating blow by the stock market crash.

Albuquerque's Fascination with Flying

The people of Albuquerque had always had an interest in flying. The first local flight was actually a gas bag and basket that made a free ascension from Second Street between Railroad

1821
Signing of Plan of Iguala brings independence under conservative leadership of President Iturbide and the arduous task of creating a new independent nation begins.

México reaffirms with the Plan of Iguala that, "Inhabitants of Nueva España...are citizens."

1822
Population 2,302 (not including outlying villages).

1824
Bureau of Indian Affairs established by U.S. Government.

and Gold avenues on July 4, 1882. The bag was filled from the city gas plant and reached an altitude of 14,207 feet before landing in a cornfield near Old Town. The next balloon flight was twenty-five years later, at the Territorial Fair of 1907. A balloon carrying Joseph Blondin ascended shortly before noon and landed near sunset, four miles northwest of Corrales. The most dramatic flight to date was in 1909. On October 19, Blondin and Roy Stamm made a free flight through Tijeras Canyon and across the Estancia Valley to the vicinity of Clines Corners, where cowboys helped them recover their balloon and basket. The two aeronauts returned to Albuquerque by train.

The first heavier-than-air flight was made on October 11, 1911. Pilot Charles F. Walsh took off in his Curtiss biplane from the state fairgrounds and flew for twenty-seven miles to the Barelas Bridge, east to the railroad tracks, then northwest across Robinson Park before landing back at the fairgrounds. This flight took ten minutes. In succeeding days he made more exhibition flights, some with passengers, including Roy Stamm. In 1913 Roy Francis piloted another biplane, carrying as a passenger Roy Stamm, who took the earliest known aerial photographs of New Mexico.

Almost twenty-five years later, air flight had proved to be more than a novelty, and the city saw the start of construction of an airport. Railroad employees Frank Speakman and William Franklin, perhaps seeing the future, leased 140 acres of relatively flat mesa on the present site of Kirtland Air Force Base and began grading a runway. By mid-May 1927, interstate aircraft began arriving regularly. Within a year, Western Air Express (WAE) and Transcontinental Air Transport (TAT) began serving the airport regularly, thanks to its excellent airfield and the city's central location. In 1929 one could fly from Albuquerque to Los Angeles for a fare of ninety dollars. Longer trips required a combination of air and rail travel because of a ban on night flying, yet one could still get from Albuquerque to New York City in less than forty hours. Shortly before the stock market crash, WAE moved its operations to a second, newly-constructed field closer to downtown on the West Mesa, approximately where West Mesa High School stands today. By 1930 Albuquerque had two transcontinental airports, one on each mesa.

Government and Service Buildings

More than a half million dollars in bond issues were approved by voters between 1912 and 1919, and the resulting building expansion continued into the next decade. Schools were rapidly erected to serve the growing population. In the fall of 1916 APS had 2,252 pupils; by October 1927 this figure had doubled to 4,500. Expansion was going on at such a fast pace, officials were unsure how funds would be obtained for further expansion.

Several hospitals and hospital additions were also under construction in the '20s, including Santa Fe Memorial Hospital, the Nazareth Sanatorium, the expansion of St. Joseph Hospital, a Veterans Administration Hospital complex, and the U.S. Indian Public Health Hospital. Meanwhile Albuquerque had achieved greater prominence as a regional economic center. The increase in federal agencies and their employees necessitated a new six-story federal courthouse and office building.

First American Pageant

Albuquerque had no important early fall tourist attraction after the discontinuance of the state fair during the war. Meanwhile leaders wanted to capitalize on the growing national interest in the Gallup Inter-Tribal Indian Ceremonials. Several prominent members of the Chamber of Commerce organized the First American Pageant in April 1928.

Six months of intense preparation followed, including contracts with the Pueblos, Navajos, Apaches and local Hispanics for daily parades and performances on the pageant grounds near present-day Wyoming and Central. Promoters constructed a grandstand and a four-story papier-maché Pueblo village stage set and contracted for twenty 9-by-20 foot tipis from New Mexico Tent and Awning Company. The massive public relations effort included volunteer speakers dispatched throughout the state and the railroad's distribution of thousands of brochures featuring their own cut-rate promotional fares.

Opening day in September saw schools and businesses closed and Central between Fifth and Seventh roped off for a free street dance. The Hotel Franciscan held a formal Montezuma Ball. Citizens and visitors enjoyed daily pageant performances, agricultural and industrial exhibits and Indian artisans selling wares and competing for cash design prizes.

The First American Pageant grew in popularity and increased in numbers of tourists every year until the economic pressures of the Depression ended its run. Although their efforts had been inadequate to lessen the effects of the Depression, local

1841
Governor Armijo thwarts an attempt by Texans to take eastern Nuevo México.

U.S. annexes Texas which México declares an act of war.

1846
U.S. invades México under direction of General Kearny and places Nuevo México under United States military rule, starting The Mexican-American War.

Lt. James Abert and Lt. William Peck enter the city during their 3-month government survey of Nuevo México.

Area claimed as a U.S. territory when an army post was established in the city.

leaders had learned important lessons about organization that would benefit the city in the rough times ahead.

Albuquerque During the Depression and World War II

The onset of the Depression brought about a chain reaction of bad economic events in Albuquerque. By the end of 1933, livestock values, mining production and the volume of wholesale business trade had experienced catastrophic declines. As a result, the AT&SF Railroad saw its operating income dip and was forced to cut work weeks and lay off almost 40 percent of its workers. The MRGCD had to stop dredging and levee construction because farmers couldn't pay the assessments and bonds weren't selling. As the largest city in the area and a major stop on the way west from the Dust Bowl, Albuquerque attracted a large number of transients who added to the population of people looking for work.

Because federal Social Security and unemployment insurance did not exist, local governments tried as best they could to cope, but their meager resources were quickly depleted. The grave unemployment situation intensified with a steep decline in the local building industry, affecting not only workers but lumber and materials manufacturers and dealers as well. Around this time a "Hoover Village," a shantytown for the transient unemployed, formed on the city's southern fringe.

The arrival of President Franklin Delano Roosevelt and the New Deal in 1933 started the slow process of recovery. An enormous amount of money was soon available to the state, which was used through federal programs designed to put people to work in new construction and public works projects, including landscaping, renovation of water lines, improvement of the municipal sewer system, creation of parks and playgrounds, and highway improvement. During the first year of the National Industrial Recovery Act, New Mexico received $5,792,000 for highway construction, which would also be an important source of work relief. The Federal Emergency Relief Administration (FERA) funded a program to augment state and local relief for "unemployables."

The development of Roosevelt Park was begun in November of 1933. Federal funds paid artists to paint murals in the Bernalillo County Courthouse. Some women were hired to sew mattress covers for needy families, while others rendered fat into soap for families on relief.

The Civilian Conservation Corps (CCC) greatly benefited the state. Not only did the CCC provide employment; by February of 1933, it was giving almost $3,000 a day, or $3 million a year, to the state's economy. Around Albuquerque the CCC improved most of the public parks and picnic areas still enjoyed today. The railroad, lumber, and clothing industries were all stimulated by constantly changing needs of the CCC.

In addition to the $3 million a year from the CCC, state government received $2.4 million in Civil Works Administration (CWA) funds and another $3.1 million from FERA. By the summer of 1934 over 5,000 farmers driven from their lands by drought were employed on drought-relief labor projects. School districts that had been suffering from increased enrollments and lack of funds for expansion began receiving FERA money. These and other federal initiatives would continue to provide relief and promote modest growth for the rest of the thirties.

The next year brought the Social Security bill, which included three important measures: unemployment insurance, matching grants to the states for relief for unemployables, and a federal system of old-age insurance. That year also saw the creation of the Public Works Administration (PWA), which was even more important in the short run for New Mexico.

Meanwhile the Albuquerque Chamber of Commerce was busy promoting Albuquerque projects, including reviving the State Fair, establishing an Army air base, constructing a civic auditorium and working to provide a larger supply of water to the city. Federal funds became available in 1936 for construction of a new municipal airport on the Southeast Mesa. The State Fair opened in the fall of 1938 at its present location. Work on water reclamation to provide the city with more water and alleviate flooding was begun. The auditorium, however, was postponed until over a decade later.

Local organizations and individuals learned to exploit the availability of public funds, permanently changing Albuquerque's physical and cultural landscape. University of New Mexico president James F. Zimmerman was especially aggressive, spearheading procurement of funds to enact a massive building program at the university. Over the next decade, renowned architect John Gaw Meem would design an average

1854
Gadsden Purchase averts another war with Mexico and adds 45,000 sq. miles to southern New Mexico and Arizona.

1856
First ferry across Rio Grande.

1857
Beale's Wagon Road established between Albuquerque and California; Camels quartered at Army stables in Albuquerque.

1858
Army creates wagon road through Tijeras Canyon.

of one new major building a year, all in adaptation of the Pueblo Revival architectural style. Older buildings were renovated and improved, and smaller projects, such as faculty housing, were constructed. In addition, federal money was used to employ students and "professional workers" in the arts, archaeology and political science. Because of federal programs, UNM experienced substantial growth during what should have been hard times for the university. More than $1,600,000 of federal money for building projects, student aid, faculty research and housing left UNM with an expanded faculty, a growing student body, and a campus larger than was even imagined by James Zimmerman when he started his promotion of the university. The federal subsidies of students coupled with the later G.I. Bill made it possible for many more students to attend.

The Albuquerque Public Schools also reaped the benefits of public funding. Several new school buildings were constructed and improvements were made on existing facilities. School officials learned how to make use of federal monies and accept gifts of land from promoters and developers for future school sites, knowledge that would be put to use as Albuquerque continued to expand into new suburbs.

The Works Progress Administration (WPA) also helped fund civic improvements, including the construction of the Albuquerque Little Theatre, the Veterans' Community Center, a new fire station, the Buena Vista Community Playground, the Heights Community Center and improvements to Rio Grande Park. Relief workers were also employed in construction of new water and sewer lines, street improvements such as gutters and sidewalks, and construction of underpasses under Central and Tijeras and a viaduct over Coal. The street, sidewalk, sewer and waterline improvements were continued into the suburbs. For all these projects the city only had to pay for the materials; federal projects paid for the labor, a great deal for the city since the ratio of labor to material costs was about four to one.

Development of the suburbs was encouraged by another federal program, the newly established Federal Housing Authority (FHA), which made low-cost loans available and stimulated a housing boom, especially in the eastern heights subdivisions. As developers expanded they would make available parcels for schools and parks.

Bernalillo County also reaped the benefit of federal funds, which made possible improvements to county roads, creation of flood-control dams, renovation of *acequias* (irrigation ditches) and additions to Old Town Plaza. They also brought construction of new schools and renovations to older school buildings not part of Albuquerque Public Schools, as well as the creation of a library with repaired books and even a free hot lunch program for needy children.

The MRGCD was able to take advantage of a massive PWA investment in the construction of El Vado Dam and Reservoir on the Chama River, which, along with its subsidiary dams, levees, canals, laterals and ditches, brought flood protection as well as irrigation water to the Albuquerque area. The WPA also funded conservancy work on the Pueblo Indian land around Albuquerque. The New Mexico Department of Public Health used federal funds to eliminate malaria by draining and filling swamps and ponds, eliminating mosquito breeding grounds and rehabilitating the land for farms.

Two other Depression-era changes involving transportation had a profound effect on the future development of Albuquerque. The first was a change from the major highway orientation of north-south following the route of the Camino Real to an east-west orientation, taking advantages of changes in Route 66. Before 1931, travelers on Route 66 going west had to turn north at Santa Rosa, travel northwest to Santa Fe, then pick up Highway 85 south to Albuquerque. From Albuquerque, travelers continued on 85 south to Los Lunas before turning west on State Route 6. At this time no maps even showed a road between Santa Rosa and Moriarty. After Albuquerque's heavy promotional efforts, the Bureau of Federal Highways changed Route 66 to run straight through Albuquerque on Central Avenue. All of this highway construction brought money and jobs to the city and the state.

The effects of the new highway were profound. By 1938, New Mexico attracted more visitors than any of the other five mountain states. Hotels, tourist camps and restaurants were kept constantly busy by tourists and travelers on their way east or west. Developers rushed to plan new subdivisions along the new east-west route. Reliance on the railroad decreased as interstate trucking gained importance.

The second major transportation change was the new Albuquerque airport. The city had entered the decade with two

1863–1866
U.S. Army campaigns against Mescalero Apaches and Navajos; 8,000 Navajo and 450 Apaches prisoners are forced to make "The Long Walk" of 300 miles to Bosque Redondo reservation. Hundreds die in the process.

1864
President Lincoln affirms 1620 Spanish Land Grants and presents "Lincoln Canes."

1866
Congress creates six regiments of African-American troops to serve on the frontier of the west; the mounted units are nicknamed "Buffalo Soldiers" by the Cheyenne and Comanche as a sign of respect for their fighting spirit; others say it was because their hair resembled the coat of the buffalo which were highly respected.

Hilia Lowly Emerson and Mike Lowly at the Albuquerque Airport, before 1945 (30s-40s). J.R. Willis, Ward Hicks Collection. Photo courtesy of the Albuquerque Museum, Image # 1982.180.026.

1867
US Army abandons Albuquerque post, creating a deep local recession.

1870s
African-Americans begin migration to Albuquerque to work for the Santa Fe Railroad; Buffalo Soldier John Collins plants many trees along Railroad (now Central) Avenue.

private airports, one on each mesa, serving competing airlines, Transcontinental Air Transport and Western Air Express. These companies merged and formed Transcontinental and Western Air (TWA), which acquired the coast-to-coast airmail route with Albuquerque as one of its stops. They used the small private airport on the West Mesa, which was quickly proving inadequate for the enormous increase in air traffic. The Chamber of Commerce began lobbying Washington for a new federally financed municipal airport and an Army base.

All the efforts paid off, and the new airport was ready for flights in 1939. It not only greatly improved air service for travelers; it also helped attract the desired Army base. Lobbying efforts intensified, aided by the Army's interest in constructing a bombing range in the southern part of the state, and construction on the million-dollar Albuquerque Air Base (renamed Kirtland Field in 1942) began in 1941. The initial occupants, the 19th Bombardment Group, required barracks for 2,000 enlisted men as well as housing for officers and other personnel. The housing demand continued to increase during the war, and money continued to be awarded for improvements to the base.

Everyday life carried on with vigor during the 1930s. Churches, clubs and social organizations mobilized to help the less fortunate with sewing for the needy and fund-raising activities such as bridge games, dances and galas. They supported a well-baby clinic, the Salvation Army and the Red Cross. Holidays brought donations of presents for children. Generous individuals treated poor children to movies and circuses. The Women's Club initiated a fund drive to pay for health care for the indigent.

Other activities went on with relative normalcy. Children took piano, dance and other music lessons. Federally financed community centers offered recreation for both children and adults. For fifty cents or less, families could spend hot summer afternoons swimming, canoeing, taking boat rides, or just relaxing at Conservancy Beach west of downtown. The Albuquerque Zoo saw a huge expansion of its animal population. Eight movie theaters entertained with the latest Hollywood offerings. The city's second radio station, KOB, went on the air in 1932. By 1939 table radios could be purchased for as little as $9.95, and radio-phonographs, which played the new improved 78 r.p.m. records, sold for under $100. The *Albuquerque Journal* and the *New Mexico State Tribune* moved into a joint central facility, each retaining its individuality but sharing circulation services, billing, printing and classified advertising. This was the first such newspaper plan in the country. The repeal of Prohibition in 1933 brought back bars and dance "gardens."

Albuquerque's economy in the late 1930s and early 1940s was booming, although not in every part of the city. The downtown and Rio Grande Park area had benefited from very large relief projects. The middle- and upper-middle class suburbs expanded rapidly, especially with the aid of the new FHA mortgage loan guarantees. Homes were going up at the rate of almost one a day. City water, sewer and street-paving activities likewise gravitated to the new areas. Meanwhile, in the older neighborhoods nearer downtown, owner-occupied dwellings gave way to rentals and the "house trailer" appeared, along with trailer camps or parks with spaces to rent.

In addition to all the other activity surrounding the military presence in Albuquerque, railroad business increased

1874
Bilingual newspaper, *The Republican Review*, is started by William McGuinness; Old Town becomes an "island" as it is surrounded by Rio Grande flooding.

1875
"A New Englander" sinks the first well in Old Town's Plaza and people come from as far as Los Lunas to get cold, clear water.

1875–76
The 9th Cavalry Regiment, "Buffalo Soldiers," is transferred to the New Mexico District."

1876
First telegraph arrives.

Crowds swarm Central Ave., 1929. Milner Collection, Milner Studio, Museum Purchase, G. O. Bonds. Photo courtesy of the Albuquerque Museum, Image # 1992.005.074.

1878
Central Bank,
Albuquerque's first,
opens doors.

1879
Railroads come to
New Mexico.

during the war, especially the repair yards, working to keep everything in good shape. The first government contractors, mostly involved in manufacturing related to the war effort, came to the state. In an unrelated development, new treatments reduced the threat of tuberculosis, causing some sanitoria to change to modern health facilities and others to close their doors. The draw of Albuquerque as a promise to defeat respiratory illness faded, but by this time many newcomers were arriving for other reasons.

Albuquerque Since the War

Although the end of the war brought many military activities to an end, changes came from a development in the nearby city of Los Alamos. Los Alamos National Laboratory, home of the Manhattan Project and the development of the atomic bomb, underwent reorganization, and one division was moved to Sandia Base, near Kirtland Field. This was the beginning of Sandia Laboratory, which became a completely separate organization with almost 2,000 employees. Kirtland began to be used for storing weapons, and Manzano Base was added in 1952.

Other nonmilitary-related businesses also were attracted to Albuquerque. This led to an increase in commercial building. The Nob Hill Business Center, Albuquerque's first shopping center, opened in 1949. Partly because it had become a tourist attraction, Old Town was finally incorporated into the city in 1951.

The fifties saw a radical change in the downtown skyline. The Commercial Club was leveled to make way for the 13-story Simms Building. Several more tall buildings followed, including the 17-story First National Bank Building and the 18-story National Building (now the Compass Bank Building).

An exciting change in outdoor recreation took place during these years. Bob Nordhaus, who had organized the Albuquerque Ski Club in 1936, formed La Madera Company and installed the nation's longest T-bar lift at Sandia Peak. Sandia Peak Ski Area began modern operations in 1963, when co-owners Nordhaus and Ben Abruzzo added a double-chair lift and a mountain-top restaurant. A year later they began building the Sandia Peak Tramway, the longest single-section tram in the world. Tourists can ride the tram up the steep mountainside, enjoy mountain vistas while dining at the restaurant, then ride the tram back down.

Recent History

The early sixties showed a need to diversify the economy still further, instead of relying so heavily on Kirtland and Sandia. A group of businessmen, including Nordhaus and Abruzzo, backed by the Chamber of Commerce, formed the Albuquerque Industrial Development Service, to entice other businesses to move to the city. They were successful in drawing several, including Sparton Southwest, Boeing's Aerospace Division, EG&G, Levi Strauss and General Electric. Activities at Kirtland, which employed some of the nation's top laser experts, attracted related work such as laser, sensor, component and instrument manufacturing.

The population had doubled during the fifties, rising to 201,189 in the 1960 census. New shopping centers and indoor malls became popular, including Winrock Shopping Center, Northdale Shopping Center, Eastdale Shopping Center, Indian Plaza, and a few years later, Coronado Shopping Center. The higher population led to expansion of health care facilities,

1880
Santa Fe Railroad extended into Albuquerque. Over the next few years, this would create an influx of new residents and further broaden the ethnic makeup of the city.

African American populations settle here to work on railroad; Northern Italians work on railroads then enter business and ranching; Italian stonecutters build St. Mary's School, Old Town Courthouse and UNM's Hodgin Hall. Chinese settle here to work on railroad. Pueblo Indians negotiate for jobs in exchange for railroad rights of way.

Railroad brings urban culture. Horsedrawn streetcars run on Railroad Avenue (later named Central Avenue) to Old Town Plaza; first daily paper lasts only two issues then Albuquerque Publishing Company takes over to print the *Albuquerque Daily Journal*.

Huning Highlands Addition platted to become the city's first residential development.

1880s–1890s
Large Jewish merchant community forms around the railroad.

including St. Joseph Medical Center and the expansion of Presbyterian Hospital.

By 1966, two major interstate highways, I-25 and I-40, were completed through Albuquerque. This encouraged more building activity on the west side, including the beginnings of Paradise Hills, Taylor Ranch and Eagle Ranch.

Urban development during this period saw many historical buildings being torn down to make way for progress. Even the landmark Alvarado Hotel fell to the wrecking ball. During a decade of urban renewal, federal funds were used to level entire blocks.

The high-tech industry began in the 1970s. Albuquerque was the birthplace of the first personal computer, when H. Edward Roberts, a former Air Force engineer, developed the first practical, affordable home computer, the Altair. Two young men working for Roberts' company were Paul Allen and Bill Gates, who started Microsoft in Albuquerque in 1975 but later moved to Seattle.

During these years, the Albuquerque area began attracting electronics companies from California because of lower costs, a bigger labor pool and room to grow. Among the companies relocating were GTE Lenkurt and Motorola. Sandia became a national laboratory in 1979. Lovelace became the area's first HMO with the Lovelace Health Plan. Presbyterian Hospital followed suit and organized its own HMO health plan. As was the case nationwide, rail traffic was down, causing the Santa Fe to close its Albuquerque shops and turn passenger operations over to Amtrak.

Meanwhile, Albuquerque became a major annual national tourist destination with the launch of the Balloon Fiesta. Some 20,000 people showed up for the first hot-air balloon rally in 1972. By 1978, the Albuquerque International Balloon Fiesta had become the world's largest ballooning event, drawing balloonists and crowds from all over the world.

The eighties brought major changes in the skyline, including the tallest building in New Mexico, the 22-story Albuquerque Plaza. Another wave of businesses came into the area including Signetics and Honeywell.

This new business expansion altered again the city's pattern of growth, as many of the newly arrived high-tech businesses constructed their plants along the northern route of I-25. Businesses were moving north and west. Rio Rancho, originally a bedroom community northwest of Albuquerque, incorporated as a city in 1981 and began attracting industry. Intel Corporation located there in 1980, triggering a tremendous period of growth for Rio Rancho.

Over the next years, rapid growth continued, especially in the north and west. Rio Rancho's population continued to explode, with Intel expanding and the city adding about 4,500 additional jobs associated with the call-center industry. Its population increased from 9,985 in 1980 to 51,765 in 2000 with no end in sight.

The nineties and turn of the century saw changes in the Albuquerque business lineup. Major companies locating in the city included General Mills Inc. and U.S. Cotton. New biomedical and biotechnological companies started up. Eclipse Aviation Corp. will produce a six-seat commercial jet in Albuquerque. St. Joseph Healthcare System and Lovelace Health Systems combined as Lovelace Sandia Health System.

With its dramatic physical setting, beautiful light, pivotal spot on transportation routes and available land on all sides, Albuquerque has long been a place for dreams and opportunity. Countless people, attracted by its rich, diverse culture and open spaces, came here looking for a different, more individual way of life. Others came for jobs as more companies choose to locate here. Tourists visit and wish they could stay. Many do. Yet despite this remarkable growth, Albuquerque remains a frontier that is both new and old—and forever unique.

1882
First telephone service started; first permanent bridge built with five cent toll to cross Rio Grande.

First Black church, Grant Chapel African Methodist Episcopal, established; B'nai Brith Jewish fraternal service organization started.

1883
Grant Opera house opens; St.Vincent Academy founded.

1885
Albuquerque is incorporated, Henry Jaffa, a Jew, elected first mayor.

Census lists 33 Chinese living in Albuquerque.

Sources

Albuquerque Tricentennial Committee, official Tricentennial website: http://www.albuquerque300.org. Used history matrix and other miscellaneous information.

Biebel, Charles D. *Making the Most of it: Public Works in Albuquerque during the Great Depression, 1929–1942, An Albuquerque Museum history monograph* (Albuquerque: Albuquerque Museum, 1986).

Boles, Edgar, ed. *Albuquerque-Area Archaeology: Sites and Stories* (Albuquerque: TRC Mariah Associates, Inc., 2001).

Holmes, Richard D., *Albuquerque-Area Archaeology: Sites and Stories* (Albuquerque: City of Albuquerque Planning Department, 2001).

Johnson, Byron A. and Robert K. Dauner. *Early Albuquerque: A Photographic History, 1870–1918* (Albuquerque: *Albuquerque Journal*, 1980).

CULTURAL OVERVIEW

The Albuquerque Museum of Art & History

By Jim Moore, Former Director

The Albuquerque Museum of Art and History presented a series of three exhibitions in 2005 and 2006. *El Alma de España* dealt with the "Golden Age" of Spanish painting in the seventeenth and early eighteenth centuries. *Fortuny to Picasso: Prelude to Spanish Modernism* brought together, for the first time in the United States, work by Spanish Impressionist and post-Impressionist painters that rivals that of their much better-known contemporaries in France. *Picasso to Plensa: A Century of Spanish Art* addressed the pivotal role that Spanish artists have played in the evolution of the modernist idioms that still dominate thought-provoking art around the globe. The scale of this project, and its concentrated focus on a particular national culture, was unique in the history of the museum, but it was also a fitting tribute to the founding of Albuquerque as a city in 1706 and the Tricentennial celebration of that pivotal event.

Though part of the mission of The Albuquerque Museum has always been to research and celebrate the history of this city and the Middle Rio Grande Valley, the mission is broader and more complex than that description might suggest. The founding of the city was an important milestone, yet we are much more than a colony on the remote northern frontier of New Spain. The uniqueness of our history and the art of our region is truly found in the diversity of our cultural expression. The museum's permanent collections are intended to represent this diversity, while the breadth of programming in exhibitions has brought the world to Albuquerque.

People everywhere are quick to simplify definitions and to stereotype others as cultural norms, even while recognizing the complexity of their own lives and histories. A museum is one of those places where such assumptions about identity can be examined and subjected to closer scrutiny, and in this process the real stories of who we are can be revealed. For the past century and a quarter, tourists have come here to encounter "Indians," yet what they find if they reach out to individuals are cultures that speak different languages and have different points of view on issues, as people do everywhere. On the other hand, one can readily find in New Mexico that the fact of sharing the Spanish language does not result in a shared set of common cultural values. To point out the obvious, the same can be said of those who share English as a common language.

Sheepherder, sculpture by Lincoln Fox, beside the Albuquerque Museum. Photo © Marcia Keegan.

When the museum moved from its original quarters in the WPA building of the old Albuquerque Sunport to its new location in Old Town, one of the first exhibitions we developed was called *New Town and the Railroad Boom Years*, an examination of the business district that grew up in the 1880s about a mile and a half east of Albuquerque's Plaza Vieja. The establishment of Albuquerque as a major stop and repair depot for the AT&SF Railway brought a major influx of people from far and wide. There were African-American, Asian and Latin American residents here. Many newcomers were from Western, Eastern and Northern Europe. Those of non-English European origin soon became characterized as "Anglos" (perhaps because of speaking English), yet they were Irish, German, Italian, Scottish, French, Polish, Lithuanian, Norwegian, Danish, Austrian. The list could go on. For over a century, Albuquerque, like many cities in the U.S., has been a multicultural city.

Park Place, sculpture by Glenna Goodacre along side entrance to the Albuquerque Museum.
Photo © Marcia Keegan.

Outside view of the entrance to the Albuquerque Museum. Photo © Marcia Keegan.

We have, however, synthesized this complexity into our own unique cultural stereotype, the result of an advertising campaign in the 1930s; in the mid-1980s, the museum documented this in an exhibition titled *Tourism in New Mexico.* When Clyde Tingley became governor, he sought to promote economic development by encouraging automobile tourism, and in doing this he hired the Ward Hicks Agency in Albuquerque to "re-brand" (as marketers would say now) the image of the state. Thus, the "tricultural" image of New Mexico was created, our ethnic diversity reduced to "Indian, Spanish, and Anglo." Successful advertising seeks to simplify the message and to make it memorable. The fact that this image of us survives to this day is a testament to the effectiveness of the Ward Hicks campaign, although many New Mexico residents today recognize this as an amusing, and occasionally frustrating, fiction. Again, the museum provides an appropriate setting for the discussion and understanding of such issues in communities.

These two exhibitions are simply examples in which the museum directly addressed issues of our identity as a community. More often, over the years we have sought to celebrate the diversity of the community by providing a "window on the world" in our selection of exhibition topics.

1890
Albuquerque Commercial Club founded.

Laguna Indian Colony established in Barelas neighborhood near rail yards.

1890s
Syrian-Lebanese Arabs flee poor economic conditions and Ottoman Army conscription; some come to Albuquerque (Budagher, Bellamah, Hyder, Maloof).

1891
Albuquerque
incorporates as a city
with population of
3,785; public library
opens; public school
system (APS) begins.

St. Paul's (German)
Lutheran Church
established.

1892
University of New
Mexico opens on its
present location.

1897
Jewish Congregation
Albert established,

1898
First chemical fire
engine; Albuquerque
Elk's Lodge begins.

U.S. declares war
against Spain: Spanish-
American War. Teddy
Roosevelt recruits
Rough Riders from New
Mexico into the war
effort; fourteen officers
and 242 enlisted men
are mustered into The
First New Mexico
Cavalry.

Treaty of Paris signed
ending the Spanish-
American War.

Between 1979 and 2006 the museum has presented over 460 temporary exhibitions on a great range of subjects: Japanese masterworks, European and American paintings, Chinese ceramics, the role of the horse in the American West, Tibetan art, contemporary Native American art, pre-Columbian sculpture, the U.S.-Mexico Boundary Survey, Chicano art, the Ottoman Empire, Southeast Asian jewelry, internationally acclaimed contemporary artists, and much, much more. Our goal has always been to support and encourage responsible and accurate research, to present examples of the highest quality of human achievement in the arts, and to illuminate our history in ways that look beyond the obvious stereotypes.

As we celebrate this Tricentennial it is important to acknowledge the efforts of Governor Francisco Cuervo y Valdés and the settlers who envisioned this place in 1706 as a city. But it is just as necessary that we recognize that we are, like many cities in this country, a widely diverse community of immigrants, and our vigor is derived from that diversity. Albuquerque recently has been acknowledged as one of the primary centers of the newly emerging "creative class," and that cultural shift is seen to be one of the keys to building robust and vibrant communities. Perhaps the best place to examine and celebrate that strength is in a museum that reveres our past, identifies who we are and pushes forward to envision our future.

About 20 million years ago in this area, geological forces pulled the Earth's crust thin, creating the Rio Grande rift, where large blocks of the existing land dropped downward and the margins lifted up to form the Sandia and Manzano Mountains. Photo courtesy of the museum.

Albuquerque, Land of Volcanoes
The Museum of Natural History & Science

By Jayne Aubele, Larry Crumpler and Tim Aydelott

When we look around Albuquerque and see the gorgeous sunsets on the Sandia Mountains, the West Mesa volcanoes and Petroglyph National Monument, the troublesome pass through Tijeras Canyon and the lovely Rio Grande and bosque, we are tempted to think this is the way it has always been, but, geologically speaking, the landscape in and around Albuquerque is quite young, the result of active and dynamic geological forces. When we look out of our windows, the landscape we see is telling us a geological story that explains why Albuquerque is located where it is.

We could go back about a billion and a half years to when the Sandia granite (not the mountains, just the granite rock) and the rocks of Tijeras Canyon and the Rincon Ridge were formed by ancient mountains and volcanoes. Tijeras Canyon is actually the site of a very, very old fault in very, very old mountains. The modern canyon has been eroded along the trace of

1900s
Albuquerque becomes known as "health city" for tubercular patients; many Americans suffering from tuberculosis migrate to Albuquerque to try to recover their health. Central School built at Lead and Third. Social and economic conditions worsen causing many Mexican citizens to migrate to the U.S., particularly during the Mexican Revolution. Opportunities in mining and railroad continue to draw many Italians who later enter business and ranching. Japanese immigrants begin to arrive and settle in Albuquerque.

Jurassic display at the Museum of Natural History and Science. Photo courtesy of the museum.

1902
Alvarado Hotel opens as
showcase of Fred
Harvey chain at a cost
of $200,000.

1903
First powered, sustained
airplane flight at Kitty
Hawk; President Teddy
Roosevelt visits
Albuquerque.

1904
Most disastrous flood in
New Mexico history
takes many lives.

this old forgotten fault, and some of the rocks from these early mountains are still on view as you drive through the canyon, but the old mountains are long gone. They were beveled down to a flat plain during a long period of erosion over almost a billion years.

We could go back 300 million years to when Albuquerque was at the bottom of a sea that flooded that flat plain. The ancient seafloor formed the fossil-rich rock layers you see today at the top of the Sandia and Manzano Mountains. This is not to say that sea level was 10,000 feet higher then than it is now. No, that long ago, there was no Rio Grande and there were no mountains. It was just flat and the bottom of the ocean.

However, those ancient rocks formed long ago play a less important part in our present-day story than events that began happening 20 million years ago.

Let's rewind to about 20 million years ago, give or take a few million years. That is when the crust in this location began to stretch and crack and pull apart in the middle of the vast North American continental plate. This region of thinning crust is called the Rio Grande rift, and it is one of only five known young continental rift valleys on Earth—a very special place geologically. As this rifting occurred, large blocks of the

Front door of the Museum of Natural History and Science. Photo courtesy of the museum.

existing land dropped downward and the margins lifted up to form the Sandia and Manzano Mountains. These mountains are geologically young, and they and the rift are still forming today. This faulting and uplift also created a series of interconnected basins. As the basins formed over millions of years, they slowly filled with sediments (rocks, sand, gravel and clay) washed down from the surrounding mountain tops and brought in by early rivers, most of which flowed from the west to the southeast. The Llano de Albuquerque, the flat plateau on the top of the west mesa of Albuquerque, is actually the floor of the rift valley that formed as the basin filled with sediments. The Rio Grande and Rio Puerco, both of which developed around one to two million years ago, cut down through this floor and formed their respective modern river valleys, leaving the former rift valley floor as Albuquerque's West Mesa.

In fact, the Rio Grande is the gift of the rift. Without the prior development of the rift valley, the Rio Grande might very well have flowed in a different direction. Instead, the river took advantage of the low area of interconnected basins and flowed down the center of New Mexico, providing year-round water to support the modern bosque and human settlements. Albuquerque is a city in the middle of a rift valley, and the rift

1905
Oreste Bachechi builds Savoy Hotel, then considered to be Albuquerque's finest.

1906
Occidental Life Insurance Company established here.

1908
Fred Harvey opens Indian Museum at the Alvarado Hotel; Southwestern Presbyterian Sanitorium opens, now Presbyterian Hospital

Ford introduces the Model-T. Automobile speed limit set at 8 miles per hour; eight passenger trains run daily.

1908–1909
Severe droughts cause
decline in sheep
industry.

1909
First tethered balloon
flight in Albuquerque

1910
U.S. Hamilton Enabling
Act allows New Mexico
and Arizona to form
separate governments
equal with other states.

Census shows 1,958
foreign-born Italians in
New Mexico; small
number of Filipinos
arrive after Dewey
defeats Spanish in
Manila.

Mexican Revolution
begins with major
political and social
revolt.

1910-1940
Scandinavians arrive in
New Mexico and
Albuquerque.

1911
First airplane flight in
Curtis Biplane at old
Fairground; New Mexico
Alien Land Act prohibits
Asians from owning
land.

valley has provided a sheltered and prosperous region for biological diversity and for human history.

Remember that the West Mesa may be the west side of Albuquerque, but it is the center of the rift at Albuquerque. And the rift is a very unusual place where the crust of the Earth is thinning and pulling apart. About 150,000 years ago, molten magma came up from the mantle through some of the cracks in the crust created by the rifting, and the Albuquerque Volcanoes erupted lava along a 17-mile-long fissure. The line of volcanoes, visible from everywhere in Albuquerque, marks the middle of the rift. The lava flows traveled toward the river, and today's modern escarpment along the eastern edge of the lava flows developed when erosion of the valley sediments encroached on the flows and left them high-standing. This escarpment provided a focal point for the Native Americans who came to the area.

Throughout the geologic history of the Albuquerque basin there have been other volcanoes, too. Many are visible to the north and south of the city, from San Felipe Mesa to Isleta Volcano. There are even some that were buried early in the history of the basin as it filled with sediments; one visible example is Cerro Colorado, south of I-40, west of Albuquerque. Albuquerque is a city surrounded by young volcanoes, and the rift is still volcanically active. So volcanism in the Albuquerque basin may not be just a thing of the past, but may shape Albuquerque's future someday.

Throughout its history, the Rio Grande meandered back and forth across the Albuquerque area; evidence of river gravels has been found as far east as Eubank and as far west as Coors. The modern river channel of the Rio Grande may have been cut as recently as ten thousand years ago at the end of the last North American ice age. The Villa of Albuquerque was established where the Rio Grande meanders to the west in a large sweeping river bend. The Villa was settled close to the river in order to ensure a supply of water for irrigated fields. And the fields were possible because of the flat flood plain that developed around the river, where it was relatively easy to divert river water through acequias for irrigating crops. But the Villa's exact location within this inner channel may have come about because it was a convenient place to ford the river to the Atrisco side, at the south end of bluffs that lie on the west side of the channel. And eastward there were convenient arroyos leading up to a pass through the Sandia and

Walking through the Museum of Natural History and Science. Photo courtesy of the museum.

Manzanito Mountains, and Tijeras Canyon, which provided easy access to the eastern plains.

The bend in the river had a very important effect on the history of our city. Believe it or not, this one river meander, developed thousands of years ago, played a role in the location of modern downtown Albuquerque and the preservation of Old Town Albuquerque. When the railroad came to New Mexico in the late nineteenth century, the construction proceeded from north to south following the east side of the inner valley of the Rio Grande. At about Alameda, the river swings westward, but the builders of the railroad just continued straight south, thus ending up passing about a mile east of Old Town. The development of New Town or downtown, located near the new railroad, actually took place east of Old Town. Old Town and New Town continued to exist as separate city centers, and Old Town was preserved as an important heritage site because of a bend in the river that happened thousands of years ago.

All of these geological events shaped the land to make Albuquerque a natural geographic crossroads. In fact, since there are only a few great rift valleys on Earth like the Rio Grande rift, one might say that the regional landscape of Albuquerque is unique among North American cities. From the ancient trails following the east-to-west corridor through Tijeras Canyon to the free-flowing highway provided by the north-to-south flowing Rio Grande, Albuquerque was destined by geology to be a unique place and to prosper as a center of trade and scenic beauty.

1912
New Mexico is established as the 47th U.S. state; City of Albuquerque holds first annual First American Pageant and constructs Indian village grounds. Railroad Avenue renamed Central Avenue.

Albuquerque Independent Society Established and becomes Albuquerque NAACP in 1913.

1913
First aerial photographs of Albuquerque by Roy Stamm.

1914
World War I begins in Europe.

1915
First America Pageant closes due to WWI and financial problems; Greek immigrants come to Albuquerque.

1916
Clyde Tingley elected alderman and reigns in New Mexico politics for 38 years; JC Penney's opens.

Mexican revolutionary, Pancho Villa, raids in southern New Mexico.

National Atomic Museum. Photo © Marcia Keegan.

1917
Bolshevik Revolution
sends small number of
Russians to
Albuquerque; USS New
Mexico launched as
newest U.S. Fleet
Battleship BB-40.

Atomic Effect: Albuquerque's High-tech Beginnings and the National Atomic Museum

By Jim Walther, Director

The dawning of the atomic age in the early 1940s changed our entire world and with it, New Mexico. Even though much of the early development and discovery of atomic energy took place in Europe, California and Chicago, the real genesis of this immensely powerful discovery was here. Our state is the birth-place of the atomic era, so our cities, landscapes, people and institutions changed in fundamental ways as this age dawned. The National Atomic Museum in Albuquerque reflects and recreates this history.

In the late 1930s as World War II was taking its toll on the cities of Europe, there was a deep sense of dread that Hitler and his Nazi empire were ahead of the United States in the race to use atomic energy as a weapon. This fear was so intense that the U.S. military devised a plan to beat the Nazis to the atomic bomb, because to fail in doing so was unthinkable.

The super-secret Manhattan Project was created in the early 1940s to develop and use the bomb to end the war. A project of immense proportions, it involved theoretical physics applications as well as actual experimentation that had never been done.

Its headquarters was at Los Alamos, in New Mexico, and into that formerly quiet hilltop boys' school poured scientists and technicians from Europe and the United States. This secret project, not even known by Congress or the Vice President at the time, set the stage for New Mexico to become a center of technical discovery and scientific prowess.

Following the end of the war, work at Los Alamos expanded. Albuquerque's Sandia Base was chosen in 1946 as the site for the "Z division" of Los Alamos Laboratory, because it could offer easier access to air and rail transportation. These resources were needed to help assure that the new weapon designed by the scientists could be replicated if need be.

From that beginning, Sandia Laboratory came about as a separate laboratory in 1948. In these years, a calm came across America. The war was won, the Japanese and Nazis had been defeated and while much rebuilding was needed in Europe, at least the world was at peace. That short-lived sense of security came to an abrupt end in 1949, when the Soviet Union success-fully tested its first atomic bomb. The work of the labs at Los Alamos and Sandia immediately went into high gear as a result of this perceived parity of atomic capacity.

The work of the labs had a major impact on Albuquerque in the early part of the Cold War, attracting well-educated workers who needed new homes, places to shop and worship, schools for their children and places to play and relax. Though the actual work of the lab remained secret, other

---

1917–1919
U.S. involved in World War I.

1918
Worldwide flu epidemic, 675,000 Americans die.

1919
World War I ends with signing of Treaty of Versailles.

Prohibition begins with the 21st Amendment ban on sale and consumption of alcohol in the U.S.

1920
Albuquerque population is 15,157; Chamber of Commerce hosts New Mexico Harvest Festival; Albuquerque Country Club formed; New Mexico is the 32nd state to approve the 19th Amendment giving women the right to vote.

Armenians fleeing genocide by Ottoman Turks arrive.

companies that provided support for the lab began to come to town as well.

At that time, the laboratory and base were way out to the east of Albuquerque on the mesa just south of Route 66 as it stretched out toward the Tijeras Canyon. The Albuquerque airport also was once farther east of its current location, and the original waiting room for the airport is now incorporated into a credit union building on Wyoming Blvd. The old airstrip stretched east that far and was next to two large Quonset hut-style hangars that remain fixtures today. In fact the original building for the National Atomic Museum was built at the east end of the former runways. In these early years the lab was operating in smaller and less functional structures, but was attracting talented technical workers who would dedicate themselves to winning the Cold War.

The threat of a Soviet nuclear attack on the United States caused the labs to operate at fever pitch and the military to remain at a heightened alert for over 40 years. As their mission grew, the technical achievements of the labs spawned spin-off technology development as well: the creation of the Clean Room used in microchip fabrication, air bags used in automobiles and laser devices found in CD drives and scanners. These technologies prompted the founding of new companies and relocation of others to Albuquerque to take advantage of the technical work force and proximity to the national lab. Yet the mission of Sandia remained to protect America and the world from the Soviet Union. This led to extensive development of weapon engineering systems by Sandia scientists until the 1990s.

The Cold War ended in the late 1980s with the fall of the Berlin Wall and collapse of the Soviet Union. The cold warriors who had made our safety their life's work began to look for other missions and opportunities to keep us safe. Their work later would be used to train military personnel and test the way that weapons were deployed. In those early years, many of these items were classified and were not seen by the public, but they were saved for future generations to learn about.

The National Atomic Museum was founded at Kirtland Air Force Base in 1969 as the Sandia Atomic Museum. In the very early years it showcased a collection of nuclear weapon casings, aircraft and missiles and was known predominantly for this formerly classified display of military hardware. Nowhere else could one see material that played such a pivotal role in the Cold War era. The museum later became known as the National Atomic Museum and was officially chartered by Congress in 1991 as the official museum of its type. The museum began to diversify the exhibits displayed, offering material that depicted the peaceful uses and role of nuclear medicine and nuclear energy. New educational and community services were added as well to attract local families and increase tourism, since the museum is the only one of its kind in the world.

There was a certain sense of excitement when visiting the museum during its many years on base. To get to the museum required that a driver get a special pass and go through the security gates on the perimeter. While it was "fun" for out-of-state visitors to experience this, most residents of Albuquerque did not enjoy the scrutiny that was required to get a base-access pass—so many did not visit except when on a field trip in a school bus.

In 1997, a decision was made to move the museum to a new location that would be free of the security and accessibility issues for visitors. Work had begun to plan for this move and to secure the needed funds, when the terrorist attack on September 11, 2001 caused the Air Base to close to all visitors. The Museum was forced to close too and had to relocate to a temporary site while the final development work for a new location remained underway. Now it became imperative to find a permanent home for the museum as well as an interim one.

On May 11, 2002 the National Atomic Museum reopened in Old Town in the former REI building on Mountain Road NW. This was made possible by the generosity of the building owners and involved city officials and community leaders working with the National Atomic Museum Foundation board members and Sandia Lab staff. The museum attracted many more local citizens to the new site than before and found success with community programs, events, summer camps and outreach services.

Located now on "Museum Row," many more tourists found the museum—but now it had to compete with the well-established larger museums located in the area. In 2003, the museum moved one of the 38 static displays that had surrounded the old museum on base to Old Town in an effort to attract visitors to the location. The historic Redstone Rocket

1927
Oreste Bachechi builds the KiMo Theatre. Today, the KiMo remains one of the rare examples of the architectural style "Pueblo-Deco." The theater was named by Pablo Abeita of Isleta Pueblo.

Albuquerque Zoo opens at Rio Grande Park.

1928
First airplane landing field built on East Mesa; KGGM radio begins broadcasting.

1929
Wall Street crashes.

1930
Albuquerque Little Theatre opens.

1930–1934
Great U.S. Depression.

1931–1939
Eight year severe drought creates the Great Dust Bowl.

1932
Albuquerque Dons is first pro baseball team; Civic Symphony formed; KOB radio begins broadcasting.

1933
Depression closes First National Bank; U.S. Indian Hospital opens.

Prohibition repealed with passing of the 21st Amendment.

1934
Indian Reorganization Act institutes form of constitutional government adopted by many Pueblos over the next 45 years.

1935
Dennis Chavez named U.S. Senator by Governor Clyde Tingley. He becomes the first American born Hispanic U.S. Senator and serves for 27 years.

1937
Route 66 realigned to east and west through Albuquerque and paved end-to-end.

caused some consternation to a few neighbors, but it actually succeeded in increasing attendance. In 2003 the museum became affiliated with the Smithsonian Institution, providing its operations a higher level of credibility.

The museum is now preparing for the final move and the changes this will bring. In the next several years a new facility will be constructed to house the museum. New exhibits will be built to raise the quality, relevance and credibility of the institution. The museum will also change its name and reopen as the National Museum of Nuclear Science & History—admittedly a longer title, but one that reflects its national status and heritage of presenting both peaceful and military applications of nuclear energy.

In this new and larger museum building you will find exhibits depicting the impact of atomic discovery on Albuquerque, the United States and the world. There will be exhibits that deal with military history, medical applications, space exploration, energy production, waste concerns, food irradiation, time-keeping, and more. The museum will also attract students interested in history, mathematics and science, helping them stay excited about possible careers in technology. It will become a magnet for scholars and researchers who are exploring the nuclear sciences through our rich archive and collections programs.

The National Atomic Museum will continue operations in Old Town for the next several years and then complete a final move that will again allow the showcase of aircraft, rockets and other items that were always found at the museum, in addition to new and exciting science and technology exhibits both inside and outside.

Our atomic history but it is much more than an exploration of the past. The nuclear concerns facing our world are critical, and thus a visit to the National Museum of Nuclear Science & History will help adults and students to be better informed about these matters. A visit to the museum used to be a trip to a dusty warehouse for bombs, but now it is a place to learn about nuclear issues and technologies of all kinds. To learn more about the museum and its rich history in Albuquerque, check out our website **www.atomicmuseum.com**.

Front of the entrance at the Indian Pueblo Cultural Center.
Photo by Travis Suazo.

INDIAN PUEBLO CULTURAL CENTER
Gateway to the 19 Pueblos of New Mexico

By Tazbah McCullah, Marketing Director, and Cynthia L. Chavez, Museum Director

For 30 years, the Indian Pueblo Cultural Center (IPCC), a tax-exempt 501c3 corporation, has given many visitors their first experience of New Mexico's 19 Pueblos by sharing the Pueblos' rich history of culture and traditions still in existence today.

Located in the northern end of Albuquerque's "cultural corridor" of museums, art galleries and Old Town, IPCC is a unique tribal, cultural and economic development institution, existing within a major southwest city of the United States. Owned and operated by a consortium of 19 Pueblo

1938
New Mexico State Fair reopens in present location.

1939
Municipal Airport opens and TWA begins daily flights. U.S. Army leases land east of the airport for flight training base that thousands of New Mexico residents build under the WPA program.

Hitler invades Poland, beginning World War II in Europe.

1939–1945
Manhattan project develops and detonates world's first atomic bomb at Trinity Site, New Mexico.

1941
Albuquerque Army Air Base gets first planes and begins training bomber crews; Continental begins daily flights.

Japan bombs Pearl Harbor and U.S. enters WW II.

communities, the IPCC delivers educational opportunities via its exhibitions, research facilities, art galleries and educational programming. In their wisdom, the Pueblo leadership created a corporation, Indian Pueblos Marketing, Inc., dedicated to supporting the operations of the Center so that the mission of IPCC could flourish, thereby bringing to fruition many long-held dreams of the state's first people.

After three decades of operation, the Center has been successful in making those dreams come true by meeting the cultural, social, educational and economic needs of Pueblo people—and by providing opportunities for thousands of visitors to learn about and share in the achievement of the Pueblos through the collections and educational programs of the Center.

The Indian Pueblo Cultural Center's 11-acre campus is home to a permanent collection of artifacts and art from Pueblo cultures dating from pre-Columbian times to the present. The Children's Pueblo House Museum provides hands-on learning experiences for school-aged children throughout the year. New exhibition galleries are devoted to changing historical art and fine art exhibitions reflective of the Pueblo and other Native American people of the Southwest.

The Institute for Pueblo Indian Studies and Pueblo Archives and Research Center also has its home at IPCC. The Institute hosts a large and growing collection of various materials that document many phases of Pueblo Indian history, culture and society and is open to the public.

Other popular public attractions at IPCC include weekend tribal dance performances, art demonstrations by Native American artists and an ongoing calendar of special events featuring local and international educational and cultural exchanges.

In addition to providing a wide array of public events and venues, the center is the hub for thriving for-profit centers managed by Indian Pueblos Marketing, including a large gift shop, Avanyu Art Gallery, Pueblo Harvest Café, Facilities Leasing and Four Winds Travel Center—plus a new fuel/convenience store business.

The Pueblo people have lived in this part of the world for more than 10,000 years and continue to be willing to share their rich cultural heritage with others through the Indian Pueblo Cultural Center.

History & Literary Arts Building at the National Hispanic Cultural Center, featuring world-class art, exhibits, library, genealogy center, performing arts, a restaurant, gift shop and more. Photo courtesy of the National Hispanic Cultural Center.

Un Sueño Hecho Realidad
The National Hispanic Cultural Center

By Carlos Vasquez, Historian

In the fall of 2000, in a cold, drizzling rain, the National Hispanic Cultural Center opened with the new century. It was, and remains, an ambitious project: a center for the study of all things Hispanic, from the performing, visual and literary arts to the history of a rich and vibrant culture.

It also was *un sueño hecho realidad*—a dream made of reality—for generations of Hispanics, not only in Albuquerque but throughout the state. And it took many years and many people to bring the dream to life.

The project began in earnest in 1987 under the aegis of the Hispanic Culture Foundation. At that time, it was conceived as a center for the study of Hispanic culture in *Nuevo México*— New Mexico in its original configuration, which included Southern Colorado—southern Nevada, all of Arizona, southern Utah and parts of Chihuahua.

1945
Kirtland becomes B-29 training base; Sandia Laboratories (former Los Alamos "Z Division") is established to help support the Manhattan Project; first atomic bomb is detonated at Trinity Site rattling windows in Albuquerque; Wernher von Braun's rocket team relocated to White Sands, New Mexico.

Outdoor celebration in restaurant patio at National Hispanic Cultural Center. Photo courtesy of the National Hispanic Cultural Center.

1945
Many Japanese brides return with servicemen; New Mexico Japanese serve in 442nd Regimental Combat Team in Europe; New Mexico soldiers bring Filipino brides home; Filipino nurses, doctors, nuns, and priests also migrate to Albuquerque; nurses and doctors recruited for Public Health Service which later becomes Indian Health Service.

U.S drops atomic bombs on Hiroshima and Nagasaki; World War II ends; United Nations organization is formed.

Blue Cross begins service in Albuquerque.

However, by the time of the official opening, the foundation's leadership had determined that in order to raise federal funds and interest national corporations in donating funds, it would be necessary to change the name, and thus the mission, to the National Hispanic Culture Center (NHCC). Prominent local Hispanic business people and political figures, such as Arturo Ortega, then guided the foundation to the public funds necessary to begin construction in 1999.

Un sueno hecho realidad was the slogan that opened the NHCC and the title of an archival video produced by the Center. The video chronicles construction crews peeling away the history of the WPA-era schoolhouse, Riverside Elementary School, and the demolition of Pete Padilla Park to build the Intel Center for Technology and Visual Arts. In what was to become the History and Literary Arts building, institutional wall tile and lowered acoustical ceilings lighted by cold fluorescent bulbs were replaced with rustic sand-finished plaster, wall *nichos* were backed with tinwork and the corridors lighted by warm tin wall sconces. Exposed *vigas* made the ceiling height more impressive and reminiscent of New Mexican colonial architecture.

To appreciate the challenges met by the founders, the setting, or *coyuntura*, must be considered.

Only a few years before, Albuquerque voters had turned down a performing arts center in the downtown area. Some, including influential merchants in Old Town, saw the new Center as an attempt to circumvent that election and a threat to their businesses as well. Since the bulk of the initial funds came from the state legislature, some criticized the project as another boondoggle concocted by the "Ray and Manny Show" in Santa Fe. At the time, Manny Aragón was a strong President Pro Tempore of the State Senate, while Raymond Sánchez was an equally strong Speaker of the House of Representatives.

After much debate within the various Hispanic communities near Downtown as to where a center would be located, a site in Barelas was chosen. But complicating things was the fact that a strategic piece of the property was owned by a 75-year old widow, Adela Mártinez. She had managed to escape the massive displacement of the early 1970s in "lower" Barelas by Model Cities and Urban Renewal projects. Now, she refused to sell her property to the State of New Mexico for the Center. To build around her meant spending an additional eight hundred thousand dollars in design and grading costs. Ultimately, that was the course of action taken, for both cultural and political reasons. In addition to bringing the mechanical, electrical and plumbing systems on her property up to code, the Center has acted like any other neighbor toward her family since she passed away several years ago. In fact, her son and daughter and their respective families continue to live there and raise their children in their original homes. But at the time, the issue received an inordinate amount of negative coverage from virtually every media outlet in the city.

As a result, public opinion was less than enthusiastic about the project. But at the three-day opening in late October, 2000, more than twenty-five thousand people attended the festivities—highlighted by a visit from then-sitting Vice President Al Gore, the Prince of Asturias, Spain, many local and national dignitaries, and leading figures from the world of Hispanic arts and letters in the United States.

Funding from state and federal governments was secured through the efforts of both of New Mexico's U.S. Senators, especially Pete Domenici, who grew up in the downtown Albuquerque area. From state government the Center received

1946
Bugs Bunny first utters the famous phrase "I knew I should've taken that left turn at Albuquerque!"

Hungarian (Magyar) miners arrive in Albuquerque via Pennsylvania.

1947
Roswell UFO incident occurs.

1948
KOB-TV begins broadcasting.

1949
Old Town annexed into City of Albuquerque to boost population for 1950 census; Western Electric takes over Sandia Labs.

1950
Uranium is discovered near Grants; a bear cub rescued from a fire in the Capitan Mountains is taken to Washington, D.C. National Zoo to become U.S. Forest Service's "Smokey Bear."

Albuquerque population is 97,012. KANW begins first FM broadcast of educational shows. Indian students attend UNM for advanced studies; Arabs from Palestine, Jordan, Lebanon, and Syria flee Palestinian partitioning and Israeli expansion - some come to Albuquerque.

Korean War begins.

1951
University of Albuquerque established.

1952
City passes the nation's first anti-discrimination ordinance; Indian Relocation Act displaces many Indians to urban centers like Albuquerque; Cézar Chávez begins his 25-year campaign for civil rights for workers and Hispanos.

broad support from members of both houses, including Representative Al Otero, who passed the first appropriation for a feasibility study. But ultimately it was Senator Manny Aragón, a one-time resident of Barelas, who secured a considerable amount of state funds for construction. And the land on which the Center was built was donated to the project under the first administration of Mayor Martin Chávez. Thus the combined efforts of public officials and local business figures such as Edward Lujan, president of the Manuel Lujan Insurance Agencies, and former U.S. Ambassador to Spain, Edward Romero, led to the grand opening in 2000.

From the outset, the Center has been driven by a commitment to scale and to quality, with Hispanic history and culture as the cornerstones of public programming. It is situated between the ancient Camino Real de Tierra Adentro and a favored crossing point on the mighty Río del Norte, Río Bravo, the Río Grande—the basis for human occupation of the area throughout history. The fifty-two-acre site has buildings that represent the multicultural mosaic of Hispanic history and includes twenty acres of the *bosque* adjacent to the Center on the banks of the river. A summer high-school student program, Jardines del Bosque Research Station, assisted by local, state and federal agencies responsible for dealing with the river, have begun a restoration and replanting program in those twenty acres. The notion is to create a bio-space for native species, and a place for peaceful contemplation and community interaction.

The programs have evolved during the Center's first five years in operation. Initially, only performing, visual, and literary arts were represented. Now, distance education, media arts, technology, Spanish language classes and genealogical research have been added, with a radio station looming on the horizon. To date, none of the programs has been staffed as planned for. Yet high-quality programming, a hallmark of the Center's activities, is made possible because of dedicated staff, volunteers and docents who are largely responsible for the Center's daily operation and for providing service to the public.

The commitment to history and to the arts is highlighted in the *torreon* fresco project, in its third year of completion, by muralist Frederico Vigil. The 4,500-square-foot concave mural, done in *bon fresco* style, chronicles the history of Hispanics from La Dama de Elche, to the Olmecas, to the current amalgamation of peoples who make up Hispanics in New

Gallery installation in the National Hispanic Cultural Center Art Museum. Photo courtesy of the National Hispanic Cultural Center.

Mexico, including Apache, Navajo, Comanche and Pueblo bloodlines. It will be a focal point on the campus. It is concurrently a work of art, a monument, a sanctuary and a sacrosanct space in which to contemplate and visualize the 3,000-year history of a people.

The name of the Center's restaurant again underscores the *bosque* as pivotal to its location. La Fonda del Bosque operates under private concessionaires and serves New Mexican and Mexican cuisine.

The Intel Center for Technology and Visual Arts is dominated by nearly 12,000 square feet of gallery space. Art exhibits of the highest quality have come through the galleries, while an impressive permanent collection has been built in a few short years under the direction of Helen Lucero and curator Andrew Connors. The Spanish Resource Center, a curriculum repository for K-12 teachers, also is located in this building, as is the Albuquerque branch of the Instituto Cervantes, an agency of the Spanish government. La Tiendita, the gift shop also is here.

At the Roy E. Disney Center for the Performing Arts, three theaters offer video, film and live performances, including symphonic orchestras and large dance and theatre productions. The same complex will house a media arts program whose planning is underway. In the near future, the FM station KANW, in

1953
The United States, North Korea and China sign an armistice, which ends the war but fails to bring about a permanent peace.

1954
BIA Indian Hospital opens in Albuquerque.

1955
Huning Castle demolished, artifact of the town's railroad promoter Franz Huning; Albuquerque Academy opens; TWA Flight 260 crashes into Sandia Peak, taking 16 lives.

operation since 1951 as part of the Albuquerque Public Schools, will broadcast from this complex.

The NHCC also houses a research library with major genealogical collections, allowing people to reconstruct their family genealogies within the context of the region's history. Books, pamphlets, periodicals, manuscript archives, video, microfilm, CD and CD-ROM, audio oral histories—are all available to the public and to professional scholars alike. The collections are housed in the renovated WPA-era History and Literary Arts Building that also houses La Fonda del Bosque restaurant.

Increasingly seen as a major arts venue in the city of Albuquerque, the NHCC, through its rental of performance spaces, also provides the public with an eclectic array of programs from avant-garde theater to traditional symphonic concerts. In time, the Center will become a mainstay of the arts in the city, the state and eventually the nation.

Why, one could logically ask, does such a large, multipurpose and successful complex like NHCC exist in Albuquerque and not in major cities like New York City, Los Angeles or Dallas? Part of the answer: the thirst for preserving regional history, the political and economic strength of the Hispanic community in New Mexico, and the tremendous wealth of culture already preserved here by Hispanics and their allies in the state.

The role of the Hispanic Culture Foundation, which changed its name in 2004 to the National Hispanic Cultural Center Foundation, was paramount. With its capacity to bring private money to bear on the project, it was able to leverage public funds beyond what otherwise might have been conceivable for such a large project, and in such a poor state.

It was the foundation that was able to convince Intel, the largest computer chip manufacturer in the country; the publisher of the *Albuquerque Journal*; leading financial institutions like Bank of America and Wells Fargo, and many other businesses to fund building projects and education programs. Major scientific centers like Sandia National Labs and government suppliers like Lockheed Martin also have been contributors. The foundation has been successful because of the rich bounty of art produced by Hispanics in New Mexico and around the nation, many of whom have donated their work or performed for the center. Tapping the talent abundant among

Hispanics of several generations, the Center has become an important venue for the arts in a relatively short time,

Moreover, Albuquerque has become an increasingly cosmopolitan city in recent decades, capable of supporting a varied and rich cultural agenda. Massive migration from other states and other countries, along with a growing number of high technology industries and an improving array of two-year and four-year colleges and universities in the area have created a vibrant market for art and culture.

As Latinos rise in national prominence, areas like New Mexico, with a large historically rooted Hispanic population, will support venues like the National Hispanic Cultural Center. Clearly, financial, political and demographic power has shifted from Santa Fe, the capital city, to the Albuquerque metropolitan area, which represents fully one-third of the state's population.

Three hundred years ago, the Spanish empire, already in its waning days, founded a *villa* in the middle Rio Grande valley. Only a *villa* and not a *ciudad*, Albuquerque was originally a composite of small Hispanic settlements named after prominent families. Almost by accident, it became a leading urban center in the Southwest when the railroads were unable to reach an accommodation with landowners in Bernalillo and settled for Albuquerque as a site for their repair shops.

Later the new interstate highways came through the center of the city, making it a transit point for the tourist and tuberculosis trade. World War II, with its need for air training bases and weapons laboratories, made Albuquerque, at one point in its history, the city with the most Ph.D.s per capita in the nation.

But across time it has been the climate, the river, the fertile land, and the unique mountains that have beckoned immigrants to this beautiful place. Now, on the banks of the Río Grande, a grand experiment has been launched. Can and will the National Hispanic Cultural Center live up to all the words in its name? Will New Mexicans support a state institution devoted to researching, preserving, and disseminating Hispanic art and culture in all its varieties and all its richness? History is written by us all, on a daily basis, despite how insignificant things may appear at the time. We, together, can determine just how successful this experiment of the National Hispanic Cultural Center turns out.

1961
Winrock Mall, Albuquerque's first shopping center, opens; 16-story Bank of New Mexico building completed as tallest building in downtown. National Indian Youth Council created and relocates to Albuquerque.

1962
President John F. Kennedy visits Sandia Labs for weapons briefing.

1963
Coronado Center opens; work begins on International Sunport; President Kennedy assassinated.

1964
U. S. Civil Rights Act passes; Gulf of Tonkin Resolution allows President Lyndon B. Johnson to go to war in Vietnam; Beatlemania arrives; Bracero Program gives way to Maquiladora Program.

Anderson-Abruzzo Albuquerque International Balloon Museum. Photo © Megan Mayo, Albuquerque Convention & Visitors Bureau.

The Albuquerque Balloon Fiesta began in 1972 when Sid Cutter and Tom Rutherford gathered 13 balloonists in the parking lot of Coronado Shopping Center. A year later, the two formed World Balloon Corporation to host the first fiesta with the official name. It attracted 138 balloons.

Ballooning: A New Albuquerque Tradition

By Tom Rutherford,
Co-founder of the Albuquerque International Balloon
Fiesta and former New Mexico State Senator

It seemed really early to me when I arrived at the vacant lot at the corner of San Pedro and Menaul at 6 o'clock on Saturday morning, April 8, 1972. But at least 10,000 people had gotten there first. Sid Cutter and his pals were about to stage Albuquerque's first hot air balloon race in celebration of KOB Radio's 50th anniversary, and in addition to the world's largest birthday cake, we hoped to stage the world's largest competition among the world's largest birthday balloons. That was the idea anyway. We needed to have 19 balloons to be the biggest, but some competitors' balloons got stuck in air freight in Chicago, so 13 launched that spring morning. No one there could have dreamed where all of this would lead.

Gov. Bruce King, Slim Pickens, Rob Reiner and Penny Marshall were there, as was a balloonist from Iowa, Don Kersten, who only two weeks before had been given the job of finding a site for the first-ever World Championship for hot air balloons.

Well, none of us had ever seen a balloon race before, but we did our best. We laid out sheets of plastic so the balloons wouldn't get dirty in the dust of the vacant lot, and we had trucks to chase the balloons and crews to help. We even had a few sponsors whose names we'd painted on long sheets of oil-cloth with metal poles sewn in the bottom that were to be unfurled on takeoff. That plan didn't work so well, as the first balloon lifted off and rolled out its banner, which immediately ripped loose and hurtled to the ground.

But all in all it was a great success for pilots and spectators alike—so much so that Don Kersten asked if we'd like to make a bid to host the first World Championships. It seemed like a good opportunity for Albuquerque, so Sid and his pals put together a very nice presentation and, believing that there would certainly be lots of competition for such a prestigious award, included lots of incentives for pilots. A few months later we were awarded the right to host the race. (We learned some time later that no one else had even been invited to bid on it.) And so Albuquerque began to become the Ballooning Capitol of the World.

The first championships were held at the state fairgrounds in February of 1973. We had done a computer analysis of the weather that said February would be the best time of year, but computers were new, and we were new at this too—in fact, it snowed throughout the entire event. But the balloons flew, a world champion was named (Sid's brother Bill came in second) and plans began for the next world championship set for two years later.

In order to not lose momentum, a coyote and roadrunner balloon race was held in February of 1974, again at the fair-grounds, and again it snowed. So the 1975 World Championships were set this time for the month of October, which we know now is really the best time for ballooning. In February of 1975 it was decided that some sort of race should be held, so people wouldn't forget about ballooning, so Albuquerque's balloon club AAAA (the world's largest by the way) began the tradition of their Valentine's Balloon Rally, which is still held each year in February and sometimes it still snows.

The second World Championships were an even bigger success, with more and more balloons, sponsors and spectators,

1965
All Indian Pueblo Council adopts Constitution and bylaws.

Immigration and Nationality Act ushers in new immigration of people with needed skills or close relatives of U.S. citizens, bringing additional Japanese, Chinese, Koreans, Indians and Filipinos to Albuquerque.

1966
Sandia Peak Tramway, the world's longest aerial tram, opens; I-40 and I-25 interchange through Albuquerque completed; Sasebo, Japan becomes sister city.

1967
First Afghanis arrive in Albuquerque.

1968
Martin Luther King assassinated.

Albuquerque native, Bobby Unser wins Indianapolis 500 at a record 152.882 mph.

1969
Manuel Luján, Jr. becomes the first Hispanic Republican in the U.S. House of Representatives and serves for 10 years; Americans land on the moon; Iranian-sponsored students attend Naval ROTC at UNM.

1970
Chihuahua, México, becomes sister city; Alvarado Hotel, queen of the City's railroad heyday is demolished.

1971
Albuquerque Sunport renamed Albuquerque International Sunport..

1972
First Kodak Albuquerque International Balloon Fiesta with 16 hot air balloons, Occurring every year in October, the Balloon Fiesta is currently the largest balloon event in the world.

Roy Stamm dumping ballast at the beginning of the balloon ascension, October, 1909. Photo courtesy of the Albuquerque Museum, Image # 1980.075.013.

and were now under the management of a nonprofit board appointed by Mayor Harry Kinney. The World Championships moved on to other countries and are still held every two years. In Albuquerque we have opted for less serious competition. Each year in October, with hundreds and hundreds of balloons, the Albuquerque International Balloon Fiesta still offers the world's largest balloon race and the largest community festival. It has become the most photographed event in the world.

Albuquerque's Ben Abruzzo, Maxie Anderson and Larry Newman were the first to cross the Atlantic Ocean by balloon, and Ben, Larry and Ron Clark were the first to cross the Pacific. Although Albuquerque is home to more of ballooning's world champions, national champions, world record holders and

Balloon Fiesta/ Rio Grande Over 900 balloons float over the skies of Albuquerque at the annual Albuquerque International Balloon Fiesta® each October. Photo by Ron Behrmann.

international award recipients than any other place in the world, the fact is that Albuquerque is the Ballooning Capitol of the World and to the Anderson-Abruzzo Albuquerque International Balloon Museum. This is because of its people — the thousands and thousands and thousands of volunteers who assist the balloonists and thousands more who host pilots and spectators during the event, and the sponsors who defray the significant costs, and all of us in Albuquerque who consider it "our" Balloon Fiesta. That is what sets us apart.

Soft landings.

1972
Convention Center opens; Pete V. Domenici elected to U.S. Senate, still serving in 2006; two Albuquerqueans win Olympic medals in Munich: Cathy Carr and Janet Ely.

1973
City purchases volcanoes on West Mesa to preserve them from undesirable development.

Last U.S. troops leave Vietnam.

ALBUQUERQUE'S ECONOMIC HISTORY

By Sherry Robinson

Albuquerque has come a long way, from subsistence agriculture to computer chips, from wagons to rail to air travel. During the past three hundred years, however, some things have remained constant. The city has had a good position on transportation corridors, the stability to withstand economic ups and downs, and entrepreneurs who could seize an opportunity.

Early Economy

The earliest form of economy, as we know it, began around A.D. 500, when Pueblo agriculture began producing enough surplus corn and cotton to store. The Pueblo people also made pottery, and had domesticated dogs and turkeys.

Around A.D. 1000, Tiwa-speaking people migrated to the Río Grande Valley. They participated in an extensive trade network with other pueblos and tribes. They bartered pottery, turquoise and salt for shell, bison hides, copper bells and macaw feathers. Traders carrying products in burden baskets established trails.

After the Spaniards colonized New Mexico, the trade network changed dramatically. Spanish settlers established several dozen *estancias* in the middle Rio Grande Valley by the 1660s. Spanish requirements of tribute and unpaid labor reduced the Pueblos' surpluses, and the region suffered from devastating droughts and raids by Navajos and Apaches. Pueblo people and their allies drove the Spaniards from New Mexico during the Pueblo Revolt of 1680. Some of the original middle Rio Grande settlers returned in 1693, after the Spaniards reclaimed the area.

Settlers had brought horses, cattle and sheep, which adjusted well to the Southwest and provided an economic base. Sheep provided not only food but wool, which could be sheared, carded, spun and woven for garments and blankets. Settlers augmented their subsistence economy through trade with the Plains Apaches and the rare arrival of a caravan from Mexico.

Initially the Spanish government provided food and tools while the settlers got re-established, but in 1698 the royal treasurer declared that the

Get your kicks on Route 66 in Albuquerque. Photo montage © MarbleStreetStudio.com.

New Mexicans should now sustain themselves. This decree coincided with a severe drought, which lasted until 1704. As streams dried up, pastureland turned to dust and crops withered. Both livestock and people suffered.

When Francisco Cuervo y Valdés founded the villa of Alburquerque in 1706, he chose the place because it would be good for farming. He wrote to his superiors that it was "a good place as regards land, water, pasture and firewood," all required by Spanish law.

The new villa had another attribute that would buoy its economy. It lay along the 1,500-mile Camino Real, the Royal Road between Santa Fe and Chihuahua, and near the Cañon de Carnué (Tijeras Canyon), which provided access to the plains east of the mountains.

The governor invited settlers to join the new Villa de Alburquerque, and farmers from Bernalillo joined people who were already in the area. They began establishing farms up and down the Middle Rio Grande Valley. By this time, the estimated 15 pueblo villages in the area were abandoned. (Isleta and Sandia pueblos would be re-established in the mid-1700s.)

New residents raised corn, beans and squash, as the Pueblo people did. They also brought plants and seeds from Spain, including cabbages, onions, lettuce, radishes, apples, peaches, apricots, grapes, cantaloupes and watermelons, plus such grains as wheat and barley. Crops that came up with settlers from Mexico were chile, tobacco, Mexican beans and the tomato. And they brought a new variety of corn with a long cob and white kernels.

The Indian pueblos had irrigated agriculture, but the Spanish settlers expanded irrigation into a network of *acequias*, or irrigation ditches. The main ditch, the *acequia madre*, siphoned water from the Rio Grande several miles above the villa and carried it to tributary ditches that ran to individual fields.

Sheep ranches were successful here. By the mid-1700s, a herd might have 1,200 sheep and 100 cows. By 1800 herds numbered in the thousands. There was little cash, so sheep became the unit of exchange, at a rate of one or two pesos per animal. Textiles became Alburquerque's leading commodity, and weaving was as important as farming and stock-raising to the village economy. Cobblers formed a smaller cottage industry, selling New Mexican footwear.

Spanish governors tightly controlled the export of products, grain and cattle. The result was to depress the local economy. Alburquerqueans petitioned in 1737 to sell more woven blankets, stockings and piñons to Chihuahua.

Despite the government's prohibitions against outside trade, settlers maintained regular trade with the Apaches, even though they were often at war, and this love-hate relationship came to be accepted. They also traded illegally with the Utes as far north as the Great Salt Lake. In fact, some Spanish settlers carried loads of trade goods east to the plains and west to Utah and searched out the Apaches and Utes.

By the 1750s farms were yielding good crops of corn, wheat, chile, squash, beans, onions and the native tobacco (which they smoked in cornhusk cigarettes). There were also excellent vineyards and orchards of peaches, apricots, plums and apples. The residents raised enough for their own use and traded any surplus at nearby pueblos or in Santa Fe.

Merchants traded New Mexican blankets, woven cloth, corn, piñon nuts, buckskin and buffalo robes for manufactured products from other Spanish provinces. Every year in November, a convoy left for Ciudad Chihuahua. Anyone with goods to sell would rendezvous in Alburquerque, and a military escort would ride with them down El Camino Real. The merchants in Chihuahua knew they had captive buyers, and the Alburquerque traders didn't fare well in this exchange.

Economic Transitions

In 1821 Mexico won its independence from Spain. New Spain, which included New Mexico, became the new Republic of Mexico. This brought significant changes to New Mexico's economy, because the Mexican government no longer prohibited outside trade. New Mexicans had long desired more markets and trade goods, and they wanted to trade with the United States.

That year William Becknell left Missouri and rode west on a trading expedition, expecting to barter with trappers and Indians. On the way, he and his companions encountered Spanish dragoons. Expecting to be jailed, he learned instead that Mexico was now free of Spain. The soldiers encouraged Becknell to go to Santa Fe instead.

In Santa Fe, Becknell and his trade goods were warmly received. His profits inspired him to try again. His route

1978
Albuquerque balloonists Maxie Anderson, Ben Abruzzo and Larry Newman are first ever to cross the Atlantic Ocean in a balloon; New Mexico's Nancy Lopéz becomes first Hispanic to win the Ladies Professional Golf Association Tournament.

1979
Sandia Laboratories is designated as a National Laboratory by Congress. Many Iranians come to attend UNM and to be with friends and family already here.

between Independence, Missouri and Santa Fe became the Santa Fe Trail. New Mexico was now open for business. Items such as tools, building materials, medicines and cloth were quickly sold. The trail came to be called "The Great Commerce Road."

When Santa Fe gained access to trade, so did Alburquerque, as goods now moved south on El Camino. By 1830 trade was booming, and merchants began sending their trains south on El Camino to Mexico. Alburquerque prospered from the increased traffic.

Alburquerque's population grew to 2,547, up from 2,302 in 1821. Some of the town's land barons became traders, adding greatly to their wealth.

In 1846 the United States and Mexico went to war, and the United States claimed New Mexico. Gen. Stephen Watts Kearny and his men arrived in Alburquerque in early September. Residents were harvesting corn and grapes, and the hooves of mules crushed wheat on threshing floors. The Americans marveled at the system of irrigation ditches.

The U.S. Army established a supply depot in Albuquerque. (About this time, the name lost its second "r.") The Army needed corn, flour, beans, mutton, hay and firewood. Antonio José Otero founded Peralta Mills, one of the first mills. So began Albuquerque's first government contractors. The Army hired civilian employees and rented quarters. Soldiers patronized local merchants and saloons. The result was to introduce a cash economy where there had been only barter.

The most prominent businessmen in town were José Leandro Perea, Mariano Yrisarri and Cristóbal Armijo, who were already successful in the old economy and in a position to profit in the new economy. One of the first Anglo merchants was Simon Rosenstein, who in 1852 hired a young German immigrant named Franz Huning as clerk. Five years later Huning opened his own store on the plaza and by 1860 was a successful businessman.

In 1863 Huning bought machinery for a new gristmill and a sawmill, certain that the town would boom. His La Molina de Glorieta became the largest in the valley. In 1864 he began building a new store on the west side of the plaza. By the late 1860s at least nine other mercantile stores were operating, including one owned by Juan Cristóbal Armijo, which he built in 1857, and another owned by Salvador Armijo, who also owned warehouses with branches in other towns. Ambrosio Armijo was then a successful importer and freighter.

The Civil War created a demand for New Mexico wool. When the war ended in 1865, demand for wool increased, boosting the fortunes of men like José Leandro Perea and Mariano Otero of Bernalillo. The price of wool rose from 4 cents a pound in 1862 to 18 cents a pound by 1871. And Indian raiders were no longer a threat, so ranchers expanded their operations.

After the war more Americans began to appear in Albuquerque. Because the newcomers didn't think they could make a living as farmers and stock raisers, they became merchants, tradesmen, restaurateurs, barkeepers and hoteliers. Some doctors and lawyers also hung out shingles. If they wanted to stay in business, they learned to speak Spanish. Some improved their connections by marrying into prominent local Hispanic families.

In 1867 the Army closed the Albuquerque post, plunging the town into an economic downturn that lasted for years. Albuquerque had become a commercial center, but cash was once again scarce, so merchants accepted hides, wool and farm products in trade and then marketed them outside the area.

As the economy began to turn around, newcomers were making their mark. In the 1870s John Murphy opened the first hotel, the Atlantic and Pacific Hotel, anticipating the arrival of the railroad of the same name. The hotel's third owner was Tom Post, who also acquired the ferry business started by the Army and built the first toll bridge at the site of the present Central Avenue Bridge.

Maj. Melchior Werner, a German immigrant who came here as a musician in the army's regimental band, in 1876 opened The Centennial, which would become the first communications center. The hotel housed the post office and the telegraph office. The same year Elias S. Stover, former lieutenant governor of Kansas, arrived and established a store on the plaza, which was soon thriving.

In 1878 brothers Frederick, Jefferson and Joshua Raynolds established the town's first bank, Central Bank, on the plaza. Previously, merchants had accepted deposits, used the money in business and paid interest to depositors. In 1881 a second bank opened; it was First National Bank. The two banks merged in 1884, keeping the name First National Bank.

1981
Ben Abruzzo captains longest balloon flight in history across Pacific Ocean. Albuquerque African-American Cultural Center established. Armenian Cultural Association presents tree to Albuquerque Museum to commemorate 1915 genocide.

1983
Acoma Pueblo opens first high-stakes bingo hall; First Annual Albuquerque Gathering of Nations PowWow held; Helmstedt, Germany, becomes sister city; USS Albuquerque (SSN 706) Los Angeles class submarine commissioned.

1984
El Dorado High School girls basketball team wins 74 consecutive victories—the longest winning streak in the nation.

1985
Route 66 decommissioned as a national highway.

Railroad Boom Town

Merchants and town leaders had long hoped the railroad would serve Albuquerque, and by 1879, the Atchison Topeka & Santa Fe was approaching. Railroad representatives asked Bernalillo landowners Francisco Perea and his nephew, José Leandro Perea, if they would sell land for shops and repair facilities. The Pereas quoted an exorbitant price and refused to budge. It wasn't greed—the Pereas were quite wealthy—but the senior Perea feared the railroad would ruin the wagon freighting industry.

The railroad men continued on to Albuquerque, where they received a warmer welcome. Franz Huning, Elias Stover and attorney William Hazeldine made a quiet deal with the railroad. They began buying land in the proposed right of way, which they deeded to a railroad subsidiary for $1 and a share of profits from the sale of land the railroad didn't need. The deal clinched the railroad for Albuquerque, and the three promoters also prospered. Apparently nobody was critical of the three because everyone expected to gain from the railroad's arrival.

The tracks were actually laid two miles east of Albuquerque to accommodate north-south track alignment and to avoid washouts when the Rio Grande flooded. On April 10, 1880, the tracks reached Albuquerque.

The railroad spawned a second town, as stores and saloons sprouted along the tracks in tents and shacks. In time the new commercial district gained permanent structures of brick and brownstone, becoming known as New Town. The original community became Old Town. They were linked by the Street Railway Company, organized in 1880 by Huning and Hazeldine, with Oliver E. Cromwell. It had eight mule-drawn cars and three miles of track connecting the plaza with New Town and Barelas.

Soon after the railroad arrived, Huning began building the Highland Addition, east of the tracks between Copper and Iron. Now called Huning Highland, it was Albuquerque's first residential development. The Pereas of Bernalillo may have missed an opportunity, but they weren't out of the game. The younger Perea prospered in Albuquerque, in 1881 building his own subdivision, now called the Downtown Neighborhood District. And Huning, Stover, Hazeldine and Perea, along with others, joined to organize the Territorial Fair, which became the State Fair.

An Albuquerque Traction Company Motorette. Milner Collection, Milner Studio, Museum Purchase 1897, G.O. Bonds. Photo courtesy of the Albuquerque Museum, Image # 1992.005.081.

The railroad brought a lot of newcomers, but not all had good intentions. Sister Blandina Segale complained about the "want-to-get-rich-quick people," who were trying to cheat the native-born people out of their land. Fraud was such a problem that the priest had to go door to door warning people not to make their mark on any piece of paper.

Legitimate business people launched a variety of new enterprises in the railroad town. One of the first businesses was J.C. Baldridge Lumber Company, started in 1881. (The business was sold in 2005.) Mariano Armijo decided Albuquerque needed an elegant hotel. In 1882 he built the three-story Armijo House at Third and Railroad Avenue. Two years later local businessmen built the 80-room San Felipe Hotel at Fifth and Gold, which claimed to be the best in the territory. The San Felipe offered a reading room instead of a bar because one of its promoters disapproved of the heavy drinking then common in Albuquerque. But without liquor, the hotel failed. Both hotels burned down in the late 1890s.

1986
Guadalajara, México, and Hualien, Taiwan, become sister cities. Sandia Pueblo becomes gaming tribe.

1988
Albuquerque voted
cleanest city in America;
Manuel Luján, Jr.
becomes Secretary of
the Interior.

1989
End of Cold War sends
small number of
Russians and
Hungarians to
Albuquerque; State
Department opens
immigration from
Vietnam.

Railroad construction brought bridge contractor Angus Grant to Albuquerque. He started a construction company in 1882 and the Albuquerque Electric Light Company a year later. In 1883 he built the Grant Building, which housed the 1,000-seat Grant Opera House. (It burned in 1898.) Grant also owned the water utility—the Water Works Company, which had a city franchise to develop a municipal water system. In 1882 Miguel Otero started a telephone system, which had 34 subscribers a year later. (Albuquerque got long-distance service in 1905.) Huning and Hazeldine started the Albuquerque Gas Company and built a plant that converted coal, shipped in by rail, to gas for street illumination.

Soon after the railroad arrived, the first daily newspaper, the *Golden Gate*, appeared briefly. A few months later Albuquerque Publishing Company acquired the Golden Gate's press and began printing the *Albuquerque Daily Journal*. Huning was president and Hazeldine secretary of the publishing company. Four years later Stover was president. (The *New Mexico State Tribune*, later the *Albuquerque Tribune*, began publishing in 1923.) In 1889 Stover became the University of New Mexico's first president.

As New Town grew, Railroad Avenue (Central) became the hub of retail and entertainment with clothing stores, restaurants, hotels, theaters, general stores and plenty of saloons. The appropriately named Gold Avenue was home to most of the city's banks, real estate firms and insurance agencies.

Three years after the railroad's arrival, Huning built a 14-room mansion called Castle Huning at Railroad Avenue (Central) and Fifteenth Street. (It was torn down in 1955.)

With accessible transportation, the town's economy changed dramatically. Albuquerque became a shipping point for livestock and wool, and the lumber industry boomed. The sheep industry continued to be important—the Perea and Otero families alone had an estimated half-million head—and Albuquerque was still the center of the Southwestern wool trade. Wool warehouses proliferated along the tracks. Rio Grande Woolen Mills employed carders, spinners and weavers and produced blankets and clothing. Wool even contributed to professional sports in the city. In 1880 William McIntosh, a sheep rancher in the Estancia Valley, financed a baseball team, the Albuquerque Browns.

By 1885 New Town was mushrooming, and families were building homes there. In 1891 wholesale grocer M.P. Stamm

Castle Huning, Albuquerque, New Mexico. Photo courtesy of the Albuquerque Museum, Image # 1972-042-001.

filed a plat for the Terrace Addition to sell house lots south of Central to Hazeldine and east of the city limits to Buena Vista. Local people then considered Stamm's subdivision way out on the mesa. It took an hour by horse and buggy to get there.

The forerunner of the Chamber of Commerce started in 1892. The Albuquerque Commercial Club, which organized to attract residents and promote investment, built a handsome, brownstone building at Fourth and Gold. It featured plush meeting rooms, a ballroom, parlors and offices.

The biggest employers in the late 1800s were the Santa Fe Railway shops, the Albuquerque Wool Scouring Mills, the Albuquerque Foundry and Machine Works and the Southwestern Brewery and Ice Company.

In 1893 New Mexico suffered during the financial downturn that gripped the nation. The railroad went into receivership, although it would later recover. What buoyed the Albuquerque economy was agricultural production. Albuquerque's truck farms were then supplying mines in northern New Mexico.

1990
Ashgabat, Turkmenistan, becomes sister city; Petroglyph National Monument established, the only National Monument jointly managed with a city. There are over 20,000 petroglyphs within the Monument and several prehistoric campsites dating over 10,000 years old.

Isleta Pueblo becomes gaming tribe.

Alvarado Hotel with train. Photographer Cobb Studio, Ward Hicks Collection, gift of John Airy. Photo courtesy of the Albuquerque Museum, Image # 1982.181.096.

1991
Some Filipino
dependents of U.S.
Military transferred to
New Mexico from base
closings caused by Mt.
Pinatubo eruption.

By the turn of the century Albuquerque had surpassed Santa Fe as the Territory's commercial center. The Commercial Club raised money to buy a tract of land and gave it to the railroad for a tie-treating plant south of San José.

Construction began on the railroad depot and complex in 1901. And in 1902 the Alvarado Hotel opened. Completed at a cost of $200,000, it was considered the finest railroad hotel of its time. Charles F. Whittlesey designed the California Mission-style building, which featured towers, balconies and arcades supported by arches. It had 75 rooms, parlors, a barbershop, a club, a reading room and a Harvey dining room. It also offered electricity and steam heat, luxuries at the time. Between the hotel and depot was the Indian Building, where visitors could see Indian artisans at work and buy their wares. It was a successful early effort to promote Indian art and sparked a revival in native crafts.

In the early 1900s Albuquerque gained another industry as logging picked up momentum in the Zuni Mountains, west of Grants. American Lumber Company was soon second only to the railroad as Albuquerque's largest employer. Its 110-acre complex was built between 1903 and 1905 near Twelfth Street. Producing milled lumber, doors and shingles, American

Lumber by 1908 was the largest manufacturing company in the Southwest and one of the largest lumber businesses in the country. It employed more than 1,000 men in Albuquerque alone, more even than the railroad. It also had its own fire department and medical staff.

Col. D. K. B. Sellers was one of the busiest developers of the period. He platted and sold 700 lots in the Perea Addition in 1905. Then he subdivided the Grant Addition on North Fifth Street, selling the lots in 30 days. Next he built University Heights.

In 1905 the Albuquerque Gas, Electric Light and Power Company completed its first generator near two sawmills that provided its fuel—wood chips. It would later become Prager Generating Station.

1993
Santa Ana Pueblo opens casino; Outbreak of mysterious Hantavirus in Four Corners area.

1994
North American Free Trade Agreement goes into effect between USA, Mexico and Canada.

Statehood Economy

Railroad Avenue, the city's primary commercial and transportation corridor, became Central Avenue in 1912, the year New Mexico achieved statehood. Business and civic leaders in Albuquerque had worked tirelessly for years to shed its status as a territory.

Albuquerque continued to grow and prosper. The federal government in the early 1900s would become an increasingly large presence, marked by a new building at Fourth and Gold in 1908, a six-story courthouse and office building next door in 1930 and the 262-bed Veterans Administration Hospital built in 1932 southeast of the city.

Downtown began to fill in with more sophisticated buildings, including the Rosenwald Building (1910); the distinctive, white-tiled Occidental Life Insurance Company building at Third and Gold (1917); the first skyscraper, the nine-story First National Bank Building, at Third and Central (1922); the six-story Sunshine Building at Second and Central, the city's first big theater (1923); and the KiMo Theatre (1927).

Neighborhoods grew near the railroad's operations and continued to expand across the East Mesa, enveloping UNM and moving beyond. More than 300 subdivisions were registered between 1900 and 1940.

The lumber industry, following its peak in 1910, began a rapid descent. After harvesting millions of board-feet of timber over the previous decade, American Lumber in 1913 halted operations and went into receivership, throwing hundreds out of work. The Santa Fe Railway, on the other hand, was still growing and in 1914 began building its shops and roundhouse south of downtown.

New technology—the automobile—would threaten the old. New Mexico in 1915 had 4,250 cars and 92 dealers, and these "automobilists" demanded better roads. That year work began on the transcontinental highway system called the National Old Trails Highway, the forerunner of Route 66. In 1920 Albuquerque could boast of 60 miles of graded streets. By 1929 it had 53 miles of paved streets, much of it paved by contractor A. R. Hebenstreit.

In 1917 Albuquerque Gas, Electric Light and Power Company and the Albuquerque Electric Power Company merged to form Albuquerque Gas & Electric Company The company's offices were at 422–424 Central. Its biggest customers then were the trolley company and American Lumber. The lumber company provided wood chips for the first power plant.

Understanding that flood control was critical to Albuquerque's economy, the Chamber of Commerce in 1920 organized a mass meeting of property owners that ultimately resulted in creation of the Middle Rio Grande Conservancy District in 1923.

With the end of World War I in 1918, New Mexico suffered from a postwar recession brought on by drought and falling prices for agricultural products. With the downturn, State National Bank of Albuquerque failed. George A. Kaseman bought up the bank's assets in 1924 and used them to start Albuquerque National Trust & Savings Bank, which became Albuquerque National Bank (later Sunwest Bank).

Albuquerque was then seeing some tourists, but business people wanted more. In 1923 they raised money to build the elegant, Southwestern-style Franciscan Hotel at Sixth and Central because they thought the Alvarado was too small to attract conventions. (Both hotels became parking lots in the early 1970s.)

In 1925 business people petitioned Santa Fe Railway to begin promoting tourism. Always an eager partner in the city's development, the railroad started its "Indian Detours" program the same year. Albuquerque became a hub of the program, which relied on rail and bus to take visitors around to see the sights. Tourism got another shot in the arm a year later when the new Route 66 began moving travelers from

Chicago to Los Angeles. In Albuquerque the route initially passed down Fourth Street.

The city's electric trolley succumbed to competition from the automobile. It went out of business in 1928, and its 12 cars became rooms at an auto camp along Route 66. The trolley was replaced by a privately owned bus company.

In this period the Chamber of Commerce helped create The First American Pageant, a four-day event with parades, concerts, dances, arts and crafts, races and night dramas performed before a papier-maché pueblo. The event was intended to replace the defunct State Fair.

In 1927 Charles Lindbergh's flight across the Atlantic inspired two railroad workers, Frank Speakman and W. Langford Franklin. They leased 140 acres on the East Mesa and with city equipment loaned by Mayor Clyde Tingley after hours, graded two runways. Entrepreneur James Oxnard bought Franklin's interest and added new hangars, lights, beacons and expanded runways. The facility was named Oxnard Field. By 1929 Albuquerque's central location and good airfield had attracted two competing carriers—Western Air Express and Transcontinental Air Transport.

In 1928 KGGM became Albuquerque's first radio station. It began as a mobile station with equipment mounted on a 1.5-ton truck to broadcast a transcontinental foot race when it entered Albuquerque. KGGM later moved into a studio in the Hotel Franciscan. (In 1932, KOB became the city's second radio station.)

Albuquerque gained a second airfield in 1929, when Western Air moved to the West Mesa. It was there that Bill Cutter established a flying school and charter service. The two airlines merged and became Transcontinental and Western Air, or TWA, in 1930.

The first housing boom began in 1922 with the Country Club Addition, named for the club to the east and later known as Spruce Park. Grenada Heights followed in 1925 and a year later, Parkland Hills, Knob Heights, Monte Vista and College View. Seventeen subdivisions sprouted in quick succession on the East Mesa.

In 1928 lawyer William Keleher and contractor A. R. Hebenstreit acquired land from Franz Huning's heirs and platted the Huning Castle Addition. Swamps made much of the land unattractive for development, but that was remedied after the Middle Rio Grande Conservancy began projects to drain

1997
Indian Pueblos first major gaming compact to share revenues with New Mexico; The National Hispanic Cultural Center Act creates a National Hispanic Cultural Center in Albuquerque.

1998
New Mexico celebrates QuartoCentenario, 400 years of European/Hispanic presence; Albuquerque Philippine Historical Society established, one of 21 chapters nationally; Afghan Society established.

Albuquerque Sanitarium, 1913. Photo courtesy of the Albuquerque Museum, Image # 1980.100.003.

2000
National Hispanic
Cultural Center opens
in Albuquerque.

Sierra Grande
"controlled burn" fire in
Los Alamos burns
thousands of acres.

marshy lands and control the river. Albuquerque Country Club moved from the East Mesa to its current location in 1928, which added prestige to the development. They built just a few homes before the Stock Market Crash of 1929. (Most of the homes in this affluent subdivision, which came to be known as the Country Club neighborhood, were built after World War II.)

Health care, including TB treatment, continued to be a thriving industry. St. Joseph Sanitorium was still in operation, and in 1930 the Sisters of Charity completed a new 152-bed hospital to serve the growing city. Southwest Presbyterian Sanitorium by then had become a large complex of buildings. Other new facilities in that period included the 30-bed Santa Fe Hospital for railroad workers in 1926; the pueblo-style Veterans Administration Hospital, built in 1932 at a cost of $1.25 million; and the Albuquerque Indian Hospital, which opened in 1936.

The Great Depression

Albuquerque didn't feel the brunt of the Depression right away, thanks to its isolation, lack of major industries and a spate of construction. But after 1931, the city reeled from business failures and bank failures. It wasn't uncommon to see lines of the unemployed seeking help.

Hardest hit were the small businesses on Route 66. Tourists were replaced by the migration of impoverished job seekers immortalized in John Steinbeck's *The Grapes of Wrath*. In New Mexico, unemployed Hispanic and Indian people formed another wave, traveling north to work in Colorado or south to the southern New Mexico cotton fields.

As the economy began to shrink in 1931, the Santa Fe Railway had to cut its Albuquerque workforce by nearly 40 percent and reduce its work week to four and a-half days. The county tried to help with temporary road jobs, and the federal government provided commodities, but it wasn't enough. In 1933 the Roosevelt administration began the Civil Works Administration, which would provide a 90 percent match for public works projects. The CWA in 1933 and 1934 supported more than 30 projects in Albuquerque, including construction of Roosevelt Park and Tingley Beach, and provided hundreds of jobs.

Bank runs weren't unusual. Merchant Louis Ilfeld staved off a run on First National Bank by showing up with thousands in cash, which he made a great show of depositing. Worried depositors decided that if Ilfeld trusted the bank, they could too. Despite the gesture, the bank closed in 1933, followed by First Savings Bank & Trust Company Banker George Kaseman tried to acquire First National, but federal regulators believed Albuquerque needed two banks. First National was resurrected in six months through a loan blessed by FDR himself, plus the agreement of depositors to become shareholders. One of the board members was real estate promoter D. K. B. Sellers.

In 1934 Clyde Tingley was elected governor. New Mexico was then seeing some tourism but lagged behind all other Rocky Mountain states. In 1935 the Bureau of Tourism learned that the average tourist spent less per day here. That year Tingley launched a national advertising campaign to promote the state's mountains, Indian culture and landscapes, and provided a colorful road map. The campaign drew more visitors that year than the other five mountain states. After the first year, the state increased tourism expenditures by $6 million. Albuquerque enjoyed full hotel rooms and tourist camps, crowded restaurants and out-of-state cars on the street.

Route 66, once again delivered visitors, especially after paving was complete in 1937. The realigned route now crossed Albuquerque along Central Avenue, and diners and tourist courts popped up. The Mother Road helped not only the hospitality industry but Indian artisans as trading posts opened

2001
Isleta and Sandia Pueblos open grand casinos.

2003
Laguna opens grand casino; Albuquerque Indian Center opens.

along the route, offering high-quality rugs and pottery along with the typical tourist fare.

Meanwhile, the Chamber of Commerce was busy. The chamber had labored since the 1920s to relieve Albuquerque's dependence on the railroad. As the Depression took a toll on the First American Pageant, chamber officials agitated to restore the State Fair. To that end the chamber raised money to buy land and construction materials. It also worked to attract federal offices to the city, and in some cases members put up money to offer rent-free downtown offices.

By 1935 the chamber was seeking an Army air base but promoting it quietly to avoid conflict with rivals Santa Fe and Roswell. That year the chamber's board would begin lobbying personal friends and acquaintances in Washington D.C. The prime movers were Oscar Love, Frank Shufflebarger, Ray McCanna and Pierce Rodey, who often traveled to the capital.

The same year TWA suggested that Albuquerque have a municipal airport. With financial help from George Kaseman, chamber boosters got an option on 2,000 acres of land on the southeast mesa. The City Commission agreed to sponsor a WPA project. Gov. Clyde Tingley and two other men attended FDR's second inauguration in 1936 and returned with approval for $700,000.

By 1936 Clyde Tingley had become friends with FDR. Tingley and Sen. Clinton P. Anderson secured an additional bounty of federal funding for the State Fairgrounds, schools, UNM's library and administration building, Monte Vista Fire Station, Jefferson School, Nob Hill Elementary School, Monte Vista Junior High School, Pershing Elementary School, the old UNM Student Union, plus street and sidewalk construction, sewer and power lines and road paving.

With WPA funds pouring in, Albuquerque turned a corner. There were signs of optimism. The most important development in years was the ten-story Hilton Hotel completed in 1939 by New Mexico native Conrad Hilton. Hilton believed Albuquerque was destined for great things.

Also in 1939 the municipal airport opened with one of the longest runways in the country. Boosters said Albuquerque was the "Air Capital of the Southwest." Experts claimed the weather was ideal for flying 97 percent of the year. The city's excellent air and rail facilities were a deciding factor in the selection of a site for Los Alamos Laboratory.

Wartime Economy

By then, war had broken out in Europe. The groundwork laid by chamber representatives paid off when the Army Air Corps leased land east of the city's new airport to build a flight training base, which became Kirtland Field. In 1941, 2,000 men worked around the clock building structures on the base, for a $3 million infusion into the local economy.

The Santa Fe Railway's repair shops and yards, with 1,800 workers, were still the city's largest private employer. The military presence increased rail activity. During the war the railroad operated around the clock to keep rolling stock in condition for unprecedented demands of transportation.

The activity fueled a building boom downtown. In 1940 and 1942, 450 new small businesses opened their doors, and the city's population grew by 3,000. Home builders raced to provide new housing at a rate of nearly one house a day, with an average price of $3,200. The city added 1,200 new water meters in 1941. But as the war effort soaked up construction materials, civilian construction declined as the base continued to add buildings.

The first government contractors of the modern era appeared. The Eidal Manufacturing Company opened a factory in 1943 to assemble truck trailers and tractors for the Army. Eaton Metal Company built metal pontoons used by the military in amphibious landings. Martin Laboratories made parts for autopilot gyroscopes.

The El Rey Theater opened in 1941. It included a restaurant called The Hangar, decorated with a mural of bombers in combat. Albuquerque had eight other movie theaters by then—the Sunshine, KiMo, Chief, Rio, Savoy, Mesa, Coronado and Lobo.

In the 1940s, new antibiotics reduced the threat of tuberculosis. St. Joseph and Presbyterian evolved as modern health-care facilities, but other sanitoria closed their doors. And by then, Lovelace Clinic, which was started by two recovering tuberculars in 1916, had 16 specialists.

Post-War Economy

When World War II ended, many bases and military installations closed. Kirtland Air Field became a scrapping point for deactivated planes. Then the Cold War and the Korean War gave the base new work.

What a collection of museums can be found on the campus of the University of New Mexico—a pedestrian dream.

The Geology & Meteoritics Museum, has dinosaur bones and moon rocks.

Maxwell Museum of Anthropology, preserving the heritage of people who walked the Southwest from 10,000 years ago to the present.

In 1945 Robert Oppenheimer reorganized Los Alamos Laboratory and wanted to move some activities off the hill. He moved Z Division to Albuquerque's Sandia Base, an aircraft maintenance training site next to Kirtland Army Air Field. Z Division then provided engineering design, production, assembly and field testing of non-nuclear components of nuclear weapons. From this rib the government would create Sandia Laboratory in 1948. A year later it became a separate organization, managed by Western Electric and then AT&T. The lab then had 1,742 employees. Meanwhile Kirtland gained a new mission—weapons storage—and the Army added another installation, Manzano Base, in 1952.

The economic impact for Albuquerque was huge. By 1944 an estimated 8,000 newcomers were competing for housing and consumer goods. In 1945 a building boom began. New subdivisions began spreading toward the mountains. In 1950 the *Saturday Evening Post* wrote, "New houses go up in batches of 50 to 300 at a time and transform barren mesas before you get back from lunch." In the four years between 1946 and 1950 the city's area tripled.

In 1946 electric utilities in Albuquerque, Santa Fe, Las Vegas and Deming merged to form Public Service Company of New Mexico. The architect of the merger and PNM's first president was Arthur Prager. The company then had 58,679 customers and 914 miles of electric line. The gas operations were sold to Southern Union Gas Company in 1949.

Between 1940 and 1950 the population more than doubled, from 35,449 to 96,815. Homebuilders scurried to meet demand. Sam Hoffman built the Hoffmantown Addition north of Menaul and east of Wyoming. In 1953, Ed Snow's Snow Heights Addition followed directly south. Harvey Golightly built the Bel-Air subdivision between Carlisle, San Mateo, Menaul and Candelaria. In 1954, Dale Bellamah added the 1,600-home Princess Jeanne Park, named for his wife, between Lomas and Indian School from Eubank to Juan Tabo. Bellamah also built the Kirtland Addition just west of the airport.

West Side development also took root in the 1950s. Homebuilder Leon Watson in 1951 bought land from Florencio Baca, and the development between Central and Bridge near Coors became Los Altos. In 1949 the Black family, which owned the Seven Bar Ranch on the West Mesa, sold 8,000 acres to Horizon Land Corporation. The Blacks in 1947 also built a general aviation airport. (The airport later became the site of Cottonwood Mall.)

By the mid-1950s Sandia employed more than 4,000 people and was the city's largest single employer. Initially they lived in base housing, but soon families began buying homes in the rapidly growing new subdivisions of the Northeast Heights. The population had reached 175,000—a 500 percent increase over 35,000 in 1940.

The city didn't have enough wells to serve this new population, although the supplies of water were then ample. The City Commission, led by the influential former Gov. Clyde Tingley, was slow to extend water lines because Tingley didn't think the city could afford them. A group of Sandia employees, led by Dick Bice and Ray Powell, thought otherwise and in 1952 ran a slate of candidates for City Commission. They won. Bice then devised a strategy to fund the expansion of the water system, and Albuquerque continued to grow.

The Chamber of Commerce realized in the 1950s that Albuquerque couldn't remain dependent on the base and organized the Industrial Development Committee to recruit new industry. Gulton Industries, which opened in 1954, became one of the city's first high-tech industries. The government contractor made monitoring and remote-control devices for missiles and satellites.

Commercial building kept pace with new housing. In 1949 R. B. Waggoman completed the Nob Hill Business Center, Albuquerque's first shopping center. In 1953 the brownstone Albuquerque Commercial Club made way for the 13-story Simms Building, which then became the city's tallest skyscraper.

In 1959 Wright's Trading Post was leveled to build the Bank of New Mexico building. In quick succession more tall buildings joined the city's growing skyline, each vying to be tallest. Two more federal buildings and City Hall went up. At San Mateo and Central the 17-story First National Bank Building became the city's tallest in 1963. In 1966 the 18-story National Building (now the Compass Bank Building), at Fifth and Marquette, became the tallest. In the same period, the Bank Securities Building at Lomas and Second (now the Wells Fargo Building), the PNM building, and the 13-story federal building were also built.

As Route 66 delivered more tourists to the city, Old Town became a tourist attraction and in 1951 was finally incorporated into the city.

The University Art Museum, with a permanent collection including works by Georgia O'Keeffe and changing exhibits.

The Tamarind Lithography Institute is internationally recognized for training, research, and publication of fine art lithography.

Historic Route 66's colorful neon signs are featured prominently along Albuquerque's Central Ave.
Photo © MarbleStreetStudio.com

Concha Ortiz y Pino de Kleven was elected to the New Mexico State Legislature in 1936 at the age of 26. She was the first woman in the United States to be elected Majority Whip in a state legislature, and is believed to be the first Hispanic woman elected to a state legislature. She was re-elected twice to the New Mexico Legislature.

The post-war years also saw the rise of two individuals who would have a big impact on local tourism. In 1945 Bob Nordhaus, who had organized the Albuquerque Ski Club in 1936, returned from the war and started a rope tow at La Madera. Lift tickets were $1. Nordhaus decided to turn his hobby into a business and formed La Madera Company. He bought the club's assets, sold stock, and built a T-bar lift that was the longest in the nation. In 1957 Ben Abruzzo became ski area manager and a year later bought half the assets from Nordhaus. In 1963 they added a double-chair lift and a mountain-top restaurant and changed the name to Sandia Peak Ski Area. A year later they began building the Sandia Peak Tramway. When it was finished two years later, it was the longest single-section tram in the world.

Modern Economy

In 1960 Albuquerque was heavily dependent on Kirtland and Sandia, and that year the base's employment shrank. Realtor Gene Hinkle thought the city needed to diversify and rounded up a handful of like-minded people to form a new group focused on attracting new industry. They included developer Jack Clifford, Bob Nordhaus, Ben Abruzzo, developer Elmer Sproul, homebuilder Coda Roberson, and architect Max Flatow. The new organization, Albuquerque Industrial Development Service, agreed to work closely with the chamber, and the chamber provided funding. In the late 1960s the group raised $1.3 million to recruit industry.

In the 1960s new companies included Sparton Southwest, Boeing's Aerospace Division, EG&G, Levi Strauss and General Electric. Sparton Southwest in 1961 opened a plant on the West Side to make switches for military applications. GE Aircraft Engines in 1967 became the first major aerospace company with an Albuquerque plant; it produces components for commercial and military aircraft engines.

In the 1960s Kirtland's research lab planted the first high-tech seeds. The base then had some of the nation's top laser experts. Their work spawned the city's optics industry, which evolved from government contractors to an independent industry segment whose activities include laser, sensor, component and instrument manufacturing. (The oldest of these companies is CVI Laser Corp., which started in 1972.)

By 1960 the population had reached 201,189, more than double the 1950 census. Shopping centers proliferated to serve new neighborhoods. In 1961, Winrock Shopping Center opened. The same year Dale Bellamah built the Northdale Shopping Center in the North Valley and the Eastdale Shopping Center in the Northeast Heights. Elmer Sproul built Indian Plaza at Indian School and Carlisle. Coronado Shopping Center opened in 1965. They were popular, but it was the beginning of the end for downtown retail.

Activity also increased on the West Side. In 1961 Horizon Land Corporation began developing Paradise Hills. Taylor Ranch and Eagle Ranch followed in the 1970s.

By 1966, I-25 and I-40 were completed through Albuquerque. From the 1950s on, cars, trucks and airplanes began to replace the train for both passenger service and freight.

Health-care facilities grew to meet the needs of a larger population. In 1960 Presbyterian Hospital expanded, and the early complex was largely demolished. In 1966 the Sisters of Charity began building St. Joseph Medical Center, a 12-story facility.

In 1974, H. Edward Roberts, a former Air Force engineer, designed the first practical and affordable home computer—the Altair. His Albuquerque company, MITS Inc., dominated the new industry in the mid 1970s. In 1975, he hired two young men to write computer software: Paul Allen and Bill Gates.

Bill Gates and Paul Allen founded Microsoft in Albuquerque in 1975, and moved the business to Bellevue, Washington in 1978.

Of the 22 heads of household who originally settled in Albuquerque, five were identified as Negro or Mulatto.

A UFO was sighted over Albuquerque during June and July 1947. The Albuquerque reported UFO sightings repeatedly. Residents reportedly watched "space ship" maneuvers from their front lawns.

If the 1960s were an era of construction, the 1970s were an era of destruction. Albuquerque lost its most prominent and best loved landmark when the Santa Fe Railroad demolished the Alvarado Hotel. During a decade of urban renewal, federal funds were used to level entire blocks.

New companies continued to appear. In 1970 the Singer Co.'s Friden Division used the city's first industrial revenue bond to build a plant on north I-25 to produce business machines. Singer soon employed 1,300 people in Albuquerque but in 1976 closed the division and left town. That year Digital Equipment Corp. moved into the plant.

Computers and software—the industry that would later be called information technology—began to take shape in the 1970s. Along with corporate giants Singer and Digital, startups made their mark. Albuquerque was the birthplace of the first personal computer. H. Edward Roberts, a former Air Force engineer, made the first practical, affordable home computer—the Altair. His Albuquerque company, MITS Inc., dominated the new industry in the mid-1970s. In 1975 he hired two young men to write software: Paul Allen and Bill Gates, who started Microsoft here. Roberts sold his company in 1977. Gates and Allen moved their company to Seattle in 1978.

By then the first wave of electronics companies began leaving California in search of lower costs, bigger labor pools and room to grow. One of the few to choose Albuquerque was GTE Lenkurt. It opened a massive plant on the city's East Side in 1971 to make electronic communications devices. By 1982 the company had 1,400 employees.

Other new companies in the 1970s included Amity Leather, Elastimold, BDM, Motorola, the Social Security Administration data operations, and a second Levi Strauss plant. Also building a second plant was Sparton Southwest, which in 1977 opened an operation in Rio Rancho to assemble circuit cards for computers and memory-storage equipment. (That plant moved to Albuquerque in 2004.) Sandia became a national laboratory in 1979.

During the 1970s Lovelace launched managed care in Albuquerque with the Lovelace Health Plan. In 1975 the clinic and hospital merged. Presbyterian Hospital continued to grow, adding Kaseman Hospital in the Northeast Heights. Presbyterian also organized its own HMO health plan and expanded statewide.

Located in the heart of Downtown, Civic Plaza hosts many festivals and special events throughout the year. Photo © MarbleStreetStudio.com.

The 1970s would deliver the biggest boost to tourism since the railroad arrived. In 1972 Sid Cutter organized the first hot-air balloon rally in New Mexico. That April, 13 balloons rose from the dirt parking lot west of Coronado Shopping Center. KOB announcer Tom Rutherford had stirred up excitement, and 20,000 people came to watch. Cutter and Rutherford then organized World Balloon Championships Inc. and submitted a bid to the Balloon Federation of America to host the first world hot-air ballooning championship. The next year Albuquerque hosted its second Balloon Fiesta in conjunction with the first World Hot Air Balloon Championship at the State Fairgrounds, with 138 balloons flying from 13 countries.

Cutter continued to organize and provide financial support to the Balloon Fiestas until he could no longer sustain the financial loss. Mayor Harry Kinney appointed the first Balloon Fiesta Committee, which subsequently incorporated. By 1978 the fiesta had become the world's largest ballooning event.

The 1970s were not good to railroads. The Santa Fe closed its Albuquerque shops, which had employed over a thousand

The Indian Pueblo Cultural Center opened in 1976 to benefit Pueblo people and educate the community about Pueblo Culture. Its main building was modeled after Pueblo Bonito in Chaco Canyon.

In 1922, the All Indian Pueblo Council was organized representing all nineteen Pueblos in New Mexico.

On May 6,1966, Bob Nordhaus and Ben Abruzzo completed the Sandia Peak Tramway. It took two years to build and cost nearly $2 million. It's the longest single span tram in the world.

The Albuquerque Convention Center has high-tech capabilities including high-speed Internet access and computer networking capabilities. Photo © Pat Berrett.

workers for decades. And it turned passenger operations over to Amtrak. (The depot burned in 1993.)

The 1980s saw new changes in the downtown skyline: The First Plaza complex on Second St., PNM's Alvarado Square, the 11-story city-county building, the 15-story Marquette Building, and the Sunwest Bank Building. Construction began in January 1988 on Albuquerque Plaza, a 22-story office tower and neighboring 20-story Hyatt Regency Hotel. The office tower remains the tallest building in New Mexico.

Albuquerque Industrial Development Service had been very busy. As the 1980s began, Albuquerque still didn't have many large manufacturers. But then a second wave of companies expanded outside of California. (The organization changed its name to Albuquerque Economic Development in 1986 and became independent of the chamber in 1992.)

The two biggest high-tech catches were computer chip makers Intel and Signetics. Other major developments included Johnson & Johnson subsidiary Ethicon, a maker of surgical sutures and devices; Sperry Flight Systems Defense and Space Systems Division, a maker of aircraft flight control systems; General Dynamics; Olympus Corporation, a Japanese electronics company producing fiber-optics equipment; Plastech, a maker of plastic component parts for local electronics plants; Roses Southwest Papers Inc., a maker of paper products; and Honeywell, making energy-saving devices.

The city also drew the first back-office operations, including two J.C. Penney operations (credit-card processing center and a catalogue center), Citicorp Credit Corporation, and Baxter Healthcare's billing, collections and financial services.

Signetics, Sperry and Motorola anchored a new high-tech concentration in the north I-25 corridor. Motorola built an 89,000-square-foot plant in 1981 to make communications components and devices. Signetics built a 467,000-square-foot plant to produce semiconductors for the U.S. domestic industry. (The name changed in 1992 to reflect its parent company, Royal Philips Electronics.) Ethicon Endosurgery built a 230,000-square-foot plant on the city's south side. In 1987 Digital Equipment Corporation designated its Albuquerque plant a showcase operation. By then 1,000 local employees produced workstations, video monitors, high-volume printed circuit boards and cables, and harness assemblies.

The early 1980s also saw a worldwide downturn in the computer industry, which prompted Intel and Signetics to delay their plant openings. When Signetics opened its doors in 1982, it had 5,000 applications for 400 jobs. GTE laid off 450 workers, and Pertec Computer Corporation closed its plant.

In 1984 St. Joseph Healthcare added its West Mesa Hospital, followed in 1985 by the Northeast Heights Medical Center and in 1988 by the St. Joseph Rehabilitation Hospital and Outpatient Center (now the Rehabilitation Hospital of New Mexico). In 1987 Lovelace razed its old facilities and built the Lovelace Hospital and Medical Center.

In the 1990s, major companies locating here included General Mills Inc., which makes 100 million boxes of cereal a year; U.S. Cotton, which makes cotton balls and cosmetic supplies; Sumitomo Sitix Silicon (now called Sumco USA), which makes silicon wafers; and Xilinx, which makes programmable

Albuquerque was one of the first cities to pass an ordinance barring discrimination in public places because of race, creed or ancestry. The law was passed on February 12, 1952.

Albuquerque had one of the first chapters of NAACP. The Albuquerque Independent Society organized in 1912 and was renamed the NAACP a year later.

Historic Route 66 was first commissioned in 1926, and the first alignment ran north-south through Albuquerque to include Santa Rosa, Santa Fe, Los Lunas and several Indian reservations. This was mostly unpaved. To make the road straighter, in 1931 federal money was designated to realign it to a now east-west direction. Many parts of the old highway can be seen just beside I-40.

Some Albuquerqueans of note are award-winning author Tony Hillerman; Santa Clara Pueblo-born award-winning artist Pablita Velarde; country music star Glen Campbell; the famous Unsers of Indy 500 fame—Al Sr., Bobby, and Al Jr.; and World War II correspondent Ernie Pyle.

logic chips. Goodrich Corporation acquired Gulton Industries Inc. in 1997. And Southwest Airlines opened a call center. However, Siemens (the former GTE) and Digital closed their plants. In 1993 Lockheed Martin Corporation took over management of Sandia National Laboratories from AT&T.

By this time the biomedical and biotechnology industry, which had started in the 1980s, had become a sizable segment involved in everything from pharmaceuticals and medical technology manufacturing to bioinformatics (specialized software used in drug discovery). Many of the companies were startups or spinoffs from Sandia or UNM.

In 1991 Lovelace Hospital and Medical Center and the Lovelace Health Plan were sold to a private health-care provider, and the Lovelace Foundation spun off as The Lovelace Respiratory Research Institute.

New companies since 2000 include Sennheiser Electronics, which makes communications devices; The Gap, which opened a services center; and Tempur-Pedic, which opened a 750,000-square-foot mattress factory in 2006. However, Philips Semiconductors closed, as did one of Honeywell's two operations. Eclipse Aviation Corporation chose Albuquerque for its headquarters and manufacturing plant and will produce a six-seat commercial jet, the Eclipse 500.

In 2002 Ardent Health Services acquired St. Joseph Healthcare System, which that year celebrated its 100th anniversary. A year later it acquired Lovelace Health Systems and joined the two organizations as Lovelace Sandia Health System. Presbyterian Healthcare Services continues to be a not-for-profit corporation with seven acute-care hospitals, a long-term care facility and a managed-care health plan.

Today Albuquerque enjoys a diverse economy with a stable government sector, healthy manufacturing and call-center segments and a budding aviation industry. The city is home to a growing number of high-tech companies that include aerospace, biotech, electronics, information technology, micro- and nanotech, and optics.

Sources

Biebel, Charles D. *Making Most of It: Public Works in Albuquerque during the Great Depression 1929–1942* (Albuquerque: Albuquerque Museum, 1986).

Bunting, Bainbridge. *Early Architecture in New Mexico* (Albuquerque: UNM Press, 1976).

Davis, Mary. *Albuquerque's Environmental Story.* www.cabq.gov/aes.

Fergusson, Erna. *Albuquerque* (Albuquerque: M. Armitage, 1947).

Fitzpatrick, George and Caplin, Harvey. *Albuquerque: 100 Years in Pictures, 1875–1975* (Albuquerque: Modern Press, 1975).

Garcia, Nasario. *Albuquerque: Feliz Cumpleaños! Three Centuries to Remember* (Santa Fe: La Herencia, 2005).

Sánchez, Joseph P. *The Río Abajo Frontier 1540–1692: A History of Early Colonial New Mexico* (Albuquerque: Albuquerque Museum, 1987).

Sanders, Jeffrey C. *McClellan Park: The Life and Death of an Urban Green Space* (Albuquerque: Albuquerque Museum, 2004).

Sando, Joe S. *Pueblo Nations: Eight Centuries of Pueblo Indian History* (Santa Fe: Clear Light Publishers, 1998).

Segale, Blandina. *At the End of the Santa Fe Trail* (Milwaukee: Bruce Publishing Co., 1948).

Simmons, Marc. *Albuquerque: A Narrative History* (Albuquerque: UNM Press, 1982).

Elfego Baca, a Socorro candidate for sheriff who survived a one-man stand against 80 Texas cowboys in 1884, became a lawyer and district attorney. In 1907, he moved his law practice to Albuquerque and had his combined office and home on Gold Street. Walt Disney Studios created "The Nine Lives of Elfego Baca." Historian Howard Bryan wrote a book about him titled *The Incredible Elfego Baca.*

University of New Mexico was founded in 1889 and held classes in a building at Railroad Avenue (now Central) and Edith.

THE SOUTHERN PUEBLOS THREE HUNDRED YEARS AGO

By Joe S. Sando
Historian and author from Jemez Pueblo

There were few, if any, Pueblo Indians in the Albuquerque area at the time of its founding. The year following the revolt by the Pueblos in 1680, Governor Antonio Otermín returned to the scene of his eviction and destroyed and burned Isleta Pueblo, although that Pueblo did not take part in the revolt. Some of the Indians were taken prisoner and the rest fled to the Hopi country. On his return trip to El Paso, Otermín took the prisoners with him to join those who were taken the year before. Sandia Pueblo also was burned and destroyed, and those Indians fled to the Hopi country.

During the 1681 trip Juan Dominguez Mendoza was second in command to Otermín. Mendoza took his troops as far north as Cochiti but did not destroy any of the Pueblos they visited. Thus Otermín blamed Mendoza for the failure of the punitive expedition.

Meanwhile, Pueblo Revolt leader Po'pay was replaced by Luis Tupatu of Picuris Pueblo, who became the new leader, at least of the northern Pueblos. In July 1683, Tupatu sent an emissary, Juan Punsilli of Picuris, to El Paso del Norte (present-day El Paso). There was reportedly unrest among the Pueblos, as well as continuing drought. The Apaches and Navajos had intensified their raids on the villages. After learning that the Spaniards were gone, they attacked the Pueblos, intent on appropriating the livestock left behind by the Spaniards as well as the villagers' field crops.

Once in El Paso del Norte, after presenting gifts to Otermín, Punsilli stated that the new Pueblo leader, Don Luis Tupatu, had sent him to negotiate peace with the Spaniards and to say that if they should again return to New Mexico, Don Luis Tupatu would aid them in their entry, provided they came peacefully and did not kill the people or burn their homes. That was the Pueblo leaders' hope, but it did not happen that way.

In fact, other Pueblos suffered from the Spaniards' return visitations. In 1687 Governor Pedro Reneros de Posada arrived late in the summer and attacked Tamaya (Santa Ana). The Pueblo's leaders were executed and others taken prisoner and sold as slaves for ten years and were forbidden to return to their homes.

Isleta Pueblo today. Photo © Marcia Keegan.

In 1689 Governor Jironza Petris de Cruzate arrived and destroyed Zia Pueblo. Six hundred Zias were killed and 70 prisoners were sentenced to ten years of slavery. Most of the others fled to Mesa, Colorado, west of Jemez Pueblo. A Zia man, Bartolome de Ojeda, was wounded and taken to El Paso del Norte to be healed. While there he learned to speak and write Spanish. Thus he became a trusted and true friend of the Spaniards.

In 1692 Governor Diego de Vargas came to Pueblo country and reclaimed the territory for Spain. The following year de Vargas returned with colonists, with his friend Ojeda at the point, arriving in Santa Fe October 4, 1693.

The year 1694 may be classified as a fateful year, as many unexpected disasters took place in the Pueblo Indian country. On April 17, 1694, de Vargas, with help from Ojeda and his followers from Zia, Santa Ana and San Felipe, attacked Santo Domingo, Cochiti, and La Cienega Pueblos, all of which were Keresan speakers. On July 24th de Vargas and his troops attacked the Jemez people on San Diego Mesa. In August they attacked San Ildefonso at Black Mesa. Considering the turbulence in the area, members of Cochiti, Santo Domingo and La Cienega fled to Acoma for their safety. The Acomas placed them at Cocima, the mesa north of Acoma.

Meanwhile, following their defeat on San Diego Mesa, the Jemez people were split into three groups. Those taken prisoner were taken to Santa Fe, along with much captured corn and livestock. Once in Santa Fe the men had to help de Vargas fight the Tewas on Black Mesa. The second group fled to the Hopi country. The third group fled to the Northwest near the Navajo country the Jemez called Boulder Canyon. Anthropologists call it Navajo Pueblitos, which is incorrect. Many Jemez married Navajos, so today many from the Navajo Coyote Clan and Young Corn Clan are of Jemez blood. Much of Jemez beliefs and culture is seen within the Navajo culture, and their language is peppered with Jemez words. In fact, the Navajo Code Talkers' word for "P" is a Jemez word. Each November during the Jemez Feast, thousands of Navajos visit the Pueblo to continue long family ties.

On August 14th and 15th, 1696, de Vargas, with help from his friend Bartolome, attacked Cocima, the 375-foot-mesa where the three Rio Grande Keresan peoples had fled. But the attack did not succeed in reaching the summit.

Pedro R. Cubero replaced de Vargas as governor in 1697. In 1698 he and interpreter Joseph Naranjo of Santa Clara and later Santa Cruz went to Cocima to try to return the refugee Keresans to their homes. They succeeded in bringing the refugees from the mesa. They traveled as far as a beaver pond full of water, a *laguna*, where they stopped to rest. The

George Montoya of Santa Ana Pueblo. Photo © Marcia Keegan

refugees liked the place so they asked the governor if they could build their new home there and not return to the old place, which did not have as much promise of freedom. Permission was granted, and on July 2, 1698, the newest Pueblo, Laguna, was founded.

In 1702 more Isleta Tiwas returned from Hopi country and settled at Alameda. In 1708 they were moved to Isleta Pueblo by Fray de la Pena and settled at an area they named Oraibi. They also established a new church, San Augustin.

In 1716 many of the Rio Grande Pueblo refugees in the Hopi country returned, after some Jemez people had traveled from Hopi to ask if they could return. So Acting Governor Captain Felipe Martinez gathered an army of Pueblo men from many villages to challenge the Hopis if they put up a resistance. After waiting for a favorable report on rainfall to the west, the army set to try to return the Pueblos to their former homes. The size of the expedition alone may have caused the Hopis not to challenge them. It was a peaceful adventure, and many—mainly Isleta Tiwa and Jemez— returned to their homes, bringing a new dance the Isletas call Evergreen Dance and the Jemez call Hopi Dance.

The Sandia Tiwas returned to the Rio Grande valley in 1742. Earlier, in 1733, they had petitioned Governor Gervisio C. Gongora for permission to return but with no results. When they finally returned in 1742, they were temporarily placed at neighboring pueblos. They were called Moquinos because, according to the Spaniards, they had returned from Moqui land. On January 23, 1748, the Sandias were granted permission to reoccupy their former home, and on April 5th, they were granted title to their land.

The time period described was indeed a time of turmoil, but eventually peace was restored. Gradually many of the remaining Pueblo Indian refugees returned to their homes. By the early-to-mid-1700s, the Pueblo Indians and their Spanish neighbors had begun to cooperate in the face of their common enemies, the Apaches and Navajos.

So this is the story of what was going on with the Southern Pueblos during the time the city of Albuquerque was founded. At that time, the Tamaya from Santa Ana had two farming communities in that area, *Buria cana* (Butterfly Place) and *Queisti Ha* (Hane-east). With their loss of farming land, the Tamayas first purchased irrigable farmland from Manuel Baca in 1709. Later they purchased more land, which they call "Ranchito," where they live today.

Living as they did, the two groups called one another *vecinos* (neighbors) and became *compadres* as they celebrated christenings, weddings, feast days and victories over the raiders. The celebration of saints' feast days in both the Indian and the Spanish communities continues today. This is the origin of the unique New Mexico culture, which is a combination of Indian, Spanish, and Anglo cultures. Spanish became the trade language, and the Spanish and Indians adopted each other's tools and farming practices.

In 1820 Acting Governor Facundo Melgares granted the Pueblos equal citizenship in the province. The following year, after Mexico had gained its independence, the government, through the Plan of Iguala, again granted equal citizenship to the Pueblos. So the Pueblos were equal citizens when the first Americans arrived in 1846. In 1855, however, the United States Territorial Legislature took the right to vote away from the Pueblo people. It would not be restored until 1948, when Miguel Trujillo of Isleta Pueblo won a court case that provided Indians with the right to vote.

Despite their tribulations, the Pueblos were most fortunate that it was Spaniards who colonized this area, because the Pueblo people were granted full citizenship and rights to their lands. In addition, they were included under the Guadalupe Hidalgo Treaty, which protected the Spanish land grants to the Pueblos. After the Americans settled the area, however, the Pueblos lost much land through the Homestead Act and the Taylor Grazing Act, as well as by decisions by the Pueblo Lands Board, on which

San Antonio Church at Sandia Pueblo. Photo © Marcia Keegan.

the Pueblos were misrepresented. However, the Pueblos are still today living where the Spanish invaders found them, while other Indian tribes,
which met the English, French and Russians, were moved to less desirable
areas and lost much of their language and native religion. Although the
Pueblos accepted Roman Catholicism from the Spaniards, they maintained
their native religion, which they still practice today.

OLD TOWN

By Tomás Atencio

Adapted from the forthcoming book A Tale of Two Towns: from Alburquerque to Old Town

Toward the end of the nineteenth century, Albuquerque was much like other small cities located along the Rio Grande. Adobe buildings clustered around a central plaza, anchored by a Catholic church. Farm and ranch land surrounded the town and provided food. The Army depot, established there in 1846 to help contain the Indian tribes, had left in 1867, and a simple, agrarian trade-dominated economy had returned. The pace of life was slow, flowing with the seasons and the river.

All this changed with the coming of the railroad. The Atchison, Topeka and Santa Fe Railroad had organized the New Mexico and Southern Pacific Railroad company and begun building south towards Albuquerque. By early 1880, however, it became clear that the railroad was not going to go through the town but instead run about one-and-one-half miles to the east. The land further away from the riverbed was more suitable for tracks; going through the town would have passed though an area that was frequently flooded. Almost overnight, makeshift buildings went up alongside the tracks and New Albuquerque ("New Town") was born. The original Albuquerque became what we know as Old Town.

In the meantime, the boom and bust pattern that had characterized Old Albuquerque since the territory's annexation to the United States was in a boom phase. Up to 1881, Old Albuquerque still had doctors and lawyers and a plaza full of activities, with pedestrians, burros and freight wagons stretching miles up and down El Camino Real. Streets were crowded, as vendors from nearby villages peddled their fruits, meats, vegetables and cheese. Old Town seemed to be intact. It had continuity and order, something New Town with its board shacks definitely lacked. But by the fall of 1881, New Town achieved an air of permanence, and the exodus from the Old Plaza began.

In its infancy New Town was known for its board shacks, sandy streets, bars, speakeasies, brothels, English-speaking Catholic churches, Protestant churches, private and public schools, expanded commercial activities and much more. The people running New Town in its early days were a few pre-railroad entrepreneurs and civic leaders: Franz Huning, William Hazeldine, Elias Stover and E.K. Wilson. Huning had arrived in Old Albuquerque in the early 1850s. Hazeldine and Stover followed the

Native American artists selling jewelry and pottery under the portal at La Placita Dining Rooms, on the Plaza in Old Town. The building housing La Placita is the former Casa de Armijo, one of the oldest structures in Albuquerque. Photo © Marcia Keegan.

scent of good business opportunities linked to the prospects of a railroad passing through Albuquerque. Wilson came with the Raynolds Central Bank in the late seventies. Their visible control of civic and political affairs eventually subsided, but in their active lifetimes they did not yield their status as principal directors of almost every major capitalist venture in the area. They had one Mexican associate, whose relationship with them varied, depending on his political ambitions. That associate was Santiago Baca from Old Albuquerque.

The railroad opened the territory to many more people than had ever before ventured into Albuquerque. These newcomers differed from pre-railroad Anglos in many ways. Many were insensitive and prejudiced towards the native Mexican population. Eventually this set the stage for relationships between the old and the new society. Old Town was a physical symbol of the traditional Mexican community that inhabited the mid-Rio Grande Valley—the community of shepherds and subsistence farmers. It was the counterpart to New Town, and the two towns were destined to be in constant conflict with each other.

As the new residents of Albuquerque created their New Town, the Mexicans retreated into their Old Town enclave. In New Town, business leaders grouped around the Aztec Club, a social club that had no Mexicans among its members and only Hazeldine, Stover, and Wilson of the pre-railroad Anglos. In Old Town, Mexicans and the pre-railroad Anglos who sympathized with the Mexicans united around such cultural buttresses as the San Felipe de Neri Church.

A one-and-a-half-mile space gap and an immeasurable cultural chasm separated the two towns, which were connected by a horse-drawn railroad street car driven by a Mexican and owned by Huning, Stover, Hazeldine and Wilson. On a piece of land located on the eastern edge of the Old Town district and the western edge of New Town, Franz Huning built a Germanesque dwelling known as Castle Huning. He claimed that when he stepped out the east side of his house he was in New Town; on the west side he was in Old Town. Thus, he was part of the past and part of the emerging present.[1]

By the time Albuquerque New Town was an incorporated town, Old Town had already lost the right to the name Albuquerque. Three years before incorporation, New Town had acquired a post office. The original Albuquerque post office in Old Town continued, causing confusion and delay of mail. The federal office inspector resolved this by closing the Old Town post office. Angered, the people from Old Town petitioned and won back their post office, but lost the name Albuquerque. The post office was officially called the Armijo Post Office. Later it became known as the Old Albuquerque Post Office, and today it is the Old Town Branch of the Albuquerque Post Office.

ALBUQUERQUE OLD TOWN

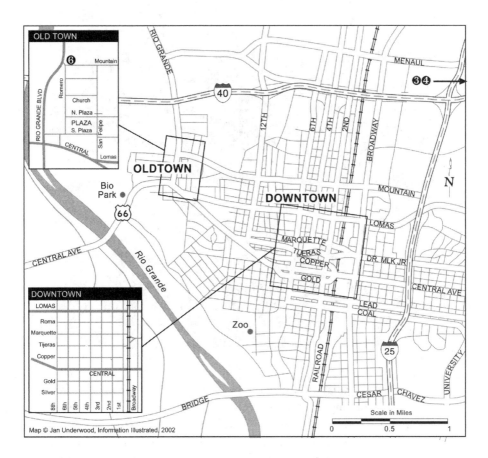

Map © Jan Underwood Information Illustrated, courtesy of Albuquerque Convention & Visitors Bureau, **www.itsatrip.org**.

Santiago Street [now Romero Street], ca. 1880, Cobb Studio, gift of John Avry. Photo courtesy of the Albuquerque Museum, Image # 1982.180.843.

From its original composition of board shack structures, rowdy saloons and gathering places for the un-ambitious, New Albuquerque grew into a railroad town much like any other American town. In time, it displayed elegant residences and two-story, hewn-stone buildings, where the young, sophisticated men and women graduates from eastern universities lived and conducted their business affairs. The dry, sunny climate attracted many Easterners suffering from tuberculosis. To meet their needs, sanitariums were built, and business enterprises evolved around the emerging health industry. New Town soon claimed two private schools and four ward public schools. The University of New Mexico silhouetted the horizon beyond the town's eastern boundaries. Closer to the center was the Ada Philbrick Kindergarten. By 1900, there were sixteen churches, most of them Protestant, and one synagogue. Social activities evolved around the Commercial Club, where the young ladies' Merry-go-Round Club and the men's Bachelor Club gathered for festive occasions and good times. New

Town had the Grant Opera House and other playhouses and theaters. The Alvarado Hotel served as a political and social center.

As New Town progressed, Old Town declined. The disparity between the two meant more than a New Town leaving its aging parent behind. Racial and ideological nuances permeated the split. An example of this was a statement during the early days of New Town's existence by the *Albuquerque Morning Journal*: "The decadence of old Albuquerque is only additional proof of the fact that where the Anglo Saxon meets the Latin race, the latter falls behind and soon ceases competition."[2]

The Rio Abajo Elites

Old Town was home to subsistence farmers, cattle tenders, and sheep-herders who characterized the Mexican community of *Rio Abajo*, that portion of the Rio Grande Valley that stretches between Albuquerque and San Marcial, including the present-day towns of Belen, Los Lunas and Socorro.

It was also the bulwark of Rio Abajo elites, heirs of those post-Pueblo Revolt soldiers—*estancieros* who traversed through several generations to become freight managers, brokers between United States and Mexico trade, political leaders during the Mexican National period and finally ushers of the rail cars into Albuquerque.

Ambrosio Armijo, Sr. died in 1881. He was owner of the Casa de Armijo, which went through many incarnations and is now La Placita Dining Rooms. His widow, Candelaria Griego de Armijo, remarried, becoming the wife of Bernard Ruppe, a New Town immigrant in the

Old Town Plaza, 1890. Photo courtesy of the Albuquerque Museum, Image # 1977.133.001.

Above: part of Casa de Armijo. Casa de Armijo and the San Felipe de Neri Church are believed to be the oldest structures in Old Town. The first owner of Casa de Armijo was Don Juan Armijo y Maestas, who sold the house to Ambrosio Armijo, a relative, around 1844–45. Ambrosio added what is now La Placita Dining Rooms to the west around 1882. When Juan Zamora purchased it from Armijo's widow in 1906, he envisioned a movie theater of silent movies and a gathering place for youth. The enterprise did not generate enough money even for maintenance. He sold the run-down building to Brice and Nelda Sewell in the fall of 1930, when it was restored under the direction of UNM architectural and art teachers and students. Photo © Marcia Keegan.

patent medicine and retail drug business. The large hacienda-like dwelling on the east side of the plaza slowly declined as Candelaria's resources dissipated. In 1906, she sold the run-down historic *plazuela* to Juan Zamora. Ambrosio's eldest son, Perfecto, thrived in county politics and joined his brother, Mariano, in real estate development in New Town.

In 1884, Juan Cristóbal Armijo died. He made news in the 1850s when he killed an Anglo in his store in Los Ranchos during a confrontation stemming from a political dispute over the question of statehood. He was acquitted. Juan Cristóbal's son, Justiniano, known as Justo or J.A., was a founding director of the First National Bank and after a stay in New York returned to New Town. He served as New Town's postmaster for a period.

Salvador Armijo, the largest farm-worker-employer in the area, with sheep ranches and fertile farmlands from the Rio Grande valley to Arizona, died in 1879. He left his daughter, Piedad, and her husband, Santiago Baca, financially secure.

Manuel Armijo died in 1882. His obituary described him as a man who helped make at least part of the history of this territory. Manuel and his brother Rafael fled to Texas with General Henry Hopkins Sibley's retreating invaders after their month-long siege of Old Albuquerque in 1862. Armijo's property was confiscated and sold at auction, but when he came home, he lived his last years in a one-story house near the old court-house and died at age 80 among friends, esteemed by all who knew him.

Cristóbal Armijo, Ambrosio and Salvador's cousin, outlived all the Old Town Dons. A man whose wealth became legendary and the source of much folklore, Armijo was said to have traveled frequently to Mexico, where he banked his money, although he was a founding director of the First National Bank. He was fond of playing the guitar and was an avid gambler. Cristóbal was married to Juanita Romero, probably of the Romero family that later did well in the slaughterhouse business. They had one natural daughter, Flora, who, some say, supported the Mexican Revolution of 1910. Few facts are known about Cristóbal Armijo's wealth, but lore about Flora, who inherited his wealth, abounds. It is said that what she did not lose in the revolutionary effort had been hidden by the old patrón in the walls of his big house on the southeast corner of the plaza.[3] The house was purchased by Florencio Zamora, Juan's older brother, around 1910. Legend has it that Florinto, Zamora's laborer, uncovered the cache while digging an outhouse. Zamora ran a butcher shop, and in 1941 his house served as office of the *Old Town News*. Heirs of Zamora still own the house, which now houses Plaza Primorosa and Plaza Indian Trading Post as well as the Casa Fiesta Restaurant.

Henry Springer, the Prussian immigrant businessman, died in the early 1880s. Destiny deprived him of the opportunity to test his business

In 1910 Florencio Zamora bought this building from Cristobal Armijo and moved his business there. This shows the *portal* part of what is today called Plaza Primorosa and Plaza Indian Trading Post. Also under the portal is the Casa Fiesta Restaurant, and to the south are curios shops and other commercial outlets. The property is still owned by Florencio's descendants. Photo © Marcia Keegan.

in the 1870s–80s, this was the location of Henry Springer's Mint Saloon. Springer, who had immigrated from Bavaria after the Civil War, had land holdings that stretched to Arizona. Springerville was named after him. His empire collapsed after the floods in the mid-seventies. He recovered but died at the beginning of the railroad boom. In 1910 Henry's son Manuel built a two-story Queen Anne mansion, with a dwelling on top and apartments and other businesses on the ground floor. Some time after the resurgence of Old Town in the mid to late 30s, Springer sold his Queen Anne to J.R. "Dick" Bennett and his wife, who had a restaurant called La Cocina. The property is now rented to the Covered Wagon, a very well known Indian curio shop. Photo © Marcia Keegan.

acumen and affable personality in New Town developments. His sons, Manuel and Luis, continued in the general store and grocery business in Old Town's South Plaza. In 1914, Manuel built a two-story Queen Anne building next to his store. It is currently owned by Mrs. J.R. Bennett and serves as an upstairs dwelling and a curio shop complex at the ground level. Henry Springer's daughter, Mary (Meres) married Jesús Romero, who was to serve as Old Town's *patrón* for the first three decades of this century.

William McGuinness, the journalist-publisher whose advocacy for Old Town persisted, lived almost two decades into the twentieth century. One of his sons, M. J. (Miguel) McGuinness, became a well-known New Town attorney. A daughter, Nellie, married Eliseo Sánchez, a recent immigrant from the Rio Abajo subsistence farms.

Santiago Baca, Salvador Armijo's son-in-law and the one Old Town resident to straddle the Old and New Town economic and political boundaries, died in 1909. In 1885, while county sheriff, he conducted the controversial pre-election survey of eligible voters for New Town's incorporation election. In 1887, the land bequeathed to his wife, Piedad, by her father was placed in trust to the Bernalillo County Commission pending Baca's "full accounting" of money collected as sheriff and ex-officio collector for the county. After various legal maneuvers, in 1893 his daughter

Francisquita Baca de Chávez purchased the family inheritance at public auction. Baca spent his last days in the stately Salvador Armijo house and remained active in county politics until his death. That house at Rio Grande Boulevard and Mountain Road most recently was the Maria Teresa Restaurant.

Franz Huning saw his business, the first Anglo mercantile store in Rio Abajo, benefit from the fall of Manuel and Rafael Armijo. Huning lived into the twentieth century. An Anglo who lived in Old Town before and after the railroad, Huning arrived in Old Albuquerque in the early 1850s, brought his German wife from St.Louis about ten years later and established their residence near the plaza. Franz Huning died in 1905.

Change Comes to Old Albuquerque

The elites had died. The wealthier of their offspring had left town. The rest stayed. Among them were the descendants of the rising middle class of the 1870s, the children of such men as Manuel García, Gregorio García, Manuel A. Romero, Henry Springer and Vicente Romero. The subsistence farmers, the sheepherders, and cattle tenders all stayed. Old Town was made up of people bearing names such as García, González, Gutiérrez,

Up until less than a decade ago this was the Maria Teresa Restaurant, still owned by descendants of Salvador Armijo who built and lived in the house until he died. He was one of the wealthiest landowners in the Old Town area and one of the the largest employers of farmworkers. His son-in-law, Santiago Baca and his wife Piedad, inherited the house and the businesses. Photo © Marcia Keegan.

These buildings stand between Cristobal Armijo's and the Springers' structures. Now they house shops and galleries. Photo © Marcia Keegan.

Durán, Lucero, Chávez, Candelaria, Nuanes, Moya, López, Trujillo, Anaya, Perea, Zamora, Ruiz, Griego, Gabaldón, Carbajal, Romero, Ortiz, Sánchez, Martínez, Armijo, and a sprinkling of others. Hispanicized Anglos such as Springer, Vau, Werner, McGuinness, Pohl, Pohmer, Murphy and Hunick added to Old Town's population as the nineteenth century came to a close. These Old Town residents continued at the tasks of the small farmer, cattle tender, sheepherder, grocery store operator and bartender, or as wage earners in the enterprises growing out of New Town developments.

Old Town Immigrants

As New Town welcomed the Easterners, Old Town drew its own immigrants. There were some Anglos who escaped the New Town hustle and bustle in Old Town but did not Hispanicize. Some Mexican Nationals moved to Old Town, as others before them had in pre-railroad years. But most of the newcomers were New Mexican subsistence farmers from the Rio Abajo region seeking employment.

Rio Abajo immigrants to Old Town usually worked in the Blueher or Mann truck gardens or at the American Lumber Company Mill and Manufacturing plant (commonly known as the Sawmill) northeast of the Old Town settlement. A few Old Town residents worked for the railroad. Most of the railroad workers were drawn to Barelas, however. It borders the railroad tracks south of New Town and assumed an air of progress and urbanism much earlier than Old Town. Bareleños were industrial wage earners, who, as opposed to Old Town farmers and sawmill workers, perceived themselves at the upper rungs of the Mexican social class ladder. But the cultural value orientations of both neighborhoods did not differ.

Those who came to Old Town, many of them *genízaro* descendants, carried the traditions of subsistence lore and folk Catholicism that had dominated their lives in the isolated villages. In Old Town the traditions found re-enforcement for a while, as the life styles of the villages and of Old Albuquerque coincided. Gradually the influences of the growing American city a mile away caused the traditions to begin to give way to modernity.

The cultural props found in Old Albuquerque were important for a gradual transition from the farm to a neighborhood adjoining a city. But the immigrants' introduction to quasi-city life was not pleasant in other respects. They were poor and brought almost no resources to Old Town. They accommodated themselves with relatives or acquaintances living in the area, settling down temporarily in the small, flat-roofed adobe houses strung along the back streets and alleys off the old historic plaza.

The area between Church and Charlevoix Streets north of the church was one of those receiving neighborhoods. These new arrivals shared their patios and back yards with roving animals during hot summer

The Aceves Old Town Basket and Rug Shop was built by Florencio Zamora in the early 1900s; he ran a butcher shop there. Around 1910, he sold the place to Charles Mann, who ran a grocery store. The building is now part of a large complex known as Plaza Don Luis. Photo © Marcia Keegan.

The Blueher Queen Anne mansion built in 1892 sits behind the Pueblo-like structure added in a 1950 renovation. This part of the building is now La Hacienda Restaurant and Indian Gift Shop. Photo © Marcia Keegan.

nights. In the winter months, families squeezed into one or two rooms, sleeping on rolled-out mattresses on dirt or bare wooden floors. As men found jobs, they purchased land in the surrounding area and continued in the Rio Abajo farming tradition. Those who could not afford to buy property rented indefinitely around the Plaza at reasonable prices. The largest "apartment complex" was Casa de Armijo, then owned by Juan Zamora.

La Plaza Vieja (Old Town), bruised and tattered by the force of change, remained alive and vital in its own way, peripheral to a growing city a short distance away. From within, Old Town was a community unto itself, sustaining its own identity and individuality.

Old Structures and New Leaders

The Truck Gardeners

Herman Blueher and the Mann brothers came to Albuquerque in 1882. By 1896 Herman Blueher had leveled off an old adobe structure that had been rented by the Army from Cristóbal Armijo in the vicinity of today's Albuquerque Museum and turned the surrounding land into a thriving garden. He also built a Queen Anne mansion in 1892. Now part of La Hacienda Restaurant and Indian Gift Shop, the building underwent Pueblo renovation modification in the 1950s.

The Bluehers enjoyed good relationships with the native Mexican community. They employed many Old Town residents and sold garden products to their neighbors at reasonable prices. Old Town children used the Blueher irrigation pond as their swimming hole. And the small patch of grass at the center of the plaza in later years was kept alive with water from the Blueher well.

Just north of the Blueher gardens was John and Henry Mann's garden. On the current site of the New Mexico Museum of Natural History, John built a two-story house that was destroyed in the 1940s. The Manns are remembered more as storekeepers than farmers, since Charles ran a grocery store on the plaza in the old Zamora store, today's Basket Shop.

One of the most successful of the Mexican truck gardeners during the first part of the twentieth century was Eliseo Sánchez. The Sánchez farm covered the area between Rio Grande Boulevard and Montoya Street to the west and between present-day Dora Avenue to Mountain Road. At the western end of the farmland, Sánchez had his farmhouses, where the family lived in the summer months. Eliseo Sánchez died in 1946 and his wife, Nellie McGuinness Sánchez, in 1951. The plaza property was sold after Nellie's death and the farmland was developed as the Jake Baca Addition. Eliseo and Nellie's, daughter, Lucila Baca, resided in the Baca Addition until her death in 1990. Eliseo's grandson, Rudolph Baca, a state legislator from the Old Town District in 1970, was a leader in the 1966 Church renovation dispute and the 1980 Liquor Controversy.

There were many other such farms in and around Old Town. The Jesuits had an orchard and vineyard extending eastward along Marble Street and Old Town Road from San Pascuale Street. Known as the Priest's

Entry to Old Town Plaza from the east, just south of the Albuquerque Museum. This was the site of the Reagan and Messick Gardens in the 1880s, subsequently purchased by Herman Blueher. The Blueher gardens extended from this site north to where the Albuquerque Museum is today. To the east, the property included Blueher pond, where Tricentennial Tiguex Park is today. Photo © Marcia Keegan.

This was Jesús Romero's general merchandise store. His brother-in-law, Luis Springer and his wife Luciana lived there after Jesús died in 1935. It now houses the Some' Gallery and other galleries and shops. The building includes a large house with a courtyard. Photo © Marcia Keegan.

Garden, the place was sold to the Roehls around 1919. The Pereas, Zamoras and Garcías also had farms near the Plaza. The Lewis orchard, contiguous to Sánchez's property near present-day Mountain Road, was later owned by Luis Springer, Henry's son. In addition to these twenty-or-so acre farms, many more people owned smaller parcels, where subsistence farming in the Rio Abajo tradition continued. These part-time farmers had steady jobs at the sawmill or were wage earners in the larger Old Town truck gardens. Later on some worked in the New Town services industry.

Gradually the farmland has been filled with buildings. In some places the outlines of irrigation ditches allude to the earlier farming days. In the Blueher Garden site now stands the Albuquerque Museum, where photographic archives revive in older people remembrance of days past. The Blueher pond and village water hole is the City's Tricentennial Tiguex Park, a grassy monument in memory of the area's first inhabitants, the Tiwa Indians. John Mann's farm, the inactive old *camposanto* (cemetery), fittingly now hosts the New Mexico Museum of Natural History.

El Patrón

With the demise of the Rio Abajo elites, Old Town lost one kind of *patrón*. Those *patrones* owned most of the economic resources and had considerable power and authority over the lives of the rest of the residents of the community. In their place emerged a new patrón. He shared some characteristics with the elites, yet the new patrón was more like the "City Boss" who had economic power, but his visible power was generated through a political machine sustained by patronage. In Old Town the new patrón was Jesús Romero.

Between the turn of the century to the mid-thirties, Jesús Romero was legend. He was both respected and feared. To some people he was known as Don Jesús; to others *el cacique* (chief); and to others, he was *tío* (uncle), whether he was in fact an uncle or not.

Romero was born in 1859. Although he was educated at St. Michael's, the Christian Brothers' college in Santa Fe, some people report that Romero could neither read nor write and that his wife, Mary Springer, conducted his correspondence and bookkeeping. Mary was Henry Springer and Placida García Saavedra's daughter. She had been a student at the Albuquerque Academy in the 1870s.

Don Jesús displayed his political power as head of the Old Town Republican machine and a leader in the Bernalillo County and State Republican Central Committee. He also held several important county government posts. These positions and his retail store business enhanced his social status and eventually transformed him into one of the wealthiest men in the Old Town area. In the early 1890s, Romero worked in the county coroner's office. In 1895 and 1896, he was county commissioner. In

Built by Jesús Romero between 1915–17, this was the last dwelling to be built on the Plaza itself. Now it hosts the Amapola gallery, an ice cream and yogurt place and other shops. For a time in the mid-1900s, the Romero home was the Francis Lynn Home for unwed mothers. Photo © Marcia Keegan.

1897, Jesús Romero became chairman of the Bernalillo County Commission. He later served as Bernalillo County probate judge. Between 1909 and 1913, Romero was county sheriff and the last man to preside over a public hanging in Albuquerque.

Jesús Romero left a memorable impression on everyone who knew him. He was slim, about five feet, six inches tall, with a dark complexion. His daily attire consisted of a black suit and tie, and a wide-brimmed hat that narrowed at the top. People remember him in his later years strolling around the plaza jingling silver coins in his pocket. Some describe him as a very astute businessman who held to the tenet, "Don't hold on to property if it can make you a profit." Yet he is also remembered as compassionate toward the many small farmers, sheepherders, cattle tenders and poor people throughout the county.

Others describe him as a patrón who distributed food and money to the poor in return for their votes on election day. He was a founder and leader of *La Sociedad Nuevo Mexicana de Mutua Protección*, a mutual aid and burial society in Old Town. Members of the Society received financial benefits when chronically ill, and surviving members received food when a covered member of the family died.

Romero's mainstay in the Plaza was a general merchandise store on the corner of Romero and South Plaza Streets. There he allegedly ran a successful "banking" business. He extended credit and loaned money to people in exchange for property as collateral. He often foreclosed; gradually his own land holdings grew. If he could realize a profit, he sold the land to anyone who could pay the price. Some people remember Romero's practice with disfavor, but most small businessmen in merchandising enterprises commonly used it. Jesús Romero was one of the more successful ones.

Romero died a wealthy man in August, 1935. Old Town was his domain. He never relaxed his hold on Old Town in the face of a growing city next door. He lived long enough to see the Democrats sweep the state in the 1930s, and he also witnessed the beginning of the erosion of his powerful machine by the New Deal's emergency relief programs and Work Projects Administration. But he did not see the day when New Town at last engulfed Old Town and made it part of the municipality.

The final irony about Jesús Romero's life and wealth was that his empire collapsed after his death, as relatives fought over his estate. The living memorial to his wealth is the former Frances Lynn Home (now houses shops) on the west side of the square in Old Town. The last residential structure erected on the plaza itself, Romero built it between 1915 and 1917. It was an elegant home; it was a "New Town" home in Old Town in its declining years.

Other Old Town Businessmen

Other businessmen in Old Town shared the general merchandising arena with Jesús Romero and Charles Mann. One such person was Manuel Springer. He was Mary Springer's brother, and he continued in the general store and grocery business of his father, Henry Springer. Manuel operated a store on the south plaza. In 1914, he constructed a two-story Queen Anne mansion next to his store. Manuel Springer also served on the Bernalillo County Commission, when he was appointed to the unexpired term of a man who lost his post when Sandoval County was carved out of Bernalillo in 1904. He married Carlota García, daughter of Manuel García, who was county sheriff in pre-railroad days and later served on the Bernalillo County Commission. García was a freighter and frequently bought property, leaving his widow and children significant holdings in the Old Town-Duranes and North Fourth Street areas. García's grandchildren, Gaspar, Jr., and Nick García, were successful adobe builders and Old Town property owners. Henry Springer, Manuel and Carlota's son, lived in Old Town until his death in the 1990s.

Another prominent merchant in Old Town during this period was Florencio Zamora. His brother, Juan, was not a merchant but engaged in related enterprises. The Zamoras were linked to the rising middle class through the Romeros on the maternal side. They were related to Jesús Romero and also may have been related to Juanita Romero, Cristóbal Armijo's wife. Florencio and Juan's mother was Jacoba Romero Zamora. One of her brothers was Manuel A. Romero, the father of Jesús. Her other brothers, Vicente and Cristóbal, ran a slaughterhouse operation. The Romeros had two major outlets for their products. Andrés, Vicente's son, operated a meat market in New Town at Gold and Second Streets near the railroad. In Old Town, Florencio Zamora ran a butcher shop, first in what is now the Basket Shop that he sold to Charles Mann, then in the old Cristóbal Armijo house he bought around 1910. The Cristóbal Armijo house on the southeast corner of the plaza is still in the possession of Florencio's great-grandson, Tito Chávez, Old Town's district State Senator in the 1980s.

Juan Zamora, a year younger than Florencio, attended school in St. Louis. In Old Town he was known for his fiddle-playing and dexterity and skill at repairing mechanical farming equipment, which was coming into prominence in the mid-Rio Grande valley. In 1906 Juan purchased the run-down Casa de Armijo and Ambrosio Armijo's house from Ambrosio's widow. He envisioned a contained business enterprise that could host dances, show silent movies, and attract tenants to the small apartments. Though his dream materialized, the project never realized the profits he desired. He offered dances for the poorer folks, while the better-off had theirs at the old San Felipe Club at South San Felipe Street near Central Avenue under the auspices of the mutual aid society. The second story of the Armijo house was used for silent movies, but talking movies soon made their advent, and New Town developed those facilities. The disintegrating Casa de Armijo did attract tenants—the poorer folks who could not afford to buy property. In the fall of 1930 Juan sold Casa de Armijo, by then even more run-down than it was when he had purchased it. Juan Zamora drifted into obscurity, while the Armijo house became the link between Old Albuquerque's elite past and Old Town's tourist commercial success.

Culture in Old Town

The San Felipe de Neri Church, still the Mother Church, emerged as a strong and viable spiritual and social center for Old Town and surrounding villages. The church building was maintained and kept beautifully. In 1908–09 new pews were installed. Traditional ceremonies endured. The San Felipe de Neri fiesta, celebrated annually since the founding of Albuquerque, continued with the commitment of years past. People still came from as far as Tomé and Bernalillo as well as the surrounding ranches and mountain villages. They came prepared to stay from Friday until Monday, sharing homes with friends and relatives, who rolled out mattresses on the floors to accommodate everyone. It was a festive occasion where old acquaintances were reunited and good food and good times were shared. The feast of Corpus Cristi was always a special occasion, with its solemn procession visiting colorful altars decoratively constructed by faithful parishioners in front of their homes around the plaza.

As the Church thrived, so did another organization that shared its membership with the Church, *La Sociedad Nuevo Mexicana de Mutual Protección*. Organized in 1896 as a mutual aid and burial society, the Society's first lodge house was in the San Felipe Club, located on the west side of San Felipe Street near Central Avenue in the old Thomas Post Exchange Hotel. Until 1862, the rambling adobe building was Manuel and Rafael Armijo's store. Post and others after him used it as a hotel, and under his widow and heir's ownership it later housed the Sunnyside Inn and the San Felipe Club. The Society Hall served Old Town for many years, sponsoring fund-raising activities to sustain its primary mission, burials and help for the survivors. Renowned throughout Rio Abajo communities and surrounding Hispanic settlements, the Society Hall featured well-known bands, and its dances attracted both young and old from near and far way.

San Felipe de Neri Church, the "Mother Church," founded in 1706. The original building fell into disrepair and the present structure was built between 1790–93. In April 1868 the Jesuits came to San Felipe and were there until 1966, when secular priests from the Archdiocese of Santa Fe assumed pastoral duties. The Jesuits made lasting changes to the church structure.Photo © Marcia Keegan.

Social life in Old Town, centered around the Society and the church, was enlivened by the musical talents of some of its residents. Old Town had had musicians since Albuquerque's founding. The 1850 Census listed six musicians in the Bernalillo-Albuquerque area. One of them was Juan Gutiérrez. He married Jesusita García, a sister of Aniceta, Jesús Romero's mother. Juan and Jesusita's daughter, Rebecca, also married a musician, James Devine, founder and director of the first Indian Band in Arizona. In Albuquerque, Devine directed the Albuquerque Orchestra. Three of James Devine's grandsons are E.A. Mares, a New Mexico poet and play-wright, Michael Mares, a distinguished biologist, and Chris, their brother, an Albuquerque musician. Other Old Town musicians with the Albuquerque Orchestra were Juan Zamora, later the owner of Casa de Armijo, and Andrés and Cristobal Moya, one-time members of an Indian band in Kansas. Feliciano Zamora had another popular band in Old Town during this period. The band was composed of Feliciano's sons and Clara Blueher, daughter of the truck farmer who lived on the plaza. Zamora taught music to the youth and, along with other music lovers in the community, enjoyed operatic and other musical productions in New Town.

The proximity of Old Albuquerque to New Town, its core of elite residents between the 1820s and the 1880s, its place on the Chihuahua-Santa Fe trade route during the Colonial and Territorial periods—all affected development of la Plaza Vieja toward more cosmopolitan tastes. This distinguishes Old Albuquerque from other rural Mexican villages in New Mexico that were more isolated. It also influenced cultural productions such as *santos* (traditional hand carvings of saints) and *retablos* (traditional hand paintings of saints). Old Town, unlike the northern villages, did not seem to have had traditional *santeros* (carvers of santos) during this period; the statuettes found in church and home were probably brought in from Europe, Mexico or were made by local religious statue artist Dionisio Guerra, who used a mold and plaster medium. He lived in la Plaza Vieja in the late 1800s. His daughter married Abel Durán of the Durán founding families of Old Albuquerque. Abel and Refugio's son, Pedro Durán, was a long-time pharmacist and businessman in Old Town. Under different ownership, Durán's Pharmacy is still a thriving business at Central Avenue near Old Town.

While Old Town may not have had traditional *santeros*, by the late 1920s it had a few painters, something alien to the more remote rural villages. At Central Avenue and Seventeenth Street, on or near Franz Huning's first home, Esquipula Romero had a colorful gallery that later became a well-known nightclub and is now part of the Manzano Day School. Esquipula was a painter and a well-known character in the Old Town art scene later on. Vicente Pacheco painted oil portraits and landscapes as a hobby. Two of his works of Christ and the Sorrowful Mother are still on view at San Felipe de Neri, where he also did the fine gold leaf work. His wife, Aurora, also from the Rio Abajo region, was Old Town's postmistress from the Depression days until the post office became a station of Albuquerque's main post office. They had three children, Catalina, Consuelo and Joe. Consuelo, who is my wife, is an art therapist, still lives in the Old Town area, and is active in preserving the cultural and spiritual legacy of San Felipe de Neri church in the midst of the growing commercialization. Another painter was George Gallegos, who was married to Julia Bottger, granddaughter of Thomas Post, an early

Altar at San Felipe de Neri Church. Photo © Marcia Keegan.

Old Town settler. Artist Luis Moya, who worked on the church with
Vicente Pacheco, had three children also involved in the arts. Emma
Moya is an artist and Old Town historian, and Luis and Ricardo Moya,
both deceased, were artists and musicians.

Social Life in Old Town

In the 1860s the Old Town plaza included a low building, erected during
the United States Army occupation period, where a man who doubled as

dentist and barber practiced his profession and trade. By 1900, the plaza, enclosed with a white picket fence and the home of a few struggling cottonwoods, was a barren, dusty place. In time, a small patch of grass graced the center and the cottonwoods reached maturity. Then, in the early 1930s, the Works Projects Administration (WPA) changed the plaza. Following plans drafted by an Old Town committee, the WPA uprooted the trees and erected a small bandstand and a stone wall around the plaza. Critics immediately complained that the wall, constructed of large reddish colored rocks held together by white cement, was an eyesore, looking more like a fortress than a historical plaza. In addition, the bandstand was not large enough to accommodate a band. This construction was later torn down and replaced by the Old Albuquerque Historical Society.

Old Town, almost solid adobe, didn't compare with New Town in appearance. New Town's painted exteriors and beautifully hand-hewn stone or brick residences, with their fresh, green lawns, were a mystery to Old Town youngsters, whose playgrounds were earthen yards, dirt roads, alleys, the Blueher pond, irrigation ditches and puddles of water from rain and irrigation run-offs.

Those who grew up in Old Town during the early 1900s remember their hometown from within. "There facing the park was 'el Parrillán,' an open market place. The fresh meat to be sold was hanging from the porch of 'el Parrillán' and the women would sit on the ground to sell their fresh fruits and vegetables."[4] The park was a place for people to stroll or sit under the trees to chat or listen to the band that entertained on Sunday afternoon. Children, meanwhile, played about. To Mrs. Carolina Paiz, who grew up in Old Town after having moved from Socorro, "era muy bonito" (it was very pretty).[5]

To other people, especially those viewing from a New Town vantage point, Old Town was an unattractive and immoral village made up of people with loose morals—drunks, gamblers and whores. Saloons and cantinas had lined Central Avenue south of the plaza since the 1880s. The Sunnyside Inn, housed in the Old Post Exchange Hotel and a favorite drinking and gambling hangout, was the place Billy the Kid allegedly shot up when he and Elfego Baca, the infamous sheriff of Socorro County in later years, were carousing partners in their late teens. Other places of ill repute for the drinker and gambler during this period were the Gold Star Saloon and Pat's Place. After prohibition, Eliseo Sánchez had his tavern in that area. At the west end of the row of saloons was the "el faite Corral." Named "faite" for fight, the place was a fenced-in area where men gathered to settle discords exacerbated by gaming and too much drink.

During prohibition, Old Town gained color and infamy for its bootleggers, speakeasies and brothels. Manuel Springer's Queen Anne dwelling

Sitting in Old Town Plaza are two small howitzer cannons of eight captured by Confederate forces from the Union Army when they took the area for 36 days in 1862 during the Civil War. This is a reminder that Old Town was under siege for over a month, when General Sibley retreated to Texas. In the background is San Felipe de Neri Church. Photo © Marcia Keegan.

turned into a brothel after his death. Some of the bars on Central Avenue were said to be brothels. When Juan Zamora vacated the Armijo house, the second story of the north end building was partitioned into small cubicles, each with a woman's name on the wall. While children were stringently prohibited from roaming close to those places, some young boys found excitement and entertainment stealing bootlegged liquor from the large limousines parked along the street while their owners took care of other business inside the houses. Other youngsters delighted in viewing the colorfully dressed women chatting under the *portales* as men of stature in the community nonchalantly patronized the area. A campaigning candidate for sheriff in the late 1920s finally rid Old Town of some of its colorful activity, and by the early 1930s the social environment began to change. Old Town's infamous years became history.

Ironically, Old Town was the center of law and order for Bernalillo County because it held the courthouse and the jail. The courthouse gave Old Town official legitimacy; la Plaza Vieja was the county seat. To Mexican people this was extremely important, for when they had to transact official business, they came to a familiar place where the dominant language was Spanish and the inhabitants were their friends and relatives. When *las cortes* (the courts) were in session, people who came from the outlying villages turned business into visits similar to the annual San Felipe de Neri fiestas. Travelers into town accommodated themselves in

Old Town residences, receiving warm and friendly hospitality, while their horses were fed and watered in Old Town stables. They were good times, and some people view the transfer of the courthouse from Old Town to New Town in the late 1920s as the last blow against the Mexican village by New Town interests. The courthouse removal also denied people the opportunity of mixing business and fellowship in a familiar and comfortable environment.

Old Town also had the county jail. It was located on the southwest corner of Rio Grande Boulevard and Central Avenue. The jail attracted its share of excitement. One incident was a jail break of international significance. General José Inez Salazar, a Mexican revolutionary, was detained while awaiting trial for charges arising out of the violation of neutrality laws. The Victoriano Huerta forces, where Salazar was a division commander, fled into the United States after a crushing defeat. Salazar escaped and in January 1914 was arrested. General Huerta hired Elfego Baca, by then a seasoned lawman and political broker—and already a legendary fast-draw and deadly accurate pistol shooter. At night on November 20, 1914, while Elfego Baca was publicly visible at the Graham Bar in New Town, the phone rang in the jail. A woman was in distress. The guard immediately left to answer the call. Charles Armijo, the jailer, was overpowered and tied up, while Salazar was set free and escaped to Mexico. Baca and his aides were indicted and tried for complicity in Salazar's escape but were acquitted. Some believed Baca did well for his client and had an airtight alibi. With the relocation of the courthouse to New Town, the jail also relocated next to the new courthouse. La Plaza Vieja lost another institution.

Before World War I, the Territorial Fair annually provided Old Town residents with major entertainment. Discontinued during the war, the fair was resumed east of New Town in 1938 as the New Mexico State Fair, never to return to its original site. The Society Hall and the Old Town Public School took up part of the space left by the fairgrounds.

Change altered not only the town's physiognomy but also its social environment. Sheep-herding, cattle-tending and even subsistence farming had declined by the 1930s, as more Old Town residents became employed in New Town service industries, the sawmill and the railroad. And although older residents protected their traditions, younger generations were influenced by New Town values.

Education played a major role in the change. With the decline of subsistence agriculture, educational demands increased, and the Old Town School expanded with the purchase of the old courthouse in 1928. With education receiving higher value, those of the growing middle class sent their children on to St. Mary's High School in New Town. Finally, in 1930,

Casa de Armijo was purchased by people committed to restoration and preservation of native arts and crafts, who saw the building's future as a place for artists to live and paint.

Something new was in store once again for the historic village. The persisting cultural traditions that had sustained Old Town in the face of progress next door were ironically confronted once again by the forces of change that had been responsible for its economic demise a century earlier. The double irony was that those elements in Old Town's culture that were once derided by newcomers now became the new assets. Tourists and artists were discovering the charms of the old plaza area. Albuquerque officials became aware of its promotional potential and suddenly took an interest in making sure it was historically preserved.

New Mexico Revitalized

Forty years before Old Town was "discovered" in 1930, a young man, Harvard-educated and fired by his zest for understanding the essence of what made things happen, had already documented and reflected on the historical and cultural landmarks that were to make the old plaza attractive to artists. He was Charles F. Lummis. Within six years after graduating from Harvard, Lummis had helped launch a newspaper in Los Angeles, had lived in New Mexican villages among Penitentes, and had settled in Isleta Pueblo. In *The Land of Poco Tiempo* (1983), a compilation of some of his earlier articles and feature stories, Lummis wrote: "Sun, silence and adobe—that's New Mexico in three words....It is the United States which is not the United States...Here in the land of *poco tiempo* the 'pretty soon' of New Spain is better than the 'Now! Now!' of the haggard States."[6]

Long before Lummis's descriptions, artists had sketched New Mexico scenes and writers had recorded their perceptions of people and places. Not until the 1880s and after, however, were painters drawn in greater numbers to the area's natural beauty and ethnic charm. At a time of uncertainty and threatening world chaos, writers came in search of new models and new modes of expression in the context of regional experiences—and of "guidance from the alleged superior wisdom of the 'primitive people.'"[7] Around the turn of the century, artists had found at least two places spared by what they saw as the heavy-handed God of progress—Taos and Santa Fe. By 1900, Taos was on its way to becoming the first art colony in New Mexico, founded by Joseph Henry Sharp and two colleagues, Bert Greer Phillips and Ernest L. Blumenschein.

Although not as "primitive" as Taos, Santa Fe shared with it natural beauty, a unique social environment and isolation. Around 1900, Carlos Vierra, a California-born painter and photographer, moved from New

York to a Santa Fe sanitarium to recuperate from tuberculosis. He stayed in Santa Fe and was joined by Kenneth Chapman, a New York illustrator, who had originally come to New Mexico to teach at New Mexico Normal, now known as New Mexico Highlands University. In 1912, another tubercular, Gerald Cassidy, moved to Santa Fe from his first stop in New Mexico, Albuquerque. The three made up the core group of the Santa Fe art colony. The two cultural centers attracted international attention, and other aficionados, artists and art patrons gravitated to the region. Tourism likewise became very important in the area.

In northern New Mexico, the artists knew northern New Mexico people of Spanish heritage as Spanish-American. Grabbing on to a name that would distinguish themselves from more recent Mexican immigrants coming north and victims of extreme discrimination, New Mexicans perceived the new nomenclature as a class delineation as well.[8] This caused Erna Fergusson to apologize for republishing articles written before the "twenties...[when] it was just becoming imperative to use Spanish-American instead of Mexican: a word that had been used with utmost respect of gentlemen and ladies of distinction and social standing."[9] She never meant disrespect in calling her friends Mexican. Notwithstanding the ideological implication of this new awareness among "Spanish people," the change in name became important to the artist and the New Mexico Spanish heritage promoter.

In Albuquerque, the interest in native cultures and their aesthetic contributions had been confined to a small group of intellectuals. Between 1901 and 1909, adaptation of indigenous culture to architecture at the University of New Mexico ended badly for Dr. William George Tight, its promoter and president during that period, who was fascinated by native adobe construction and the whole Pueblo culture surrounding Albuquerque. He transformed the physiognomy of the university buildings into replicas of Pueblo-style structures. This met with heated opposition from local residents, who thought his designs were primitive. Partly as a result of this, in 1909 Tight was removed as president. His legacy lay dormant for two decades, when it suddenly became an important architectural style. In 1927 the Board of Regents of the University of New Mexico formally adopted the Pueblo architectural style for the campus. Dr. James F. Zimmerman led the renaissance of Pueblo design, and the future buildings were constructed in that style.

Art and commerce in New Mexico intertwined through the tourism industry. The artists brought new life to both Santa Fe and Taos. They were followed by an influx of tourists with money in their pockets. The local business community, of course, was delighted.

Cultural Revival in Albuquerque

Enhanced by the presence and activities of two art colonies in its midst, northern New Mexico had turned the "primitive" cultures and the stark beauty of its terrain into a commodity. The Atchison, Topeka and Santa Fe Railroad and various tour companies promoted the region heavily. Gallup was attracting national attention with the Intertribal Indian Ceremonial. Noticing this, Albuquerque, the state's commercial center and already attractive to health seekers, turned its energies to attracting more tourists' attention. Tourism and "chasing the cure" went hand in glove. The Albuquerque Civic Council, organized to project this image, created a promotional brochure published in 1928 that portrayed Albuquerque and its environs as a healthy and culturally unique place to visit and even settle. Albuquerque also was presented as the wholesale and banking center of the state. The brochure announced the beginning of the Middle Rio Grande Conservancy Project, the massive reclamation project of 1929 that would bring more land into cultivation and make it available to newcomers.

Challenging the general "literary" description of barren mesas and deserts, the brochure flaunted the prehistoric ruins north of Santa Fe and presented an enticing picture of a mountain playground with trout-filled streams. The University of New Mexico's claim to uniqueness in America was its "old Spanish and Indian architecture." The intellectual and aficionado were reached by presenting Willa Cather's *Death Comes for the Archbishop* as central to understanding the "feeling of reverence for New Mexico that permeates the work" of artists. The published brochure also described the "tiny adobes with red chiles hanging from flat roofs, wagons standing idle after the day's work, women drawing fresh baked bread from the ovens.... There is only one New Mexico in the world... Albuquerque is much like the cafés in Paris where one can sit and watch the world pass by."[10]

Albuquerque's first actual participation in the commercial aspects of New Mexico's "ethnic charm" was advanced with the business community's production of the First American Pageant in 1928, held consecutively for five years. Billed as the great Native spectacle of America, the pageant was Albuquerque's response to preservation of native cultures. More important, it used the Native performing arts of both Indians and Spanish-Americans to attract attention and encourage tourists to visit the city. In 1931, according to a count of license plates seen at the show, the pageant attracted tourists from twenty-seven states. A facsimile of Taos Pueblo was constructed in the vicinity of present-day Central Avenue and Wyoming Boulevard and used as a stage for Indian dances and individual acts. Around five thousand spectators, spellbound in the open, heard "the piping of weird native flutes; the soul stirring rhythm of Navajo Night Chant." [11] Attracting national attention through the airwaves and printed media, the pageant was described as one of "the most famous of American Tourist Acts." [12]

Although primarily an Indian show, The First American Pageant also included Spanish-Americans. The Montezuma Ball held at the newly constructed Franciscan Hotel on Central Avenue was described as a brilliant event, with guests attired in costumes from the days of the Spanish King Ferdinand. The pageant itself featured the Señoritas Dancing Chorus directed by Senora Lucía Sánchez de Rael. The 1931 show presented the *Spanish Episode*, Spanish-American men dressed in conquistador costumes and replaying the conquest of the Indians. It also featured a female vocal group and Tiburcio Hernández's Típica Band of Albuquerque.

Attitudes had changed in Albuquerque. By 1930 new names, mostly those of recovered tubercular patients, had filled the city's business and professional roster. Local architectural styles had become acceptable, even encouraged. The ethnic charm that had initially attracted artists, who in turn attracted tourists to Taos and Santa Fe, was now seen as an asset. Within this social context, Old Albuquerque was rediscovered.

La Casa de Armijo

The gateway to Old Town's rediscovery was Casa de Armijo. The large plazuela-like dwelling, probably named for el Colorado, Don Juan Armijo y Maestas, was purchased around 1844 by a relative, Ambrosio Armijo.

After Armijo's death, the charming and elegant house gradually fell into disrepair. After Juan Zamora purchased it in 1906, the building deteriorated further; he finally sold it to Brice and Nelda Sewell in the fall of 1930. The Sewells were from Missouri and came to Old Town by way of an art school in Philadelphia, a turquoise business in Utah, a sculpturing period among Indians in Farmington, New Mexico, and studying in the Art Department at the University of New Mexico. After completing his academic work at the university, Brice Sewell remained as an art instructor there. The Sewells were a young couple surviving the early days of the Depression. In one of their earlier trips to Albuquerque, on the urging of Carl Taylor, an English instructor at the University and a writer of Hispanic themes, they visited Old Town during the San Felipe de Neri Fiesta. The Sewells had already seen the Intertribal Indian Ceremonial in Gallup, New Mexico. Delighted and impressed by the ceremonial and won by the charm of Old Town, the Sewells sought to buy a place in the plaza.

When they purchased Casa de Armijo, it was in shambles. The second story at the north end of the house facing the plaza still had the small rooms in the state that transient paramours had used only days before. Other rental

Elegantly restored hall and staircase in the La Placita restaurant complex, formerly Casa de Armijo. Photo © Marcia Keegan.

units in the complex were hastily abandoned even before the new landlords could meet the old tenants. The restoration of Casa de Armijo began.

William Lumpkins, an anthropology student turned architect, and his professor of architecture, Irving Parsons, helped the Sewells in the restoration. By the spring of 1931 the four, with manual labor provided by local residents, had prepared the historic place for a grand re-opening.

Harvey Fergusson recorded the gala event in his book, *Rio Grande*. He writes that even Albuquerque, "the best business town between Pueblo and El Paso...the obedient child of the railroad, has felt the renaissance a little. Recently an old adobe building in Old Albuquerque was made over, not to look like the First National Bank, but to look as it had a hundred

Located behind the La Placita Dining rooms, Patio Market used to be apartments and studios attached to Casa de Armijo. The well is apparently a wishing well and its image has been used for a record album cover. Photo © Marcia Keegan.

years ago. With a grand ball it was opened to the public as Albuquerque's Art Center. Here artists were to live and paint—at least so it was hoped and said. There have never been many artists in Albuquerque but the town at least offered them a home...."[13]

"The opening costume ball was a great success. The daughter of an old Mexican family appeared in the ponderous wedding dress that had been worn in that same house half a century before. A promising young real estate man looked enough like an aboriginal Navajo....Buffalo Bill was there and Montezuma and more youth in tight Spanish trousers and girls in high Spanish combs than the floor would hold." Albuquerque was finally looking towards its past, Fergusson concluded.[14]

Artists

The grand opening of Casa de Armijo brought tradition to life. Grand *bailes* (dances) and parties filled with young people dressed in gay Spanish costumes and Indian girls in their traditional wear replicated historical happenings of the *rico* elite (wealthy Old Spanish society) period. Casa de Armijo became a popular place to entertain out-of-town guests and charm them with the local color and ethnic musical performances.

Casa de Armijo also realized the earlier dreams of its new owners; artists were attracted to live and paint there. During restoration, William Lumpkins lived there; after the completed restoration, he rented a studio and apartment and soon was joined by men and women such as Brooks and Janette Willis, later of the well-known Transcendental Painting Group, Willard Nash, Carl von Hassler, Nils Hogner, Carl Redin, Stuart Walker, Howard Schleeter, and composer Otto Amaden. Norman

McCloud, a professor in the English department at the University and Marie Wilson, a dancer and dance instructor, were also tenants. Ben Turner, Clark True, Dorothy Prussian, Ted and Lee Schuyler, and Celene Cleaver, a mural painter, were in Casa de Armijo in the 1940s. Sam Marino, an assistant to Diego Rivera in Mexico City, spent a brief period in exile in Old Town but did not live in Casa de Armijo. Through his contacts and the help of an art patron, William Lumpkins set up a Diego Rivera exhibit in the old Armijo house.

Although a true art colony never actually emerged, some artists held art shows in the patio on Sunday afternoons and participated in many interesting discussions as they shared the large complex in the early 1930s. Artists' interest in Old Town as a place to live and paint endured into the 1950s, and some painters lingered on until later days. Von Hassler and Schleeter maintained studios on Romero Street in the fifties. By 1948, Casa de Armijo had gained regional and even national reputation for its fine restaurant, La Placita Dining Rooms.

Old Albuquerque Historical Society

Soon after Old Town's resurgence at Casa de Armijo, another dwelling in the plaza was purchased by an outsider. Manuel Springer's Queen Anne house was bought by J. R. "Dick" Bennett. He turned property adjacent to the house into apartments, renting them to out-of-town tenants, some of whom were with the soil conservation projects in Albuquerque. Eventually the Bennetts opened La Cocina, a restaurant catering service in the first floor of the house. Currently the building houses the Covered Wagon.

In the mid-1930s, the new commercial leaders around the plaza attempted to form the first Old Town Historical Society. Dubbed the Old

The gazebo in the center of Old Town Plaza today. Compare this photo with how the plaza originally looked in the image on page 101. Photo © Marcia Keegan.

Town Chamber of Commerce by Erna Fergusson, the goals of the emerging group were to develop the town's commercial potential. The Old Town Historical Society never fully developed, and the efforts died at the beginning of World War II.

In February 1947, the Old Town Historical Society, now called the Old Albuquerque Historical Society, had a fresh beginning; this time cultural and historical interests were paramount. The stated goals were to restore buildings and landmarks of historical significance to their original period and style and to eventually establish a museum. Elizabeth Arnet Bennett, wife of an originator of the first effort, was the new society's first president. Within a year the Old Albuquerque's Historical Society's membership had grown to one hundred and forty-nine. Historical exhibits and educational sessions were conducted.

One job undertaken by the Old Albuquerque Historical Society was supervising the renovation of the Old Town Plaza, especially its "fortress-like appearance" undergone during WPA days. The Springer Transfer Company voluntarily removed the wall and bandstand, selling the rocks to a local contractor. The next step was securing funds for the rest of the Plaza renovation. Irene Fisher, president of the Old Albuquerque Historical Society in 1948–49 and former owner of the *Old Town News*, developed an ingenious plan linking the present with the past, raising money, and getting publicity for Old Town. She devised a plan to issue "loafing permits" in exchange for contributions to redo the plaza. The loafing permit was a new twist on the old curbstone society (1880s), a term used pejoratively by New Town residents against Old Towners who enjoyed passing the time of day around the park. Loafing permits were issued widely. In May 1949, Clinton Anderson gave one to President Harry Truman, who evidently was too busy to use it. Nevertheless, the land of *poco tiempo* gained some publicity for its one characteristic the aggressive New Town found impossible to embrace—the art of taking it easy.

Donations from local citizens accomplished much of the rest of the renovation. Albuquerque resident Albert G. Simms provided funds to purchase cast iron benches from Chihuahua, Mexico. Families with long ties to the area purchased the lampposts.

The Historical Society took part in the San Felipe Fiesta parade, through its float bringing historical awareness to fiesta participants and spectators. By the mid-1950s, the energy of the Old Albuquerque Historical Society had spent itself and interest had waned. In 1961, in another awakening, it became the Albuquerque Historical Society. By then, other areas of Albuquerque had reached their golden years, and their own historical preservation rivaled Old Town's.

Annexation of Old Town

As Albuquerque expanded in growth, Old Town's size diminished. In 1940
Old Town had 2,593 inhabitants, representing 7.3 percent of the city's population. Albuquerque bordered Old Town on three sides. Old Town had
become related to the city in other ways as well. It was a growing tourist
attraction that could profit the city; its residents were almost totally
dependent on Albuquerque for jobs; it used city facilities and had police
protection, street sweeping, and garbage collection services from the city.

At the same time, many Old Town residents, having benefited from
increased employment opportunities, abandoned their homes in Old Town
and moved to the new northeast heights or moved out of state, while
Anglos began occupying the older areas. This occurred as commercialization of Old Town increased. By 1948 the Casa de Armijo had gained acclaim
for La Placita Dining Rooms, and its earlier apartments and studios in the
old building had been turned into a series of attractive shops, the Patio
Market. Apartments next to the old Springer house were becoming shops.
The old bank building, later Jesús Romero's store on the southwest corner
of the Plaza, was remodeled into apartments and a business place. Three
other restaurants were operating in the area. This commercialization placed
an extreme burden on the existing sewage system, which included individual septic tanks that were obstructing sewer mains, causing overflow into
the plaza. Restaurant owners believed they had to choose between being
annexed to Albuquerque or going out of business.

Annexation of Old Town seemed inevitable but it was not going to be
easy. Those behind the annexation drive from within Old Town were
members of the business community, the pastor of San Felipe de Neri
Church, Father Robert Libertini and some of his loyal followers who were
committed to progress, and, in a more subtle way, the Old Albuquerque
Historical Society. Opponents included Joe and Frank Del Frate, two retail
liquor dealers, and J. W. Hedges, a retail gasoline dealer—both of whom
feared increased taxes—and the great majority of native Hispanic members of the community, who recalled the time when the two towns wanted
nothing to do with each other.

Election for the Old Town members of the annexation arbitration
board was set for April 12, 1949. Candidates for annexation were Jake Baca,
Sherman C. Anderson, and Lesman Chávez; opposed were J. W. Hedges,
Frank Del Frate, and Pat Chávez. The six members of the arbitration
board were to select the seventh member but deadlocked on the choice.
Three District Court judges appointed Gilberto Espinosa, an attorney and
historian who had an interest in Old Town families since he was linked to
them through his maternal side. Espinosa approached his task with a

lawyer's objectivity, waiting until the City proved that it was able and willing to make available to residents municipal benefits to show his posture. He pledged to keep an open mind, although he knew Albuquerque had passed a $400,000 bond issue to expand sewer services that would include Old Town. Espinosa was elected Chairman. Old Town residents' fears that higher taxes would expel them from their homes did not sway Espinosa. When it came time to break the tie, he voted for annexation.

On Thursday, June 30, 1949, Old Town was annexed to the City of Albuquerque. Albuquerque gained about three thousand inhabitants and 169 acres. The fears of control from without that plagued Old Town residents during the annexation battle are best captured in a popular proverb: "*Nuevos Reyes, Nuevas Leyes* (New lords, New laws). And so it happened eight years later. In 1957, part of Old Albuquerque was to be governed by a Historical Zoning Ordinance, the first of its kind in Albuquerque, and Old Town was the only area to be affected by it.

Historic Old Town Zone

More than anything else, annexation demonstrated to Old Town merchants that New Town had an interest in them and their "historic community." That was important. Visitors from out of town increased and business grew. To keep up with the rapid expansion and in anticipation of problems that were bound to arise, the merchants organized themselves into the Plaza Business Association. Their first task, paradoxically, was to lure travelers from Highway 66 and at the same time protect the charm assured by the Plaza's previous isolation. On the one hand, the Association placed the first sign announcing Old Town on the corner of Romero Street and West Central; on the other, they primed the process to designate Old Town a historic zone.

The goal of the Historic Zoning Ordinance was similar to that of the Old Albuquerque Historical Society in its founding days: to promote the district's cultural and economic welfare by preserving its unique historical architectural character and appearance. The ordinance, still in force today, controls the style and size of signs and the use of buildings. It recognizes and allows the manufacturing of arts and crafts and controls retail sales, allowing for food and drink on the premises but outlawing drive-ins. It specifically defines architectural characteristics as Spanish Colonial, Territorial and Western Victorian erected prior to 1912.[15]

The historic zone encompassed much less than the area known as Old Albuquerque or la Plaza Vieja annexed in 1949. Rio Grande Boulevard bounds this historic zone on the west, Mountain Road on the north, San Pasquale Street on the east, and Central Avenue on the south. The historic

A side view of San Felipe de Neri Church, showing the rectory and church offices.
Photo © Marcia Keegan.

zone, however, also affected those living 300 feet from the exterior boundaries—generally la Plaza Vieja barrio. In the 1960s the Albuquerque Historical Society suggested enlarging the zone to include what was actually known as Old Town. It is not clear whether the Society meant Old Town as annexed in 1949 or the more extensive area defined as *la Plaza Vieja* by native residents.

The ordinance provides for an application process for building or remodeling permits as well as public hearings and appeals to the Planning Commission and a Board of Adjustments, later called the Old Town Architectural Review Board. The Board was to be composed of professional architects, landscape architects, historians and knowledgeable laymen with interest in Old Town's historic qualities. It was appointed by the mayor with the advice and consent of the City Council. In 1978 the Landmarks and Urban Conservation Commission was created. This commission was to oversee the entire city and superseded the Architectural Review Board.

Some native residents of Old Town did not support the concept of their community becoming a historic zone. To them, historic zoning was but another step following annexation and leading to more external control, which they did not want. Many community members of Old Town also sensed that when historic zoning took place, property values and subsequently taxes would increase; the natives of Old Town feared they would no longer be able to afford to live there, or if they did and their homes

San Felipe de Neri Church outlined with luminarias at Christmas time.
Photo © Marcia Keegan.

needed renovations, they could not meet the standards. Petitions were circulated to no avail. The dominant community wanted to protect the area from industrial encroachment and commercialism and ensure its continued attractiveness to tourists.

The San Felipe de Neri Church Restoration and Liquor Controversies

Unlike Old Town itself, San Felipe de Neri Church trembled with changes that were not political in the usual sense, but ecclesiastical. Some of these changes came from Rome, some from within. In the past San Felipe de Neri had swayed with the political and economic transitions of New Mexico. In the mid-1960s, it was responding to global changes deriving from the Second Ecumenical Council (opened under Pope John XXIII and closed under Pope Paul VI).

At the center of the controversy was the renovation of the church to comply with the new liturgy decreed by Vatican II, as the Ecumenical Council was popularly called. The stage-auditorium pattern that separated the priest from the congregation and the "medieval gloom and secrecy" that had dominated Catholic religious services had to give way to joyful participation by the congregation, the choir, the altar boys and the priest. The Mass was to be a social celebration. Non-ecclesiastical problems also existed at the church. The building was in disrepair and had some structural deficiencies; the parish was growing and the church's use had increased. Parking was also a problem.

The central question was whether the church should be renovated or restored. The renovation plan called for moving the east wall outwards to enlarge seating space and the removal of the twin bell towers erected by the Jesuits in their early days. A dangerous structural deficiency would be eliminated by their removal, and the historic lines of the exterior of the church would be reestablished to a pueblo style structure. As a result of this renovation, the church would look quite different.

Those favoring restoring the church reasoned that a new floor could be installed to replace the existing one of rotting wood; the roof and existing ceiling would be left and the bell towers repaired rather than removed. Needed rewiring as well as plumbing and plastering would also be part of the restoration, but the church would not revert to its original pueblo style. The City was largely in favor of renovation and adding additional parking; the parishioners wanted their church architecture left as it had been for the past hundred years and the Old Town merchants feared change would make the church less of a tourist attraction.

After much haggling and some confrontations, the church was restored in accordance with the desires of the parishioners and the Old Town merchants. A new floor replaced the rotting one and the other needed repairs were made. The bell towers were repaired. On December 17, 1972, San Felipe de Neri Church was rededicated.

In 1978, six years after the church's rededication, landscaping and work on its exterior walls had not been completed. The pastor had been replaced by George V. Salazar, who believed that church maintenance was the responsibility of the church, not the Architectural Review Board. This led to a confrontation between the pastor and the City that climaxed in police officers issuing the pastor a citation for violation of the City's Historic Zoning Ordinance. A spontaneous vocal uprising from the San Felipe Parish in support of their pastor brought about a quick resolution by a prudent mayor, David Rusk, with an apology to the pastor.

A few years later, in 1980, another dispute arose that pitted the church against the city and its increasing commercialism. La Placita Dining Rooms requested a waiver of the state statute prohibiting the sale of liquor 300 feet from a church or school. The Dining Rooms were well within 300 feet of the Church and the San Felipe Elementary School. The waiver request was based on precedence: one that had been granted to a lounge 298 feet from the San Felipe School. The dispute lasted over two years and included a State Supreme Court hearing. The Archbishop authorized the closing of historic churches, among them San Felipe, to tourists and visitors if the waiver were approved by the City Council. The dispute was finally resolved by the State Legislature with amendments to the state liquor laws that allowed the sale of beer and wine with food, giving local jurisdictions the option to implement the legislation. The Albuquerque City Council passed the local waiver request.

Twenty-some years after resolution of the waiver issue, some restaurants next to the Church are seeking to serve liquor in their patios. The decision is pending at the time of this writing. But old time residents still strive to maintain the traditional residential and cultural qualities of Old Town.

At the same time, the Old Town Plaza area remains one of Albuquerque's most popular tourist attractions. It offers more than a hundred visitor-oriented businesses including over twenty art galleries, several clothing stores, jewelers, trading posts, souvenir and gift shops, general stores, shops for antiques and Southwestern furniture, hotels, restaurants, the Rattlesnake Museum and the Albuquerque Museum. In easy walking distance are the Explora! Science Center, the National Atomic Museum, the New Mexico Museum of Natural History and Science, the Turquoise Museum and the Albuquerque Little Theatre. Six blocks away are the Albuquerque Aquarium and the Rio Grande Botanic Garden. The Rio Grande Zoo and Tingley Beach are in short driving distance. Every year in the late spring, the San Felipe de Neri Church holds a fiesta with parades, food booths and traditional Spanish and Mexican entertainment. At Christmas time, *luminarias* (small paper sacks containing sand supporting votive candles) outline the buildings and roofs with thousands of tiny glowing lights, giving the old city the appearance of a magical fairyland.

NOTES

1. Franz Huning, *Trader On The Santa Fe Trail, With Notes by His Granddaughter, Lina Fergusson Browne* (Albuquerque: Calvin Horn Publishers, Inc., 1973) 132–148; See also William A. Keleher, *Memoirs: 1892–1969, A New Mexico Item* (Santa Fe: The Rydal Press, 1969) 52, 54.

2. Terry Jon Lehman, "Santa Fe and Albuquerque, 1870–1900: Contrast and Conflict in the Development of Two South-Western Towns" (Ph.D. diss., Indiana University, 1974) 184. Lehman is quoting the *Albuquerque Morning Journal*, 15 October 1885.

3. Information about Flora Armijo can be found in the following: "Cristóbal Armijo Was One of Old Town's Leading Citizens," *Old Town News*, 5 February 1941; "La Historia et las Fabulas de una Casa Amplia," Chapter One, collected and compiled by Elinor Crans, 14 December 1938 (WPA files, Bernalillo County Folder, New Mexico State Records Center and Archive, Santa Fe, New Mexico); Huning, *Trader On The Santa Fe Trail*, 118–119. The notes of Huning's granddaughter, Lina Fergusson Browne, have some of the lore about Flora Armijo; U. S. Department of the Interior-Bureau of the Census, *Ninth Census of the United States, 1870, New Mexico, Bernalillo County* (Albuquerque: University of New Mexico Library, Coronado Room, reel 1, microfilm).

4. Pedro Durán and Rosalia Durán Urrea, "Reflections On Life In Old Town," In *From the Beginning A Historical Survey Commemorating the Solemn Rededication of San Felipe De Neri Church, 1706–1972* (Albuquerque: pamphlet, n.d.) 21; Cleto Durán, interview with the author (Albuquerque: 10 September 1980 and 5 December 1981).

5. Carolina Paiz, interview with the author (Albuquerque: 29 September 1980).

6. Charles F. Lummis, *The Land of Poco Tiempo* (New York: Charles Scribner's Sons, 1928; reprint with foreword by Paul A. F. Walter, Albuquerque: University of New Mexico Press, 1952) 3.

7. Arrell Morgan Gibson, *The Santa Fe and Taos Art Colonies, Age of the Muses, 1900–1942* (Norman, Oklahoma: University of Oklahoma Press, 1983) 179–80.

8. Antonio José Ríos-Bustamente, "New Mexico in the Eighteenth Century: Life, Labor and Trade in la Villa de San Felipe de Albuquerque 1706–1790," *Atzlán: International Journal of Chicano Studies Research* 5, no. 3 (Fall 1976): 365. Since the early Spanish colonial days, Spanish identity corresponded with a higher class. Many New Mexicans of Spanish descent have called themselves Spanish-American to differentiate themselves from Mexican immigrants. This also implies Spanish-American is a higher class. See also Arthur L. Campa, *Spanish Folk-Poetry in New Mexico* (Albuquerque: The University of New Mexico Press, 1946), 12–16. Campa addresses the problem of nomenclature and holds the Americans responsible for not recognizing the national as well as language difference between New Mexicans and Mexicans. In reaction, New Mexicans disassociate themselves from Mexicans. I suggest the artist and humanist gave legitimacy to the distinction, and the New Mexicans took advantage of it as a class distinction, and as such used Spanish-American also to mean "New Mexican."

9. Erna Fergusson, *Albuquerque* (Albuquerque: Merle Armitage Editions, 1947), 25.

10. Albuquerque Civic Council, *Albuquerque In New Mexico* (Albuquerque: pamphlet, 1928), 14–15, 18.

11. Ibid., 19.

12. "Albuquerque Given Publicity In October Conoco Magazine," *Albuquerque Journal*, 5 October 1930.

13. Harvey Fergusson, *Rio Grande* (New York: William Morrow and Company, 1967), 289–290.

14. Ibid.

15. "Historic Old Town Zone," Section 43, "Old Town Architectural Review Board," *City of Albuquerque Comprehensive City Zoning Code*, Article vɪv (Chapter 7 of Revised Ordinance of Albuquerque, New Mexico, 1974) 11 January 1976, Section 33. No. 1, 80–81.

Photo montage of Albuquerque neighborhoods © Jesse H. Garves, City of Albuquerque.

ALBUQUERQUE NEIGHBORHOODS

Albuquerque enjoys a variety of neighborhoods that reflect the city's people, history, growth and development. Some are home to ethnic communities, and others are ethnically diverse. Some are decidedly urban; in others, residents wake up to a rooster's crow. They are historic or modern, close to nature or close to the freeway. They may take their character from downtown, UNM or the volcanoes.

Oldest Neighborhoods

The city that now reaches from the volcanic escarpment to the Sandia and Manzano mountains, from Sandia Pueblo to Isleta Pueblo, started out as a loose collection of farms along the river in 1706. Not until the late 1700s were some houses built near San Felipe de Neri Church in what we now call Old Town, and people only lived in them on Sundays. After its first one hundred years, Albuquerque began to look like a village.

Atrisco on the West Side is even older than Albuquerque. It too was a collection of farms and ranches, founded in 1703 as a Spanish Land Grant.

As Albuquerque grew and new settlers entered the area, they formed tiny communities named for the most prominent family. The Candelaria family was one of the first to settle in Albuquerque in 1706. The major arterial, Candelaria Road, is named for them. Another early settler was Juan Griego, or John the Greek, who accompanied Don Juan de Oñate's party of colonists to New Mexico in 1598. (The Spanish word for "Greek" is "Griego.") His descendants settled in the North Valley, and the community **Los Griegos** was named for them, as was Griegos Road.

By 1750 Albuquerque had such satellite communities as **Alameda**, **Corrales**, **Los Duranes**, **Los Candelarias**, **Los Griegos**, **Los Montaños**, **Los Montoyas**, **Los Poblanos**, and **Los Gallegos**. Most were annexed to the city in the late 1940s.

The village of **Alameda** was west of the original Tiwa-speaking pueblo of Alameda, which was abandoned just before 1700. The pueblo site, near Fourth and Alameda, is largely underneath Alameda Elementary School.

In 1748 **Corrales** settlement began with Santa Rosalia de Corrales, or Upper Corrales, and San Ysidro de Corrales, or Lower Corrales. Corrales, named for the corrals of landowner Juan González, dates from the 1700s. It remained a Spanish farming village until after World War II, when artists and writers began to restore old adobe houses.

In 1763 Albuquerque's assistant alcalde helped establish **San Miguel de Carnué** on a Spanish land grant east of Albuquerque.

Los Barelas is typical of these enclaves. In 1809, Juan Barela bought property at a ranch called El Torreon. Around 1825 Antonio Sandoval, a rancher, dug an extension of the old Griegos-Candelaria Ditch across the valley and south along the sand hills at the valley's edge to bring water to the fields south of Albuquerque. More farmers moved in, and soon a small village was formed, called Los Barelas after the largest family in the area. By 1870 Los Barelas had a population of 400 farmers and ranchers.

We know these places now as neighborhoods. Other villages have retained their identity as communities.

Martineztown started when families in the 1800s drove their herds east to the sand hills for summer grazing and camped. The area had a large acequia. Around 1850, Manuel Martín and his wife Anna María decided to settle permanently, and the area came to be known as Los Martínes, and later, Martineztown. Today Martineztown is bounded by Broadway, I-25, Martin Luther King Blvd. and Mountain Road.

After the Railroad

After the railroad came in 1880, Albuquerque began growing quickly. As Americans moved into what had been a Spanish outpost, they began to transform the town in the image of places where they lived before.

The railroad spawned a second town, as stores and saloons sprouted along the tracks in tents and hastily built shacks. Soon the new commercial district gained permanent structures of brick and brownstone. It became known as New Town, and the original community became Old Town.

The first developers hired civil engineer Walter Marmon to design and lay out the streets of New Town. A Midwesterner, Marmon stuck with the familiar. He laid out a grid of numbered north-south streets and named east-west streets after minerals—gold, silver, coal, lead and iron. Local boosters were hopeful that Albuquerque would become a transportation center for the mines. He named the main street parallel to the railroad tracks "Broadway" because he thought a proper city should have a Broadway. The major arterial was already called Railroad Avenue (later renamed Central Avenue).

A growing community needed new housing. In 1880, the same year the railroad arrived, Franz Huning started his **Highland Addition** east of the railroad between Copper and Iron. It was Albuquerque's first master-planned suburb. Huning's new subdivision, with its Midwestern-style Queen Anne homes drew merchants, doctors and professionals. (After a

Catholic Church at Barelas, 1890. Photo courtesy of the Albuquerque Museum, Image # 1978.031.007.

period of decline, the neighborhood is now fashionable again and many of the century-old homes are renovated. Huning Highland was named a national historic district in 1979 and a city historic overlay zone in 1981.)

The second housing development was the **Perea Addition** of José L. Perea, which was better known as the **Downtown Neighborhood District**, west of New Town in 1881.

In 1881 Sister Blandina Segale wrote: "I predict this Old Town Albuquerque will not long remain the metropolis." Two years earlier when she arrived here, "there was not a house where the railroad station is but now the houses are springing up like mushrooms."

North of New Town was the **Mandell Addition**, platted in 1880. Located around Fourth and New York (now Lomas), it became known as the **McClellan Park Neighborhood**. This was a thriving turn-of-the-century residential neighborhood outside the city limits. Residents converted an old apple orchard into McClellan Park, named in 1919 by prominent citizen William McClellan for his wife and mother. The McClellans lived adjacent to the park. The neighborhood faded away as auto dealerships grew along Fourth Street, which was a part of Route 66 through Albuquerque for a time, and railroad-related warehouses went in near the tracks. You can still see a few of the modest and charming older houses tucked away on First, Second and Third streets.

In 1891 wholesale grocer Martin Stamm filed a plat for the **Terrace Addition** to sell lots south of Central to Hazeldine and east of the city limits to Buena Vista, in the area of present-day TVI. This addition includes the **Silver Hill Neighborhood** west of Yale on Gold and Silver. Local people thought it was too far away; it then took an hour by horse and buggy to get there. There were no water lines, so Stamm drilled his own well and provided water to residents.

As the century turned, one new convenience that stimulated early subdivisions and suburbs was the streetcar. Promoters in those days bought up real estate as a way to promote their transportation companies. Albuquerque Traction Company, organized in 1903, proposed a loop around the business district and land where it had lots for sale.

Early Growth

In those days a good rain in the Sandias could turn into a flash flood that plunged across the East Mesa through arroyos on its way to the river. Despite that risk, builders continued adding neighborhoods east of downtown.

D. K. B. Sellers was one of the busiest developers of the period. In 1906 he built **University Heights** south of Central from Yale to Girard. He described it as the "coming aristocratic section of Albuquerque." He too provided his own waterworks. His two-story water tank is incorporated in a house at 319 Carlisle SE. The next subdivision was the **Valley View Addition** in 1911.

Both were well outside city limits on the East Mesa. Promoters offered clean air ("Escape the Coal Smoke of Downtown") and rural life, and the automobile made commuting possible.

In the early 1900s American Lumber Company's sawmill north and east of Old Town began processing logs from the Zuni Mountains in western New Mexico. By 1908 it was the largest manufacturing company in the Southwest. It employed more than 1,000 men in Albuquerque. Nearby workers built their homes of wood or adobe. This became the **Sawmill Neighborhood**.

The railroad had a similar impact on the one-time farming community of Los Barelas. The railroad built its shops east of **Barelas** on what is now Second Street. Ultimately the railroad would employ hundreds of men, and new subdivisions sprang up to house them. To this day Barelas has two distinct types of homes—the adobes of the early Hispanic settlers and the later brick and frame homes. (For the Tricentennial, Barelas was celebrated in an opera commissioned by the New Mexico Symphony Orchestra called *Time and Again, Barelas*.)

In the same way, the **Eastern Addition**, across the tracks from Barelas, sprang up in 1888 to provide housing to railroad workers. Farther south the community of **San José** began, probably after 1880, when Hispanic and some black workers at the Santa Fe shops and tie-treating plant settled there.

After 1910 only one area bordering on downtown remained undeveloped—a swampy area between the old Barelas Road and the Rio Grande. A real estate company platted the **Raynolds Addition** between Eighth Street and the city limits (roughly at Seventeenth) in 1912, but little build-

The Nob Hill Neighborhood includes the Monte Vista, College View, Broadmoor, University Heights, Granada Heights, Mesa Grande and Mankato Additions. Pictured above is the Monte Vista Fire Station, a modern restaurant located in the historic fire station designed by architect E. H. Blumenthal and completed in 1936. Blumenthal incorporated elements of pueblo style in the building, such as the terraced building arrangement of Taos Pueblo, to reflect the station's several functions. A WPA project, the station was built with local labor and materials. It was put up for sale in 1972 because the newer and wider trucks could no longer make the turn into the Monte Vista's doors. It was remodeled and opened as the Monte Vista Fire Station Restaurant in 1986. Photo © Marcia Keegan.

ing took place until the late 1930s and 1940s because the city didn't have water and sewer lines in place. The neighborhood is now a combination of small houses built in the 1920s and Southwestern style apartment houses built in the late 1930s and 1940s.

As tuberculosis became the leading threat to health, Albuquerque emerged as a health mecca. The first sanitorium took root in 1902 on the sandy, unpopulated East Mesa, soon followed by more. The University of New Mexico, long the sole occupant of land east of town, now had company.

Housing Boom

Neighborhoods continued to expand across East Mesa, enveloping UNM and moving beyond. More than 300 subdivisions were registered between 1900 and 1940.

The first housing boom was in 1922 with the **Country Club Addition**, named for the club to the east. Later known as **Spruce Park**, this neighborhood has a variety of architectural styles from the period between the two world wars.

Development began in 1925 on **Grenada Heights** on the East Mesa. **Parkland Hills, Knob Heights, Monte Vista** and **College View** followed in 1926. Seventeen subdivisions sprouted in quick succession.

In 1928 lawyer William Keleher and contractor A.R. Hebenstreit acquired land from Franz Huning's heirs and platted the **Huning Castle Addition**, named for the mansion Huning built on Central and Fourteenth in 1883. Swamps made much of the land unattractive for development, but in 1925 the Middle Rio Grande Conservancy organized and began planning projects to control the river and drain marshy lands. Albuquerque Country Club moved from the East Mesa to its current location in 1928, which added cachet to the development. They only got a few homes built before the stock market crash of 1929. Most of the homes in this affluent subdivision, which came to be known as the Country Club neighborhood, were built after World War II.

Today, ten historic neighborhoods surround downtown: **Old Town**, the **Downtown Neighborhoods Area (Perea Addition)**, **Sawmill-Wells Park, McClellan Park, Martineztown (Los Martines)**, **Huning Highlands (Highland Addition)**, **South Broadway (Eastern Addition, San José)**, **Barelas (Los Barelas)**, the **Raynolds Addition**, and **Country Club (Huning Castle Addition)**.

Post-War Boom

The city's biggest growth spurt came after World War II. As Sandia Laboratory was born from a division of Los Alamos Laboratory and the Cold War got into full swing, a massive influx of new residents poured onto the East Mesa, bringing the city's edge to the Sandia Mountains.

Construction began in the late 1950s on two major interstate highways, I-40 and I-25, which intersected near the center of town, helping to secure the city's importance as a major crossroads of commerce. Albuquerque's population swelled from 35,449 in 1940 to 201,189 in 1960, and the once-small Duke City was feeling some big-city growing pains. Homebuilders scurried to meet demand.

In 1950, the city was rapidly annexing land east and north of its borders, and subdivisions were spreading toward the mountains. That year the *Saturday Evening Post* wrote of Albuquerque, "New houses go up in batches of 50 to 300 at a time and transform barren mesas before you get back from lunch." In the four years between 1946 and 1950 the city's area tripled.

City Commission Chairman Clyde Tingley, back from a stint as governor, urged caution against "checkerboard development" that he said would require more infrastructure than the city could afford. Building continued.

The Elena Ross clothing boutique and Satellite Toys and Coffee on Central Avenue in Nob Hill. As its name implies, Satellite Toys and Coffee offers gourmet coffees along with an eclectic selection of toys. It is also a Wi-Fi hotspot. Photo © Marcia Keegan.

In 1950, Sam Hoffman built the 800-home **Hoffmantown Addition** north of Menaul and east of Wyoming. In 1953, Ed Snow's **Snow Heights Addition** followed directly south.

The **Bel-Air Subdivision**, built by Harvey Golightly, initially wanted to incorporate as a separate village. The homes, between Carlisle, San Mateo, Menaul and Candelaria, sold quickly. The subdivision was annexed into the city in 1951.

In 1954, Dale Bellamah's 1,600-home **Princess Jeanne Park**, named for his wife, was built between Lomas and Indian School from Eubank to Juan Tabo. Princess Jeanne offered "wife-planned" homes with fireplaces, spacious patios and such new products as linoleum, Formica and Pulverator disposals.

In the early 1950s Bellamah also built the **Kirtland Addition** just west of the airport. The first residents were white officers from the base. In 1952 Bill Gooden was the first African American to move in. In a 1991 interview he recalled no problems in integrating the neighborhood: "I met my neighbors on both sides and across the street, and we got along well and we enjoyed living there."

That encouraged other black families to join them. The affordable but modern homes were a step up for most black residents. Kirtland Addition was a black neighborhood for years, but it's once again mixed.

West Side

People east of the river sometimes think the West Side just exploded in the last few years. In fact, many West Side neighborhoods are as old as much of the Northeast Heights. West Side development began in 1951, when homebuilder Leon Watson bought land from Florencio Baca, who had lived there since 1936. The development between Central and Bridge near Coors became **Los Altos**.

Two other West Side subdivisions date from the post-war boom. In 1949 the Black family, which owned the Seven Bar Ranch on the West Mesa, sold 8,000 acres to Horizon Land Corporation, and in 1961 Horizon began developing **Paradise Hills**. By 1981 Paradise Hills had 1,800 homes on 12,000 acres and 6,000 residents. The Blacks in 1947 had built a general aviation airport, which became home of Cottonwood Mall.

Taylor Ranch started when Joel and Nina Mae Taylor bought 800 acres in 1939. The Taylors, who had previously lived on the Taylor homestead in Chama, had a two-room adobe house where the La Luz subdivision is now, near Montaño Place and Coors Road. This small house became their winter haven away from snowy Chama, and there is now a street called Winterhaven there. In 1973, the Taylors sold 300 acres to Bellamah Corp., which created the Taylor Ranch subdivision. **Eagle Ranch** also began in the 1970s.

Some Albuquerque Street Names

We hurry down Albuquerque's streets without giving much thought to their namesakes. Some honor important individuals in the city's history:

- **Candelaria Road** is named for the Candelaria family, one of the first to settle in Albuquerque, in 1706.
- **Juan Tabo** is a mystery. Nobody seems to know who Juan Tabo was. According to one account, he was a shepherd who grazed his flock in Tijeras Canyon. The name may also relate to the Toboso Indians of Texas or to Jemez Pueblo.
- **Griegos Road** is named for Juan Griego, who accompanied Don Juan de Oñate's party of colonists to New Mexico in 1598. His descendants settled in the North Valley.
- **Osuna Road** is named for Dr. Elijio Osuna, who came here in the 1890s from Monterey, Mexico. He not only delivered many babies, he was also a coroner.
- **Menaul Boulevard** originally led to Menaul School, named for Irish-born James A. Menaul, who came to Albuquerque in 1881 when the population was 2,200. He organized First Presbyterian Church. In the late 1800s a Presbyterian training school was named for him.
- **Eubank Boulevard** was named for Lt. Col. (later general) Eugene L. Eubank, who was commander of the 19th Bombardment Group here. He led one hundred bombers on a flight from California across the Pacific during World War II.

The Plaza at Los Griegos, 1883. Photo courtesy of the Albuquerque Museum, Image # 1978.050.075.

- **Montgomery Boulevard** was named for Eugene Montgomery. His family homesteaded on land near what is now Carlisle and Montgomery around 1909, when there were 7,000 people in Albuquerque.
- **Spain** is named for Dr. Charles R. Spain, APS school superintendent from 1957–1965.
- **Coors** is named for Henry G. Coors, who was a district attorney and judge in the 1940s and early 1950s.
- **Moon** is named for State Senator Z.B. Moon, who served in the 1930s.
- **Unser** is named for the Unser family, who in the 1940s operated a wrecking service at Unser Garage on 7700 Central SW. The family has gone on to achieve fame in auto racing, participating in every Indianapolis 500 except one since 1964 and winning nine times. The small dirt street adjacent to their family home became Unser Boulevard.

Sources

Biebel, Charles D. *Making the Most of It: Public Works in Albuquerque during the Great Depression 1929–1942* (Albuquerque: Albuquerque Museum, 1986).

Davis, Mary. Albuquerque's Environmental Story: http://www.cabq.gov/aes/

Garcia, Nasario. *Albuquerque: Feliz Cumpleaños! Three Centures to Remember* (Santa Fe: La Herencia, 2005).

Gill, Donald. *Stories Behind the Street Names of Albuquerque, Santa Fe and Taos* (Chicago: Bonus Books, 1994).

Simmons, Marc. *Albuquerque: A Narrative History* (Albuquerque: UNM Press, 1982).

PART II

ALBUQUERQUE
Visitors' Guide

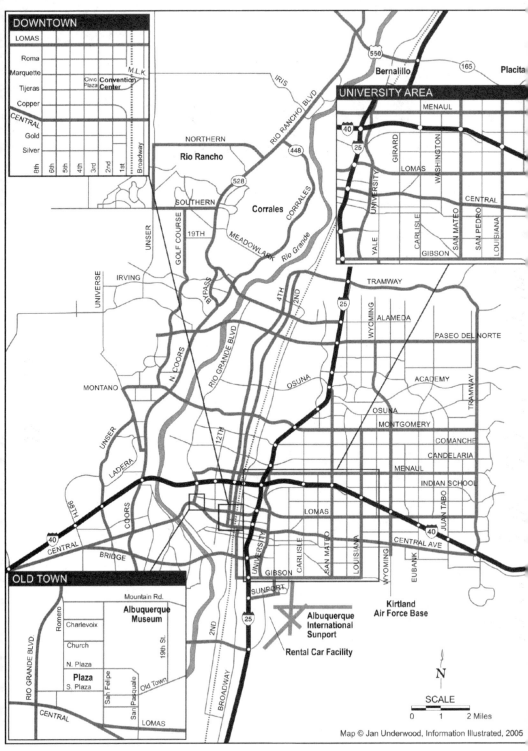

DOWNTOWN

LOMAS
Roma
Marquette
Tijeras
Copper
CENTRAL
Gold
Silver

M.L.K.
Civic Plaza · Convention Center

8th · 6th · 5th · 4th · 3rd · 2nd · 1st · Broadway

NORTHERN
Rio Rancho
SOUTHERN
Corrales
Corrales
Meadowlark
Rio Grande
RIO RANCHO BLVD
IRIS
448
528
19TH
GOLF COURSE
BYPASS
4TH
2ND

550
Bernalillo
165
Placita

UNIVERSITY AREA

MENAUL
40
25
UNIVERSITY
YALE
GIRARD
LOMAS
CARLISLE
WASHINGTON
SAN MATEO
SAN PEDRO
LOUISIANA
CENTRAL
GIBSON

TRAMWAY
25
WYOMING
ALAMEDA
PASEO DEL NORTE
ACADEMY
TRAMWAY
OSUNA
OSUNA
MONTGOMERY
COMANCHE
CANDELARIA
MENAUL
INDIAN SCHOOL
JUAN TABO
40
CENTRAL AVE
EUBANK

UNSER
UNIVERSE
IRVING
MONTANO
N. COORS
RIO GRANDE BLVD
12TH
LADERA
UNSER
H1.86
COORS
40
CENTRAL
BRIDGE

LOMAS
UNIVERSITY
CARLISLE
SAN MATEO
LOUISIANA
WYOMING
GIBSON

25
SUNPORT

Kirtland
Air Force Base

Albuquerque International
Sunport

Rental Car Facility

OLD TOWN

Mountain Rd.
Albuquerque Museum
Romero
Charlevoix
Church
N. Plaza
Plaza
S. Plaza
RIO GRANDE BLVD
San Felipe
San Pasquale
Old Town
19th St.
CENTRAL
LOMAS
2ND
BROADWAY
25

N

SCALE
0   1   2 Miles

Map © Jan Underwood, Information Illustrated, 2005

www.itsatrip.org

TRAVEL INFORMATION

Albuquerque…a name somewhat difficult to spell, but a word that conjures up curiosity, a place that offers diversity, and a destination that fulfills travel promises. The largest city in New Mexico, its blue and sunny skies mean at least 310 days of sunshine during the year! That alone means outdoor events are rarely called off due to weather.

Although over 670,000 people live in the metro area, the city spreads over 100 square miles and retains a neighborhood feel. The terrain resembles parts of Spain and Greece and has a low humidity. It is guarded on its eastern edge by the massive Sandia Mountains (10,678 ft.—3,255 m.) and is sliced from north to south by the Rio Grande. City elevations range from 4,500 ft. (1,372 m.) to 6,500 ft. (1,981 m.) in the foothills of the Sandia Mountains.

The city is now three centuries old and while it embraces its past, it is poised for its future. New attractions and venues are showing off for residents and visitors while perennial favorites like the Balloon Fiesta, State Fair, and luminaria tour continue to draw large audiences.

This guidebook offers general background about the city, its attractions and amenities, and gives readers the most current information possible through its Internet connections. Every section lists specific websites to assist trip planners with information and arrangements.

We thank the Albuquerque Convention & Visitors Bureau for generous assistance with information and maps.

Distances to Albuquerque

City	Miles	Kilometers
Dallas	655	1,048
Denver	448	717
El Paso	267	427
Las Cruces	225	360
Los Alamos	94	150
Phoenix	452	723
Roswell	202	323
Santa Fe	59	94
Taos	129	206

Seasons & Climate

Albuquerque has four distinct seasons. Mild winters and warm, comfortable summers make Albuquerque a year-round city.

Average Temperature	High/Low Degrees F
Annual	70/43
January	47/23
February	53/27
March	61/33
April	70/41
May	79/50
June	89/59
July	92/64
August	89/63
September	82/56
October	71/44
November	57/31
December	48/24

Visitor Information

Telephone numbers you might need:

Area code for Albuquerque (and all of New Mexico)	505
Albuquerque Convention & Visitors Bureau	(505) 842-9918
	or (800) 284-2282
Albuquerque Hispano Chamber of Commerce	(505) 842-9003
Greater Albuquerque Chamber of Commerce	(505) 764-3700
New Mexico Department of Tourism	(505) 827-7400
	or (800) 545-2040
New Mexico Tourism Department	(800) SEE-NEW-MEX
www.newmexico.org	or (800) 733-6396

Emergency

Albuquerque Animal Emergency Clinic	(505) 884-3433
Ambulance	(505) 761-8200
Emergency Road Service (AAA)	(800) AAA-HELP
Poison Control Center	(505) 272-2222/(800) 222-1222
Police, Fire, Ambulance or Rescue Units	911
Police Non-Emergency Dispatch	(505) 242-COPS (242-2677)
Sheriff	(505) 768-4160
State Police	(505) 841-9256

Urgent Care

Presbyterian

North Valley	3901 Atrisco NW	(505) 462-7575
Far NE Heights off I-25	5901 Harper NE	(505) 823-8888
	4100 High Resort Blvd NE	(505) 462-8888
South Valley	3436 Isleta Blvd SW	(505) 462-7777
Pediatric urgent care	1100 Central SE	(505) 841-1819

Lovelace

Far NE Heights	5150 Journal Center NE	(505) 262-3233
Far NE Heights	9101 Montgomery NE	(505) 275-4259
Rio Rancho	3801 Southern Blvd	(505) 896-8600

General

American Red Cross	(505) 265-8514
Better Business Bureau	(505) 346-0110
Crime Stoppers	(505) 843-7867
Road Conditions	(800) 432-4269
Weatherline Forecast Service (time & temperature)	(505) 821-1111

Licenses

Hunting & Fishing Licenses	(505) 841-8881 or (800) ASK-FISH
Marriage Licenses	(505) 768-4314
Passports	(800) 275-8777

Medical

Albuquerque District Dental Society	(505) 237-1412
Albuquerque Regional Medical Center	(505) 727-8000

Transportation

Albuquerque International Sunport (airport)	(505) 244-7700
Alvarado Transportation Center (train/bus station)	(505) 764-6100
Information Center for New Mexicans with Disabilities and Baby Net	(800) 552-8195
Amtrak	(505) 842-9650
City Bus	(505) 243-RIDE
Highway Hotline (road conditions)	(800) 432-4269

ALBUQUERQUE AREA TOURS

Transportation & Tours

Albuquerque is a spread-out city, bordered on its eastern edge by the Sandia Mountains and largely defined on its western edge by inactive volcanoes. But in between there is so much to see and do. You can explore on your own, or you can engage the services of a tour company to better acquaint you with the "Duke City."

A number of companies cater to group business, but some individuals may want to see more of the area with someone who handles all the driving—and parking! There are companies ready to help you. Also, if the family auto wasn't how you got to Albuquerque, a number of rental car and RV companies offer a broad selection of vehicles.

Want something more daring? Try a motorcycle! Something more classy? Try a limousine. Rentals are available for either. Shuttle services to and from the Albuquerque Sunport (airport) also are available for either individual or group transfers. Accessibility services also are available. In fact there are several companies offering specially equipped vehicles for rent so that travelers with disabilities can explore on their own, too.

While cab service is available curbside of the Sunport and at most major hotels, generally plan on a call with a short wait to engage this service.

Albuquerque Transit offers public transportation to virtually all areas of the city. Schedules are available online at www.cabq.gov/transit/ and in the information centers operated by the Albuquerque Convention & Visitors Bureau.

If you are adventurous and want to explore on your own, suggested itineraries are available in *The Official Visitors Guide and Vacation Planner* offered by the Albuquerque Convention & Visitors Bureau. The itineraries include a drive route listing distance and a suggested length of time. Each of the five itineraries is listed by theme ("Route 66," "Science and Tech," "Nature," "Arts & History," and "Sandia Mountains"). The "Jemez Mountains," northwest of the city with spectacular scenery and some outstanding sites (Bandelier National Monument), is the final itinerary in the guide.

For group transfers and arrangements, visit the website of the Albuquerque Convention & Visitors Bureau at www.itsatrip.org.

Conservatory at Rio Grande Botanic Gardens. Photo courtesy City of Albuquerque.

Train, Bus and Airplane

Albuquerque is served by Amtrak (www.amtrak.com), Greyhound (www.greyhound.com), at the Alvarado Transportation Center at First and Central SW and the following airlines: American (www.aa.com), America West (www.americawest.com), Continental (www.continental.com), Delta (www.delta.com), Northwest (www.nwa.com), Southwest (www.southwest.com) and United (www.united.com). All airline carriers are located at the Albuquerque International Sunport, 2200 Sunport SE.

Shuttle Services

Several shuttles are available that serve the Albuquerque area.

Airport Shuttle
2909 Yale SE
(505) 765-1234
www.airportshuttleabq.com

Sunport Shuttle
3223 Los Arboles NE
(505) 883-4966 or (866) 505-4966
www.sunportshuttle.com

Auto Rentals

There is free shuttle service from the Albuquerque Sunport terminal to the nearby auto rental complex.

Advantage Rent-A-Car
6601 San Mateo Ste. C-8
(505) 884-8973 or (800) 777-5500
www.arac.com

Hertz Corporation
3400 University SE Ste. 1
(505) 842-4235 or (800) 654-3131
www.hertz.com

Avis Rent-A-Car
Albuquerque International Sunport
(505) 842-4080 or (800) 331-1212
www.avis.com/local/abq

National Car Rental
2800 Girard SE
(505) 724-4500 or (800) 227-7368
www.nationalcar.com

Budget Car & Truck Rental
3400 University SE Ste Q
(505) 242-7893 or (800) 527-0700
www.drivebudget.com

Rent A Wreck
2010 Ridgecrest SE
(505) 232-7552 or (800) 247-9556
www.rent-a-wreck.com

Enterprise Rent-A-Car
40+ Locations in NM
(505) 765-9100 or (800) RENT-A-CAR
www.enterprise.com

Thrifty Car Rental
3400 University SE Ste. T
(505) 847-4389 or (877) 283-0898
www.Thrifty.com

RV and Oversize Vehicle Rentals

Visitors to Albuquerque and New Mexico frequently include excursions to rural and/or mountainous areas in their travel plans and therefore may need to rent recreational or oversize vehicles.

Capps Van Rental
2200 Renard Pl. SE
(505) 848-8267
www.cappsvanrental.com

Cruise America RV Rentals
12400 Skyline Rd.
(505) 275-3550 or (800) RV4-RENT
www.cruiseamerica.com

Specialty Tour Companies

Ancient Storytellers Tours

Take a specialized tour of the New Mexico Pueblos with Ancient Storytellers. They offer custom tours by native-owned operators.
(505) 747-6710
www.ancientstorytellers.com

B & B Photo Tours

Photo tours and seminars.
8405 Monitor NE
(505) 821-8537
www.balloonphotography.com

Follow the Sun Tours

Golf, casino, shopping.
10131 Coors Rd. 1-2 Ste 825
(505) 897-2886 or (866) 428-4SUN
www.ftstours.com

New Mexico Ghost Tours

Old Town Albuquerque Ghost Tour
Albuquerque walking tours at night.
(505) 249-7827
www.nmghosttours.com

Handicapped Services

Here is where you can rent specially equipped vehicles while you are in town.
Wheelchair Getaways of New Mexico
1015 Tramway Ln. NE
(505) 247-2626 or (800) 408-2626
www.wheelchair-getaways.com or www.ims-vans.com

Unguided Private Tours

The following area tours are detailed in the Official Albuquerque Guidebook published by the Albuquerque Convention & Visitors Bureau. These are suggested itineraries for individuals in private vehicles. They are not set tours offered by a company but rather trips tourists can take on their own.

Route 66 Tour includes Historic Nob Hill District, University of New Mexico, Downtown District, Alvarado Transportation Center, Crossroads Mall, KiMo Theatre and Historic Old Town.

Science & Tech Tour includes NM Museum of Natural History & Science, LodeStar Astronomy Center, explora!, National Atomic Museum, UNM Museum of Geology & Meteoritics and Sandia Peak Aerial Tramway.

Nature Tour includes Albuquerque Aquarium and Rio Grande Botanic Gardens, Rio Grande Zoo, NM Museum of Natural History & Science, Rio Grande Nature Center, Sandia Peak Aerial Tramway and Wildlife West Nature Park.

Arts & History Tour includes Petroglyph National Monument, Historic Old Town, Albuquerque Museum of Art & History, NM Museum of Natural History & Science, KiMo Theatre, National Hispanic Cultural Center, University of New Mexico, Tamarind Lithography Institute and Gallery and Historic Nob Hill District.

Jemez Mountains Tour includes San Ysidro and Jemez Mountains, Jemez River and Jemez Pueblo, Gillman Tunnels/ Guadalupe River Canyon, Jemez Springs and Jemez State Monument, Soda Dam, Battleship Rock, Spence Hot Springs and La Cueva, Jemez Canyon, Valle Grande and Redondo Peak, Bandelier National Monument, Los Alamos and Kasha-Katuwee Tent Rocks National Monument.

Sandia Mountains Tour includes Tijeras Canyon, the Sandia and Manzano Mountains, Turquoise Trail, Sandia Ranger Station, NM 536 and Cedar Crest, Sandia Peak and Sandia Peak Ski Area, Golden, Madrid and Cerrillos.

American Indian Cultural Tour includes Petroglyph National Monument, Coronado State Monument, El Camino Real, Indian Pueblo Cultural Center, Acoma Pueblo and Jemez Pueblo.

The Sandia Peak Tram will take you up into the clouds. Photo © Jay Blackwood.

Exploring the Routes

While there's plenty to do in the immediate Albuquerque area, there's also opportunity to explore beyond and follow one of the trails that will lead you to yet another vacation memory. Some of these trails are fabled—like Route 66—and can promise lots of geography to cover. Others are less known but no less interesting, like the Mission Route.

If a comfortable stroll is more your style, stay in town and take a walk—from the Civic Plaza downtown to the Plaza in the heart of Old Town, discovering well-established neighborhoods en route.

More information on these and other routes is available from the Albuquerque Convention & Visitors Bureau (www.itsatrip.org) and the New Mexico Tourism Department (www.newmexico.org). Maps are available from both sites with more information about sights to see and events occurring.

City Walking Tour

Some of Albuquerque's oldest neighborhoods are the setting for an easy walking excursion from **Civic Plaza** downtown to the Plaza in the heart of **Old Town**. Visit www.cabq.gov, the city of Albuquerque website, for more information and a walking tour map.

Route 66

Route 66 is considered by many to be America's most celebrated highway. It travels, as the song says, from Chicago to L.A. But the portion in New Mexico has had two different alignments over time. The first ran more north-south and included Santa Fe along with Albuquerque. The second, and current, is a straighter alignment and bypasses Santa Fe.

Church in the town of Golden on the Turquoise Trail. Photo © Marcia Keegan..

In Albuquerque, route aficionados can travel along the original alignment: Fourth Street south to Bridge, west to Isleta and south again to see some of the sites of the route. The itinerary passes through Barelas, whose commercial district is listed in the National Register of Historic Places and now includes the **National Hispanic Cultural Center**. Later the route was changed to run east-west, along Central Avenue.

Today one can also find Route 66 on a nighttime cruise up Nine Mile Hill on the west side of the city, or into Tijeras Canyon, the city's eastern gateway.

Turquoise Trail
NM-14/NM-536
(888) 263-0003

Turquoise Trail

This trail is a national scenic byway along NM-14/NM-536 on the east side of the Sandia Mountains. Former gold and coal mining towns along the route are finding second lives as artists' communities. Outstanding scenery, historical highlights, and great outdoor opportunities are reasons to take the Turquoise Trail.

The small community of Tijeras is the gateway to the Turquoise Trail, but the high point literally is **Sandia Crest**, where the mountains peak at an elevation of 10,678 ft.

www.turquoisetrail.org

Mission Route

Explore and experience some of central New Mexico's dramatic Spanish mission ruins within a 50-mile radius. **Quarai** is the best-preserved and, along with **Abo**, is an easy drive from Albuquerque. **Gran Quivira** is the farthest south, but best of all, entry to all three sites is free. (505) 847-2585
www.nps.gov/sapu

Mission Route
Quarai
Abo
Gran Quivira
(505) 847-2585

El Camino Real

Historical markers from Las Cruces in southern New Mexico to Santa Fe mark this national scenic byway. El Camino Real (The Royal Road), once the longest trail in North America, linked colonial Santa Fe with Mexico City. This 1,800-mile road was the route Spaniards traveled 400 years ago, but hundreds of years earlier, Puebloan people used the same trail. Today Interstate 25 follows roughly the same routing. Within the city it is partially Isleta Blvd. and 4th St. running north-south.

The road cuts through New Mexico and offers access to Indian lands, farming communities, and urban areas as well.
www.byways.org/browse/byways/2065/travel.html

El Camino Real
El Paso to Santa Fe

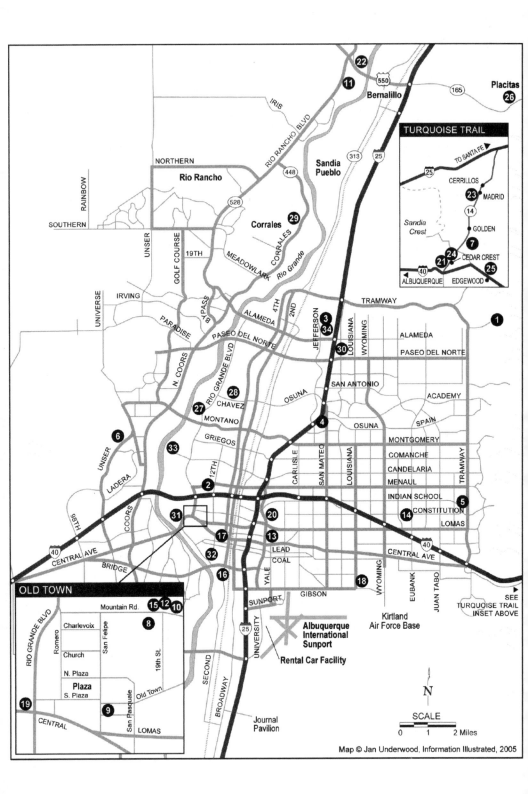

TURQUOISE TRAIL

TO SANTA FE

CERRILLOS

23 MADRID

14

Sandia Crest

GOLDEN

7

24 CEDAR CREST

21

25

ALBUQUERQUE EDGEWOOD

SEE TURQUOISE TRAIL INSET ABOVE

OLD TOWN

Rio Grande Blvd

Romero

Charlevoix

Church

San Felipe

19th St.

Mountain Rd.

15 12 10

8

N. Plaza

Plaza

S. Plaza

9

San Pasquale

Old Town

19

CENTRAL

LOMAS

Albuquerque International Sunport

Rental Car Facility

Kirtland Air Force Base

Journal Pavilion

N

SCALE

0   1   2 Miles

Map © Jan Underwood, Information Illustrated, 2005

ALBUQUERQUE ATTRACTIONS

1. Sandia Peak Aerial Tramway
2. Indian Pueblo Cultural Center
3. Balloon Fiesta Park
4. Cliff's Amusement Park
5. Hinkle Family Fun Center
6. Petroglyph National Monument
7. Turquoise Trail National Byway
8. Albuquerque Museum of Art & History
9. American Rattlesnake Museum
10. Explora! Science Center and Children's Museum of Albuquerque
11. J & R Vintage Auto Museum
12. Lodestar Astronomy Center, New Mexico Museum of Natural History & Science
13. Maxwell Museum of Anthropology
14. Museum of Archaeology & Biblical History
15. National Atomic Museum
16. National Hispanic Cultural Center
17. New Mexico Holocaust & Intolerance Museum
18. New Mexico Veterans Memorial
19. Turquoise Museum, Inc.
20. University of New Mexico Museums
21. Archeology and Material Culture Museum
22. Coronado State Monument
23. Old Coal Mine Museum
24. Tinkertown Museum
25. Wildlife West Nature Park
26. Anasazi Fields Winery
27. Anderson Valley Vineyards
28. Casa Rondeña Winery
29. Corrales Winery
30. Gruet Winery
31. Albuquerque Aquarium, Rio Grande Botanic Garden
32. Rio Grande Zoo
33. Rio Grande Nature Center State Park
34. Anderson-Abruzzo Albuquerque International Balloon Museum

Map © Jan Underwood Information Illustrated, courtesy of Albuquerque Convention & Visitors Bureau, **www.itsatrip.org**.

ATTRACTIONS & MUSEUMS

Albuquerque answers the question, "What's there to do?" by asking another one: "What are you interested in?"

This destination is a bonanza for the curious traveler. It offers outdoor recreation; it provides family-friendly activities; it showcases its history, culture and arts in a variety of museums and public arts installations; and it satisfies those wanting to experience indigenous dining and shopping. It's the hub for visitors wanting to see ancient lava flows, Indian pueblos, extinct volcanoes, and travel along fabled trails.

Yes, there are museums that extol everything from rattlesnakes and turquoise to *conquistadors* (Spanish conquerors) and nuclear science. There's an amusement park whose roller coaster is called the Rattler and a mountain tramway that's the second longest in North America. Both Native Americans and Hispanics show off everything from arts and crafts to traditional celebrations. And then there are the balloons—the hot-air balloons that have brought international recognition to Albuquerque, as both the site of the annual **Balloon Fiesta** and the **Anderson-Abruzzo Albuquerque International Balloon Museum**.

Lesser known but equally interesting attractions in the area start with the **Madonna of the Trail Monument**, one of twelve such that stretch from Bethesda, Maryland to Upland, California. These monuments started with an effort in the early 1900s to mark the Santa Fe Trail. The statue of a pioneer woman with inscriptions dedicated to national and regional history is located on the northwest corner of the grounds of the Federal Building at 4th and Lomas NW www.route40.net/madonnas/index.shtml.

Another Madonna is to be found carved in a tree trunk behind **San Felipe de Neri Church** in Old Town. And just up the street, sheltered behind Saints & Martyrs shop, is **Our Lady of Guadalupe Chapel**, open to the public for private prayer and special occasions.

At **Los Poblanos Inn & La Quinta Conference Center** in the North Valley, the public is invited to pick lavender in season (www.lospoblanos.com). Nature lovers and bird watchers are invited to **Rio Grande Nature Center State Park** where cranes winter over along the *bosque* (riverside forest).

For those interested in genealogy, both the **National Hispanic Cultural Center** (www.nhccnm.org) and the **Special Collections Library** (www.cabq.gov/library/special) offer services that specialize in Spanish records.

A look inside the Anderson-Abruzzo Albuquerque International Balloon Museum. Photo © MarbleStreetStudio.com.

Boys enjoying one of Cliff's Amusement Park's newest rides, The Falling Star. Photo courtesy Cliff's Amusement Park.

Area exploring also offers some interesting features like **Mystery Stone**, the source of conflicting explanations about the meaning of its inscriptions as well as its age, variously dated between 500 to 2000 years old. It is located in Hidden Mountain, six miles west of Los Lunas (south of Albuquerque) along an unmarked dirt road. Contact the State Land Office, (505) 841-8705, or the Isleta Pueblo Governor's Office, (505) 869-3111, for more information, or call (505) 352-3596 for a map.

Archaeological sites are evident throughout the area. One example is the *kivas* (ceremonial chambers) dating back to the 1300s found at **Coronado State Monument**, (505) 867-5351, near Bernalillo, north of the city. Tijeras Pueblo, (505) 281-3304, is today only a large, grass-covered mound half a mile south of I-40 in Tijeras at Albuquerque's eastern edge. The **Maxwell Museum of Anthropology** on the University of New Mexico campus has exhibits that emphasize the cultural heritage of the Southwest, while **Tinkertown Museum** in the Sandia Mountains offers a vast collection of miniature wood-carved figures along with an eccentric collection of Americana.

Also see the **Indian Pueblo Cultural Center** (www.indianpueblo.org), the **New Mexico Natural History Museum** and **McCall's Pumpkin Patch** for pumpkin picking in season (www.mccallpumpkinpatch.com).

Traveling with family and/or children? Explore one or all of the many museums that Albuquerque has to offer or take the kids for a little nature walk at the **Rio Grande Nature Center**. The Nature Center is surrounded by bosque and meadows, so whether you are with kids or not, embrace the tranquility of untouched bosque with more than 260 species of birds living there.

Fill the day with fun with an outing to New Mexico's only amusement park, **Cliff's Amusement Park**, with the wild rides like the "New Mexico Rattler." Between the thrilling rides and the fun Kiddieland, this park is great for anyone.

Head on over to **Hinkle Family Fun Center** to show off those fabulous miniature golf skills! Hinkle Family Fun Center is packed to the max with entertainment, with a massive arcade, two miniature golf courses, bumper boats, Go-Karts, laser tag and Nickel City (a smaller arcade).

With or without children, you should take a trip to Historic **Old Town**, the original settlement founded in 1706. Walking in the Plaza will give visitors a true feel for the offbeat eccentricity of New Mexico style. The pedestrian-friendly sidewalks are lined with jewelry and crafts sellers. Old Town Plaza has four museums within walking distance, weekend gunfights all year long except for winter and nighttime walking tours for ghosts.

For a relaxing afternoon, visit the **Albuquerque Biological Park**. There are many options here to fill the day—the **Rio Grande Zoo**, the **Albuquerque Aquarium**, featuring fish from stingrays to sharks, and the **Rio Grande Botanic Gardens**. The Zoological Park is located right near Old Town and showcases the famous and beautiful white tigers. The Aquarium allows visitors to get up close and personal with large Gulf sharks, eels, and schooling fish. The Botanic Garden boasts sixteen acres of land, including a conservatory, and is a popular site for beautiful weddings and receptions.

For a true experience of New Mexico culture and history, **Petroglyph National Monument** has it. See all of the ancient Indian petroglyphs carved into black rock made from Albuquerque's six extinct volcanoes.

Tourism reaches its peak in Albuquerque during the ever-famous **Balloon Fiesta** in October. Now, tourists can see year-round what makes the early fall Balloon Fiesta season so special. The **Anderson-Abruzzo International Balloon Museum** showcases a Balloon Hall of Fame and overlooks the balloon launch field. Located in the Albuquerque Balloon Fiesta Park, this museum is sure to teach and fascinate visitors.

When visitors are looking for a little excitement, the **Sandia Motor Speedway** satisfies every request. Located about eighteen miles west of Albuquerque, the speedway features an Indy car-NASCAR two kilometer racing oval track, a drag strip, a natural terrain road course and a motorcycle course! Fill your ears with the sound of roaring engines and shouting fans.

La Jornada, a multi-piece bronze sculpture depicting the epic journey of the first European colonists to the Southwest by Reynaldo "Sonny" Rivera and Betty Sabo at the Albuquerque Museum. Photo © Marcia Keegan.

Museums

With more than fifteen museums in Albuquerque and the surrounding area, Albuquerque is sure to have every topic covered—art, history, science and culture. Learn a little or a lot about dinosaurs, Indian and Hispanic culture, even rockets. Bring your kids, relatives or just yourself for fun and educational enjoyment!

Old Town Area

2000 Mountain Rd. NW
87104
(505) 243-7255

See art of the Southwest and 400 years of Albuquerque history.

Albuquerque Museum of Art & History

Enjoy amazing art exhibits featuring a diverse array of displays. The Albuquerque Museum of Art & History also offers tours to show off their permanent and traveling exhibits. Also offered are tours venturing out of the museum of Old Town, or even the Casa San Ysidro, a historic nineteenth century rancho located in Corrales. Tour the beautiful Sculpture Garden, which features more than fifty sculptures by artists from all over the world.

www.albuquerquemuseum.com

American International Rattlesnake Museum

Featuring the largest collection of live rattlesnakes in the world, this museum explores the myths, facts and science of rattlesnakes. If snakes tickle your fancy, come and view rattlesnakes from North, South and Central America. The American International Rattlesnake Museum even features a live Gila monster.

www.rattlesnakes.com

202 San Felipe NW, Ste. A
87104
(505) 242-6569

Also features an extensive collection of snake memorabilia and gift items.

Explora! Science Center and Children's Museum of Albuquerque

Round up the kids for an exciting and educational outing they won't forget! Explora has 50,000 square feet of hands-on and interactive exhibits that make science and technology fun. Besides the 250 exhibits, there's an Explora theater to view performing arts, and there's a fantastic Explora shop to purchase at-home science kits, books and puzzles. Don't worry—adults will enjoy this museum just as much as the youngsters.

www.explora.mus.nm.us

1701 Mountain Rd. NW 87104
(505) 224-8300

Hands-on scientific exploration fun for kids of all ages.

Entrance to Explora! Science Center and Children's Museum of Albuquerque.
Photo courtesy City of Albuquerque.

Enjoy Indian dancing at the Indian Pueblo Cultural Center. Photo © Marcia Keegan.

2401 12th St. NW
87104
(505) 843-7270 or
(800) 766-4405

Fun for the whole
family.

Indian Pueblo Cultural Center

The culture of New Mexico's nineteen Pueblos is featured at the Indian Pueblo Cultural Center, where traditional dances are performed every weekend. Enjoy the shows while feasting on authentic Southwestern and Native American cuisine, or stop by the gift shop and browse through Native American hand-crafted items. Also featured at the Indian Pueblo Cultural Center is a museum to learn about Pueblo history and culture, while the kids can go to the Children's Pueblo House museum. This cultural center is fun for the whole family.

www.indianpueblo.org

1801 Mountain Rd.
NW
87104-1375
(505) 841-5955

Visit the Natural History
Museum at the same
time!

Lodestar Astronomy Center

Located inside the New Mexico Museum of Natural History & Science, the Lodestar Astronomy Center has a fabulous planetarium and observatory to gaze up at the beautiful constellations and planets. After the planetarium, stop by the planet exhibit to venture into outer space! Before you leave, check out the StarWorks Astronomy Store for some stellar shopping.

www.lodestar.unm.edu

National Atomic Museum

Come down to learn more about the intriguing study of nuclear science and history. The National Atomic Museum features exhibits displaying the applications of nuclear energy. One exhibit offers children the chance to dive in for hands-on science activities in ZOOMzone!

www.atomicmuseum.com

1905 Mountain Rd. NW 87104
(505) 245-2137

This museum promises an educational experience for all ages.

New Mexico Museum of Natural History & Science

This extraordinary museum showcases everything from dinosaurs to outer space. Venture through the many exhibits, including The Age of Volcanoes, which allows visitors to walk through an active volcano re-creation and actually feel the heat! Take your learning experience to a whole new level with the extreme screen DynaTheater, which lets visitors see a virtual exploration of topics including insects and underwater creatures. This enormous screen measures 65 feet wide by 49 feet high. Also stop by the previously mentioned Lodestar Astronomy Center, the Naturalist Center and the Learning Garden, all inside this great museum.

www.nmnaturalhistory.org

1801 Mountain Rd. NW 87104
(505) 841-2800 OR (866) NM-DINOS

Visit the Lodestar Astronomy Center at the same time!

The New Mexico Museum of Natural History & Science offers fascinating exhibits that take advantage of the state's natural wealth. Photo © MarbleStreetStudio.com.

2107 Central Ave.
NW
87104
(505) 247-8650

Everything you want to
know about turquoise.

Turquoise Museum, Inc.

Turquoise is New Mexico's staple for authentic southwestern jewelry. Come learn all about turquoise, mines, history and lapidary, plus consumer education about this wonderful blue stone that New Mexico is famous for.

www.itsatrip.org/media/museums/#110

Northwest Albuquerque

1776 Montano NW
(505) 836-1800
(866) 258-6737

Race fans will love it!

Unser Racing Museum

Learn the history of four generations of the famous auto racing Unser family and see more than thirty racecars.

www.unserracingmuseum.com

Downtown

1701 4th St. SW
87102
(505) 246-2261

The NHCC has staged
over 20 art exhibitions
and 400 programs in
the visual, performing,
and literary arts since
2000.

National Hispanic Cultural Center

Learn about Albuquerque's rich Hispanic culture through storytelling, lectures and demonstrations. Also featured here are visual arts, drama, dance, literary arts, film, culinary arts and even genealogy. The main focus is to educate and entertain with great Hispanic culture and history. Enjoy spectacular performances, learn and review the local and traditional art, and spark those taste buds with some authentic New Mexico cuisine.

www.nhccnm.org

415 Central Ave. NW
87102
(505) 247-0606

Goal of combatting
hate and intolerance
through education.

New Mexico Holocaust & Intolerance Museum & Study Center

Exhibits about genocide, including the Holocaust, will inform and educate any visitor. There is an educational mini-theater with feature films about genocide. Admission is free.

www.nmholocaustmuseum.org

A statue of a wolf, the "Lobo," stands proud among a grove of ponderosa pines on the campus of the University of New Mexico. Photo © Marcia Keegan.

University of New Mexico Museums

Each of these museums is on the University of New Mexico campus.

Maxwell Museum of Anthropology
Exhibits cover the world's cultures, emphasizing the Southwest. Watch for the monthly sales of Pueblo bread baked on-site in a Pueblo oven.
www.unm.edu/~maxwell

Maxwell Museum of Anthropology
(505) 277-4405

Geology & Meteoritics Museum
Rock hounds will enjoy a display of mineral specimens dinosaur bones and moon rocks.
http://epswww.unm.edu/museum.htm

Geology & Meteoritics Museum
(505) 277-4204

University Art Museum
A permanent collection including works by Georgia O'Keefe, along with changing exhibits.
http://nmartmuseum.unm.edu

University Art Museum
(505) 277-4001

The Tamarind Lithography Institute
Internationally recognized for training, research and publication of fine art lithography.
http://tamarind.unm.edu

Tamarind Lithography Institute
(505) 277-3901

New Mexico Veterans Memorial. Photo courtesy of the New Mexico Veterans Memorial.

Northern area of the city

9201 Balloon
Museum Dr. NE
(505) 768-6020

Anderson-Abruzzo Albuquerque International Balloon Museum
Located in the Capital of Ballooning, this museum celebrates the art, history and science of hot-air ballooning.
www.cabq.gov/balloon

Southeast area of the city

1100 Louisiana SE
(505) 256-2042

New Mexico Veterans Memorial
This site includes a museum, an amphitheatre for special military activities and events and a visitors' center, along with special commemorative venues.
http://NMVetsMemorial.org

Outside greater Albuquerque

22 Calvary Rd.
(4 miles N Hwy. 14)
Cedar Crest
(505) 281-2005

Archaeology & Material Culture Museum
Explore archaeology over a 12,000 year generalized timeline.
www.museumarch.org

Coronado State Monument

Indian and Spanish exhibits, original murals painted in 1300s; picnic area.

www.nmmonuments.org

485 Kuana Rd.
I-25 Exit 242
Bernalillo
(505) 867-5351

J&R Vintage Auto Museum

With more than sixty-five cars, J&R Vintage Auto Museum is sure to be heaven for any car lover. It features vehicles from the 1920s and '30s, as well as some newer cars.

www.jrvintageautos.com

3650 A. Hwy. 528,
Rio Rancho 87124
(505) 867-2881 or
(888) 298-1885

Tinkertown Museum (seasonal)

Life work of Ross Ward, one of New Mexico's renowned folk artists, features hand-carved miniature Old West towns.

www.tinkertown.com

121 Sandia Crest Rd.
Sandia Park
(505) 281-5233

The animated and entertaining Rusty Wyer Band plays old-time tunes for a mere 25 cents at the Tinkertown Museum. Photo © Megan Ward.

SPORTS & RECREATION

You want to be a player on the courts, fields or at the gaming tables? Or do you prefer the spectator section? In Albuquerque, the choice is yours. And because the weather is so comfortable year-round—310 days of sunshine annually—it's virtually assured you won't be rained out.

Individual sports for the vacationer range from golf on some spectacular scenic courses to hot-air ballooning over the Rio Grande Valley. Fourteen public and private golf courses in the city and tennis courts are scattered all over town. Winter means skiing or snowboarding in the **Sandia Mountains**.

Albuquerque is a home base for more active sports in the region, including river rafting and skiing. But if a comfortable seat and a drink suit you better, consider baseball at Isotopes Stadium, men's and women's basketball by the **UNM Lobos** at "The Pit" as well as the NBA development league **Albuquerque Thunderbirds** at Tingley Coliseum, or football at UNM Stadium. The **Sandia Motor Speedway** offers Indy Car/Nascar racing, and **Albuquerque Downs** is the place for thoroughbred horse racing. Hockey in season from the pro-hockey franchise **Scorpions,** located in nearby Rio Rancho, is yet another option.

Because hot-air ballooning is so identified with Albuquerque, a number of companies are available for rides, but always weather permitting. And of course, the annual **Albuquerque International Balloon Fiesta** offers rides for individuals and groups.

Families in particular can spend time together at any of the amusement centers in the city. Hiking, fishing and hunting in the Sandias, indoor climbing at **Stone Age Climbing Gym**—take your pick and have fun.

Amusement Centers

Cliff's Amusement Park
Thrill rides, family rides, water attractions and Kiddieland.
4800 Osuna NE, (505) 881-9373
www.cliffsamusementpark.com

Hinkle Family Fun Center
Laser Tag, Go-Karts, miniature golf, bumper boats, paintball and arcades.
12901 Indian School NE, (505) 299-3100
www.hinklefamilyfuncenter.com

The New Mexico Rattler, voted one of the Top 25 Wooden Coasters in the world. Photo courtesy of Cliff's Amusement Park.

Visitors can enjoy hot air ballooning year round due to the mild climate in Albuquerque.
Photo © MarbleStreetStudio.com

Ballooning

Because Albuquerque is considered the "Hot-Air Balloon Capital of the World," a visit here frequently includes a ride in a hot air-balloon. A number of companies offer both individual and group rates and rides, along with a special "certification" ceremony.

Above & Beyond Affordable Balloon Rides
11520 San Bernadino NE
(505) 293-0000 or (800) 725-2477
www.aboveandbeyondballoonrides.com

Above It All Balloon Rides of Albuquerque
(505) 861-3386 or (800) 955-3715
www.balloonridesnewmexico.com

Albuquerque Sweet Escape Balloon Rides
216 Dogwood Trail SE
Rio Rancho
(505) 891-7634 or (800) 385-4453
www.members.aol.com/swtescap/myweb.htm

Beautiful Balloons Company
PO Box 30584
(505) 261-8249 or (800) 367-6625
www.beautifulballoonsco.com

Enchanted Winds Hot Air Balloon Company
Operated by Rainbow Ryders
11520 San Bernadino NE
(505) 843-6888 or (800) 725-2477
http://enchantedwinds.com/

Rainbow Ryders
11520 San Bernadino NE
(505) 823-1111 or (800) 725-2477
www.rainbowryders.com

Skyspan Adventures
5600 McLeod Blvd. Ste. H
(505) 250-2300 or (877) SKY-SPAN
www.skyspanadventures.com

Casinos/Gaming

Casino gaming is offered on many Indian reservations and pueblos throughout New Mexico. The Downs at Albuquerque, on the grounds of Expo New Mexico, also offers a casino with a variety of slots. Other casinos offer table games along with bingo, restaurants and a variety of entertainment. These are in the Albuquerque area.

Dancing Eagle Casino & Travel Center
Laguna Pueblo
(505) 552-7777 or (877) 440-9966
www.dancingeaglecasino.com

Downs at Albuquerque Racetrack & Casino
Seasonal live racing. Only casino not Indian owned.
Expo New Mexico, 201 California NE
(505) 266-5555
www.abqdowns.com

Isleta Casino & Resort
Isleta Pueblo
(505) 724-3800 or (800) 460-5686
www.isleta-casino.com

Route 66 Casino
Laguna Pueblo
(866) 352-RT66 (352-7866)
www.rt66casino.com

San Felipe's Casino Hollywood
San Felipe Pueblo
(505) 867-6700 or (877) 529-2946
www.sanfelipecasino.com

Sandia Resort & Casino
Sandia Pueblo
(505) 796-7500 or (800) 526-9366
www.sandiacasino.com

Santa Ana Star Casino
Santa Ana Pueblo
(505) 867-0000
www.santaanastar.com

Sky City Casino
Acoma Pueblo
(888) SKY-CITY (759-2489)
www.skycitycasino.com

Isleta Casino. Photo © MarbleStreetStudio.com.

Twin Warriors Golf Club designed by architect Gary Panks is on the Santa Ana Pueblo just north of Albuquerque.Photo © John R. Johnson/golfphotos.com.

Golf Courses

Albuquerque's climate makes golf an almost everyday opportunity. Several of the newest courses are located on area Indian pueblos, and some courses have received national recognition for quality of play and design.

Arroyo del Oso
7001 Osuna NE
(505) 884-7505
www.cabq.gov/golf/arroyo.html

Championship Golf Course at UNM
3601 University Blvd. SE
(505) 277-4546
www.unm.edu/~golf

Isleta Eagle Golf Course
4001 Hwy. 47 SE
(505) 869-0950 or (888) 293-9146
www.isletaeagle.com

Ladera Golf Course
3401 Ladera Dr. NW
(505) 836-4449
www.cabq.gov/golf/ladera.html

Los Altos Golf Course
9717 Copper NE
(505) 298-1897
www.cabq.gov/golf/losaltos.html

Paa-ko Ridge Golf Club
1 Club House Dr.
Sandia Park
(505) 281-6000 or (866) 898-5987
www.paakoridge.com

Pueblo de Cochiti Golf Course
5200 Cochiti Hwy.
Cochiti Lake
(505) 465-2230
www.santafetrailgolf.com

Puerto del Sol Golf Course
1800 Girard SE
(505) 265-5636
www.cabq.gov/golf/puerto.html

Sandia Golf Club
30 Rainbow Rd.
Sandia Pueblo
(505) 798-3990 or (800) 526-9366
www.sandiagolf.com

Santa Ana Golf Club
288 Prairie Star Rd.
Santa Ana Pueblo
(505) 867-9464 or (800) 851-9469
www.santaanagolf.com

Twin Warriors Golf Club
Hyatt Regency Tamaya Resort & Spa
1301 Tuyuna Trail
Santa Ana Pueblo
(505) 771-6222 or (800) 55-HYATT
www.twinwarriorsgolf.com

Albuquerque has spectacular year-round golfing available. Photo © MarbleStreetStudio.com.

Conservatory interior at Rio Grande Botanic Garden. Photo courtesy City of Albuquerque.

Outdoor Recreation

(505) 764-6200

Albuquerque Biological Park
City-operated facility that includes Albuquerque Aquarium, Rio Grande Botanic Garden, Rio Grande Zoo and Tingley Beach.
www.cabq.gov/biopark

2601 Central NW
(505) 764-6200

Albuquerque Aquarium and Rio Grande Botanic Garden
The Aquarium includes marine habitats of the Gulf of Mexico. The Botanic Garden offers both Mediterranean and Desert Pavilions, along with a Children's Fantasy Garden based on themes from "Alice in Wonderland." Walking distance through the aquarium and garden is about 1.6 miles.
www.cabq.gov/biopark/aquarium
www.cabq.gov/biopark/garden

903 10th Street SW
(505) 764-6200

Rio Grande Zoo
An oasis for both exotic and native species in a wonderfully designed sixty-four-acre site, the zoo has established a captive breeding program for a number of endangered species.
www.cabq.gov/biopark/zoo

Shark tank at the Albuquerque Aquarium. Photo courtesy City of Albuquerque.

Tingley Beach

1800 Tingley Dr. SW
(505) 764-6200

Open from sunrise to sunset daily. Currently open: catch and release lake, central lake and children's pond. All are stocked. Tingley Beach also features a narrow-gauge train, and work on model boat pond, food services, gift shop and other amenities is underway.

www.cabq.gov/biopark/tingley

Polar bear exhibit at the Rio Grande Zoo. Photo courtesy City of Albuquerque.

Skiing is easily accessible on the Sandia Mountains from mid-December through March.
Photo © Jay Blackwood.

For more information about all the activities at the ski area, call (505) 242-9052.

Sandia Peak Ski Area & Tram

Sandia Peak offers skiing in the winter and mountain biking in the summer. You can access the ski area by driving out I-40 east to Highway 14, then head north on Highway 14, the Crest Highway, to Sandia Peak. The distance is about eleven miles. You can also access the ski area by the Sandia Peak Tram.
www.sandiapeak.com

Sandia Peak Mountain Biking

Seasonal. Mountain bike trail system offers more than fifteen miles of trails, a full-service rental shop, bike/chairlift, scenic rides and a grill.

Ski New Mexico (800) 755-7669

Sandia Peak Ski Area

Sandia Peak offers some of the longest cruising terrain available in New Mexico, including thirty trails serviced by four chairlifts, a surface lift and a children's mitey mite. Snowboards allowed. Sandia Peak is primarily a beginner and intermediate mountain. Advanced skiing is available in other areas of the state.
www.skinewmexico.com

Sandia Peak Aerial Tram. Photo © Jay Blackwood.

Sandia Peak Tram

2.7-mile-long tram rises to 10,378 feet with an 11,000-square-mile-panoramic view. Restaurants are at the base and the top. Take Tramway Blvd. from Albuquerque.

#10 Tramway Loop NE
(505) 856-7325

Other Outdoor Recreational Sites

Coronado State Monument

Indian and Spanish exhibits as well as kiva with original murals painted in 1300s. Picnic area.

www.nmmonuments.org

485 Kuana Rd. I-25
Exit 242
Bernalillo
(505) 867-5351

Elena Gallegos Picnic Area

Albert G. Simms Park

Mountain area, hiking, biking, horseback riding, picnicking. Go north on Tramway from I-40 to Simms Park Rd.

www.cabq.gov/openspace.com

7100 Tramway NE
(505) 452-5200

Mountain biking is a favorite year-round activity in Albuquerque. Photo © Ron Behrmann.

2113 Osuna NE Ste. A
(505) 346-3894

La Luz Trail

Hiking trail on west face of Sandia Mountains in the Cibola National Forest. Take Tramway to the Juan Tabo turnoff. Turn right and follow signs to the parking area

www.laluztrail.com

(505) 841-8705 or
(505) 352-3596
for map

Mystery Stone

Hidden Mountain six miles west of Los Lunas (along unmarked dirt road). Requires permit from State Land Office for access.

www.nmstatelands.org/GetPage.aspx?sectionID=39&PagID=186

Northwest corner of
Federal Building
4th and Lomas NW

Madonna of the Trail Monument

Statue of pioneer woman with inscriptions dedicated to national and regional history. One of twelve located across the country.

www.route40.net/history/madonnas/index.shtml

6001 Unser Blvd.
NW
(505) 899-0205

Petroglyph National Monument

Walking trails with American Indian and Spanish made petroglyphs (rock carvings).

www.nps.gov/petr

The Stables at Tamaya
Hyatt Regency Tamaya Resort & Spa
www.tamaya.hyatt.com/hyatt/hotels/activities/onsite/details.jsp?onsiteActId=384

1300 Tuyuna Tr.,
Santa Ana Pueblo
(505) 867-1234 or
800-55-HYATT

Rio Grande Nature Center State Park
270 acres of riverside forest and meadows with a three-acre pond, more than two miles of walking trails and more than 260 species of birds.
www.rgnc.org

2901 Candelaria NW
(505) 344-7240

Sandia Lakes Recreation Area
Fishing, hiking, bird watching, picnicking, playground, bait and tackle shop. From Albuquerque, take I-25 north to exit 234 west, then north one mile on NM 313. Located at Sandia Pueblo.
www.sandialakes.com

Mail: 11143 Hwy. 85
NW 87114
(505) 897-3971

Stone Age Climbing Gym
Indoor facility for climbers of all ages, featuring 12,000 square feet of climbing terrain and over 10,000 square feet of floor space.
www.stoneageclimbinggym.com

4201 Yale NE
(505) 341-2016

Wildlife West Nature Park
Wolves, cougars, elk, deer, raptors, javelina. Seasonal hours and summer chuckwagon.
www.wildlifewest.org

87 ⅓ Frontage kd.
Edgewood
(505) 281-7655 or
(877) 981-9453

Petroglyphs on rock. Courtesy of Petroglyph National Monument/National Park Service.

Rafting, Skating, Public Swimming Pools & Tennis

There are public facilities located throughout the city. For a complete list of locations, hours and specific amenities, please contact the Albuquerque Convention & Visitors Bureau (www.itsatrip.org) or the City of Albuquerque (www.cabq.gov).

10140 1/2 Lomas NE
(505) 857-8640

Los Altos Skate Park

Helmet use requested at this skate park. The largest skate park in the southwest, it is designed for BMX bikes, skateboards and in-line skates.
www.cabq.gov/recreation/skate.html

Spectator Sporting Events

1601 Avenida Cesar Chavez SE
(505) 924-BALL

Albuquerque Isotopes Baseball Club

Pacific Coast League professional baseball, April–September. Isotopes Park
www.albuquerquebaseball.com

Tingley Coliseum
2325 San Pedro NE
Ste 1A1
(505) 265-DUNK

Albuquerque Thunderbirds

Professional basketball, NBA Development League
www.abqtbirds.com

EXPO New Mexico,
201 California NE
(505) 266-5555

The Downs at Albuquerque Racetrack & Casino

Live horseracing every spring and fall. Simulcast year-round.
www.abqdowns.com

Rio Rancho Event
Center
3001 Civic Center
Drive
Rio Rancho
(505) 881-PUCK

New Mexico Scorpions

Pro hockey, Central Hockey League.
www.scorpionshockey.com

Rio Rancho Events Center, Rio Rancho. Home of the Scorpions hockey team. Courtesy Rio Rancho Events Center.

The start of the Tricentennial Marathon on April 22, 2006 at Balloon Fiesta Park, part of Albuquerque's 300th birthday celebration weekend. Photo © Craig Vencill. Courtesy of the Albuquerque Tricentennial.

Sandia Motor Speedway
Paved oval and road course for a variety of local and national events.

www.sandiamotorsports.com

100 Speedway Blvd. SW
(505) 352-8888

University of New Mexico Athletic Department
Lobo teams include men's and women's award-winning basketball, football and soccer (second in NCAA in 2005).

www.GoLobos.com

UNM South Campus
1414 University Blvd. SE
(505) 925-5014 OR
(800) 955-4695

ARTS & CULTURE / SHOPPING

Galleries & Performing Arts

Some visitors are surprised at the variety and depth of Albuquerque's performing and visual arts community.

It is home to more than 100 galleries and studios, one of the oldest public arts programs in the country and a variety of indoor and outdoor performance venues. Cultural influences from its Hispanic and American Indian roots are clearly evident in the arts and crafts here, as well as the festivals, celebrations and attractions of the area. A variety of events feature the city's many other cultures.

According to the *Collector's Guide*, an impressive and in-depth source for visual arts seekers, there are thousands of artists working in the area, drawn by the inspiration of New Mexico. The guide says the area has galleries offering contemporary, traditional, Native American and Hispanic arts, crafts, and antiques.

Both the **University of New Mexico**'s several performance venues and the area casinos book all kinds of entertainment into the city, along with a varied schedule at the **Journal Pavilion**, an outdoor arena with room for 12,000 people; **Tingley Coliseum** at Expo New Mexico; and the **KiMo Theatre** downtown.

The KiMo is an ornate former movie palace in Pueblo-Deco style with architectural features that combine the spirit of the Indian cultures of the Southwest with the exuberance of America during the Roaring Twenties.

There are more than 400 works of art in the **Albuquerque Public Art Collection**; more than one quarter are in the Albuquerque Sunport and its nearby rental car facility. The program is one of the oldest in the country and is funded by general obligation bonds and certain revenue bonds.

The collection ranges from traditional to avant-garde, from "Aluminum Yucca" (made with F-16 fuel tanks) in Tijeras Canyon (the city's eastern gateway), to the locally controversial "Chevy on a Stick" at Ridgecrest and Gibson near the Albuquerque Sunport. Prominent artists like Allan Houser, Pablita Velarde, Fritz Scholder, Wilson Hurley, and Glenna Goodacre are among those whose works are part of the collection. For more information, see the official city website, **www.cabq.gov/publicart**, or call (505) 768-3289.

KiMo Theatre balcony and stairs. Photo courtesy Kells & Craig Architects.

If you happen to be in town on an evening when an **ARTScrawl** is underway, it's a fun way to tour selected galleries and meet the artists. The calendar of ARTScrawl dates is available at http://www.artscrawlabq.org. ARTScrawl and First Friday are Albuquerque's monthly self-guided gallery tours—a project of the Albuquerque Art Business Association. Each month a different area of the city hosts ARTScrawl with special events such as exhibition openings, artist receptions and demonstrations, benefits and open houses. The ARTScrawl areas are the Northeast Heights, Historic Central Avenue (Route 66) and Old Town. You are directed through each ARTScrawl with a map and information on the events at each gallery. First Friday is a citywide event happening the first Friday of each month, also featuring exhibition openings, artist receptions, demonstrations, benefits and open houses.

Albuquerque also boasts a number of indoor and outdoor performing arts venues—everything from the bandshell at the **Rio Grande Zoo**, site of summertime Zoo Concerts, to **Popejoy Hall**, whose calendar includes national touring productions along with the New Mexico Symphony. Area casinos regularly book nationally recognized acts. To find out what's happening when you're in town, refer to the Albuquerque Convention & Visitors Bureau website (www.itsatrip.org) or the weekly special entertainment tabloid sections.

The following listings represent a partial selection of the large number of galleries and shops in the Albuquerque area. For additional galleries and shops, please consult the yellow pages or check on-line.

P.O. Box 36588, Albuquerque, NM 87176 (AABA) (505) 244-0362 (AABA— Albuquerque Art Business Association)

ARTScrawl
ARTScrawl encourages casual gallery-hopping and acquaints you with Albuquerque's art and artists in a specific neighborhood. Includes special events such as exhibition openings, artist receptions and demonstrations, benefits, open houses and other special events.
www.artscrawlabq.org

P.O. Box 36588, Albuquerque, NM 87176 (505) 244-0362 (AABA)

First Friday
A citywide event happening the first Friday of each month, also featuring exhibition openings, artist receptions, demonstrations, benefits and open houses.
www.artscrawlabq.org
(First Friday info is located on the ARTScrawl website)

Galleries

Amapola Gallery

A cooperative gallery where about forty local artists local artists display and sell their work Located in the historic Romero house in Old Town, the gallery houses an eclectic collection of contemporary art and crafts.

www.amapolagallery.com

106 Romero NW
87104
(505) 242-4311

Dartmouth Street Gallery

Representing nationally known artists in different media. Extensive website.

www.dsg-art.com

510 14th St. SW
(505) 266-7751 or
(800) 474-7751

Galleria Encantada

Metal and stone sculptures, jewelry, artifacts, paintings, fetishes.

201 3rd St. NW
87102
(505) 242-5063 or
(877) 338-3200

Galleria Tamaya

Offers handcrafted jewelry, brass, copper and bronze work, artifacts, pottery, paintings from local artists and much more. Find gifts and collectibles that are truly special and exclusive to this area. Galleria Tamaya clothing store, located in the Galleria, offers apparel and accessories for any occasion.

www.tamaya.hyatt.com/hyatt/hotels/services/shops/index.jsp

Hyatt Regency
Tamaya Resort &
Spa
1300 Tuyuna Trail,
Santa Ana Pueblo,
New Mexico 87004
(505) 867-1234

Gowen Arts

Features jewelers, artisans and metal sculpture.

www.gowenarts.com

303 Romero NW
87104
(505) 242-6831 or
(800) 350-6099

Harwood Art Center

Housed in a historic building, Harwood offers exhibitions, art classes and community development.

www.harwoodcenter.org

1114 7th NW
(505) 242-6367

Mariposa Gallery, Inc.

Offers a variety of contemporary arts, crafts and jewelry.

www.mariposa-gallery.com

3500 Central SE,
Nob Hill 87106
(505) 268-6828

Mud Pony Gallery

Fine art, Native American, European, Eclectic. Featuring Ojibwa artist Sam English.

www.mudpony gallery.com

2021 Old Town Rd.
NW Ste C
(505) 243-0085

3812 Central Ave SE,
Ste 100-B
(505) 268-8952

New Grounds Print Workshop & Gallery
Works by outstanding New Mexico and international artists.
www.newgroundsprintshop.com

3015 Monte Vista
Blvd NE
(505) 268-9969

Nob Hill Gallery
Albuquerque's outstanding artist co-op.
www.nobhillartgallery.com

1919 Old Town Rd.
#6
(505) 242-0467

Old Town Frame Shop and Gallery 5
Southwestern art and prints, contemporary art gallery.
www.oldtownframeshop.com

323 Romero NW
(505) 843-7666 or
(800) 399-2970

R. C. Gorman / Nizhoni Gallery
Features the work of the famous Navajo artist R.C. Gorman.
www.nizhoni-moses.com

306 San Felipe NW
(505) 765 5869 or
(800) 234-7985

Schelu Gallery
Handcrafted pottery, stoneware, furniture, raku by local artists.
www.schelu.com

2801 Eubank NE
(Eastdale Shopping
Center)
(505) 293-6133

Weems Gallery & Framing
Featuring more than 200 artists. Affordably priced. Organizer
of annual November Weems Artfest at EXPO New Mexico, with
diverse exhibitions and artists' appearances.
www.weemsgallery.com

#1 Patio Market
206 1/2 San Felipe
NW
(505) 247-8931

Yucca Art Gallery
Original monotypes, collages, southwestern landscapes, oils,
handwoven originals, silk wearables, wall quilts and more.
www.yuccagallery.com

Performing Arts

224 San Pasquale
SW
(505) 242-4750

Albuquerque Little Theatre
75 years of community theatre. Year-round.
www.albuquerquetheatre.org

700 1st St. NW
(505) 766-9412

The Cell Theatre
Theatre and music year-round. Bi-monthly cabaret.
www.liveatthecell.com

Guillermo Figueroa, music director of the New Mexico Symphony Orchestra, conducts the NMSO at Popejoy Hall in Albuquerque. Figueroa is the tenth music director of the NMSO, which is the official orchestra of the state of New Mexico. Photo © Raymond Watt/New Mexico Symphony Orchestra.

Chamber Music Albuquerque
Presents world-class chamber ensembles in concert year-round.
www.cma-abq.org

4407 Menaul NE
(505) 268-1990

Journal Pavilion
Albuquerque's world-class outdoor concert facility, hosting 20–25 concerts annually.
www.journalpavilion.com

5601 University SE
(505) 452-5100

KiMo Theatre
Historic theatre with unique Pueblo-Deco style featuring Native American motifs. Hosts a broad spectrum of performances and events.
www.cabq.gov/kimo

423 Central NW
(505) 768-3522

Madrid Melodrama
Engine House theater melodrama. Seasonal.
www.madridmelodrama.com

2846 State Hwy. 14
Madrid
(in Old Coal Mine Museum)
(505) 438-3780

South Broadway Cultural Center. Photo © Robert Reck.

4804 Central SE
(505) 265-9119

Musical Theatre Southwest
Broadway musicals for more than 36 years.
www.musicaltheatresw.com

4407 Menaul NE
(505) 881-8999 OR
(800) 251-NMSO

New Mexico Symphony Orchestra
Southwest's premier orchestra, presenting classics, pops and education programs.
www.nmso.org

University of New
Mexico Campus
(505) 277-3824 or
(800) 905-3315
Tickets:
(505) 277-4JOY

Popejoy Hall
New Mexico's premier performing arts facility; presents touring artists.
www.popejoyhall.com

1025 Broadway SE
(505) 848-1320

South Broadway Cultural Center
Library, theater, art gallery. Preserves and educates the community about the cultures and ethnicities that define the city.
www.cabq.gov/sbcc

112 Washington SE
(505) 254-8393

Tricklock Company
Resident touring ensemble.
www.tricklock.com

Casinos

Many of the area's Pueblo casinos offer popular entertainment, including top nationally known acts. Check with individual casinos for information on current performers.

Isleta Casino
11000 Broadway SE
Isleta Pueblo
(505) 724-3800 or (800) 460-5686
www.isleta-casino.com

Sandia Resort & Casino
30 Rainbow Rd.
Sandia Pueblo
(505) 796-7500 or (800) 526-9366
www.sandiacasino.com

Route 66 Casino
I-40 West Exit 140
Laguna Pueblo
(505) 352-7866
www.Rt66Casino.com

Santa Ana Star Casino
54 Jemez Canyon Dam Rd.
Santa Ana Pueblo
(505) 867-0000
www.santaanastar.com

San Felipe's Casino Hollywood
25 Hagan Rd.
San Felipe Pueblo
(505) 867-6700 or 87-PLAY 2 WIN
www.sanfelipecasino.com

Sky City Casino
I-40 West, Exit 102
Acoma Pueblo
(505) 552-6017 or (888) SKY-CITY
www.skycity.com

Shopping

What better way to remember the fun of a vacation than the souvenirs and mementos you bring home! Shopping is a top activity for virtually everyone who travels, and the most fun may be finding those special treasures that are unique to the destination you visit.

Albuquerque and its surrounding area are home not only to American Indian artisans but also to a varied and eclectic artist community that produces Southwestern-style clothing, furniture and accessories. Whether you are looking for something unique to the area or a visit to a large shopping mall, you have plenty of choices.

Three large enclosed shopping malls offer most national retailers along with local shops and many restaurants. Two—**Coronado Center** and **Winrock Center**—are located in the northeast area of the city and are easily reached via I-40. The third and newest is **Cottonwood Mall**, located in the northwestern part of Albuquerque near Rio Rancho. All three malls are surrounded by hotels, restaurants and movie theaters.

Considered the sentimental heart of Albuquerque, **Old Town** (west of the downtown area) contains more than 130 shops, galleries, museums and restaurants. Vendors who sell primarily Southwestern American Indian-style jewelry spread their wares under the portal of one of these restaurants, La Placita, and share a view of the Old Town Plaza. Shops are tucked behind adobe walls, in museum lobbies and in

Shopping in Old Town Merchants line the sidewalks in Old Town selling unique hand-crafted jewelry. Photo courtesy of the Albuquerque Convention & Visitors' Bureau.

renovated houses. The traditional adobe style is evident in most buildings. Gift and specialty shops offer everything from hot-air balloon themed items to high-quality art.

The city has a number of smaller shopping areas, most notably **Nob Hill** on Central Avenue (Route 66) east of the University of New Mexico. Albuquerque also is home to more than 100 galleries and studios, found all over the city, exhibiting traditional, contemporary, Hispanic, American Indian and Southwestern-style art.

Visitors love to prowl through the weekend **Flea Market** (every Saturday and Sunday) at Expo New Mexico, or stroll through the aisles of the many arts and crafts shows scattered throughout the year. March features the **Annual Rio Grande Arts & Crafts Festival**, while the **New Mexico Arts & Crafts Fair** is a late June staple. **Weems Artfest**, currently ranked the state's best in this category, takes place in November, and similar events are scheduled for the December holiday period.

Shoppers can find American Indian items at many fine shops around town, including **Skip Maisel's Wholesale/Retail Indian Jewelry and Crafts** downtown, **Andrews Pueblo Pottery, Nizhoni Moses, Ltd.**, and **Palms Trading Company**, all in the Old Town area.

Both **Bien Mur Indian Market** on Sandia Pueblo north of the city, and the **Indian Pueblo Cultural Center** just north of the Old Town area, offer an incredible variety of arts and crafts.

Southwestern-style furnishings and accessories have found a wide following all over the world. The same can be said for Southwestern-style food, from salsa to piñons. All can be found in Albuquerque.

More information on galleries in the city is available in the Arts & Culture section of this guidebook. For specific information on shopping locations, hours and inventory, visit any of the following websites or go to the Albuquerque Convention & Visitors Bureau site at www.itsatrip.org.

Shopping Centers/Areas

Three large enclosed malls offer most national retailers along with a variety of local shops and restaurants.

Cottonwood Mall
Newest shopping mall in the area with major retailers. Surrounded by numerous restaurants.
www.simon.com

10000 Coors Bypass NW
(505) 899-7467

Coronado Center
New Mexico's largest mall, located in the near Northeast Heights. Accessible via I-40 East/Louisiana Exit.
www.coronadocenter.com

6600 Menaul NE
(505) 881-4600

Nob Hill Business Association
Historic shopping district on Route 66.
http://rt66central.com

2118 Central SE
(505) 265-6403

Old Town Merchants Association
More than 130 shops, boutiques, galleries and restaurants.
www.albuquerqueoldtown.com

P.O. Box 7483, Albuquerque NM 87194
(505) 248-1087

Winrock Shopping Center
Major retailers and restaurants in city's first mall. Located off I-40 E/Louisiana exit.

51 Winrock Center NE
(505) 888-3038

American Indian

303 Romero NW
(Old Town)
(505) 243-0414

Andrews Pueblo Pottery
Pottery, kachinas, baskets, fetishes, jewelry and more.
www.andrewspueblopottery.com

100 Bien Mur Dr.
NE; I-25/Tramway
Exit
(505) 821-5400 OR
(800) 365-5400

Bien Mur Indian Market Center
Jewelry, pottery, baskets, kachina dolls, hand-woven rugs, sand paintings, and other arts and crafts. Owned and operated by Sandia Pueblo.
www.bienmur.com

2401 12th St. NW
(505) 843-7270

Indian Pueblo Cultural Center
Jewelry, hand-carved Kachinas, pottery, rugs and other woven articles and numerous other craft items. Also Indian sculpture and paintings in watercolors and oils, as well as ritual sand-paintings. See also pages 49–50 and 168.
www.indianpueblo.org

326 San Felipe NW
(505) 842-1808 or
(888) 842-1808

Nizhoni Moses, Ltd.
Pottery, weaving, carvings and more.
www.nizhoni-moses.com

1504 Lomas Blvd.
NW
(505) 247-8504 or
(800) 748-1656

Palms Trading Company
Kachinas, jewelry, rugs, pottery and more.
www.palmstrading.com

1920 Central SW
(505) 242-3739

Rio Grande Wholesale
Open to the public selling arts & crafts, jewelry, furniture and clothing.

510 Central SW
(505) 242-6526

Skip Maisel's Wholesale/Retail Indian Jewelry and Crafts
Jewelry, pottery and more.

2021 Old Town Rd.
NW Ste D
(505) 242-1877

Stones & Feathers
Located next to Rattlesnake Museum, features souvenirs.

320 Romero NW
(505) 242-8822

Trader Barb's Gallery
More than 30 years selling contemporary and Native American jewelry.
www.traderbarbs.com

Visitors shop for handmade American Indian arts and crafts and other treasured items in Albuquerque. Photo © MarbleStreetStudio.com.

Warpath Traders

Traditional and contemporary Native American jewelry & kachinas. Select designer clothing.

300 AND 323
Romero NW
(505) 243-6993

Wright's Indian Arts

Jewelry, pottery, kachinas, fetishes, sculpture, Navajo and Zapotec rugs, Navajo folk art, masks and more. In business 99 years.

www.wrightsgallery.com

1100 San Mateo
Blvd. NE
(505) 266-0120

LODGING & FOOD

Accommodations

As a four-season destination, Albuquerque offers visitors everything from a bed-and-breakfast in a traditional territorial-style setting to the most up-to-date accommodations in the heart of the city. Traveling families as well as business people traveling alone can select from a variety of hotels, motels, bed-and-breakfasts and extended-stay properties.

For those bringing their accommodations along, there are RV parks, located near the major interstates.

Major chain hotels and motels are available with every amenity one could need or desire. For travelers who want more of a "local" experience there are choices too, from **La Posada** downtown or the **Hotel Albuquerque** in Old Town to the many B & B's that capture the ambience of the area. Of course, most of the major lodging chains have locations throughout the greater Albuquerque area. Specific information on locations and amenities are available from their respective websites or by contacting the Albuquerque Convention & Visitors Bureau **www.itsatrip.org**.

Travelers can find up-to-the-minute data on the internet along with options to book. Just as there is variety in accommodation types, there is variety in cost. Generally, the city offers reasonable rates. The only high season is during the Balloon Fiesta in October. This is probably the most difficult time to book, though even then, variety is still available. But be prepared to pay higher room costs at this time.

The bed-and-breakfast options in particular show off the unique architectural style of the city. The quiet and rural **North Valley**, including the nearby community of **Corrales**, is the setting for a number of B & B's, most in adobe homes with patios and outdoor hideaways that take advantage of the great year-round climate.

Downtown Albuquerque has a cluster of modern chain hotels including the **Hyatt Regency** and the **Doubletree**. Historic **La Posada**, notable as a boutique hotel originally founded by fabled hotelier Conrad Hilton, features a two-story arched lobby with a tiled fountain and hand-painted murals.

Two charming and affordable properties, recently renovated, are located on **Central Avenue** (Route 66) at the western edge of downtown as the road heads toward Old Town: the **Hotel Blue** and the **Silver Moon Lodge**.

La Posada de Albuquerque on a late Spring evening. Photo © MarbleStreetStudio.com.

There are several bed-and-breakfasts in the **Old Town** area along with the Southwestern-style **Hotel Albuquerque** with a lovely garden and wedding chapel. A block away, the **Best Western Rio Grande Inn** is also decorated in New Mexico style with an on-site restaurant. Both are within easy walking distance of Old Town.

In the **Mid-town** area, served by the "Big I" (intersection of Interstates 25 and 40), choices include everything from extended-stay and suite properties to major chain hotels. The University of New Mexico and the city's major medical complexes are in this area.

The **Uptown** area, accessed by I-40, offers the same variety along with easy access to two of the city's major shopping malls, **Winrock** and **Coronado Center**, plus many restaurants. The perimeter areas of the city are generally populated with chain motels offering reasonable rates.

Albuquerque's **airport** (Sunport) area, in the southeastern part of the city, offers a variety in accommodations from major chains. The only full-service property is the **Wyndham Albuquerque**, located immediately north of the Sunport. Properties in this area provide convenient access to the major sports venues for the University of New Mexico: the fabled "Pit," home to the men's and women's basketball "**Lobos**," and the 37,000-seat football stadium along with the tennis complex. The city's minor league baseball team, the "**Isotopes**," has its home in this area, too.

The **Balloon Fiesta** has become so identified with Albuquerque that the cluster of hotels along I-25 North nearest the event site is identified by the name of the annual celebration. The largest property in this area is the **Albuquerque Marriott Pyramid North**, so-called because of its architectural style. However, a number of other chain hotels and motels are in the immediate vicinity. These properties are also closest to **Sandia Peak Aerial Tramway**, another of the city's major attractions.

Expo New Mexico, the site of the annual **New Mexico State Fair** (September) is surrounded by several chain properties. This area is also near the major shopping malls.

One resort just outside of the city is the **Hyatt Tamaya Resort & Spa** on Santa Ana Pueblo, about 18 miles to the northwest. The newest resort is **Sandia Resort & Casino**, just off I-25 on the northern edge of the city.

The **Albuquerque Convention & Visitors Bureau** offers on-line booking at its website, and its semi-annual visitor guide provides information by location within the city.

The hotel/motel/bed-and-breakfast selections that follow are designated by one of the geographic areas identified above. The following listings represent a partial selection of the large number of lodging establishments in the Albuquerque area. For additional places to stay, please consult the yellow pages or check on-line.

Bed-and-Breakfasts

The architectural charm and diversity as well as the local hospitality are displayed in the many bed-and-breakfast locations throughout the greater Albuquerque area. Specific information about amenities, rates and availability is available by contacting the individual establishments. General information about locations is available from the Albuquerque Convention & Visitors Bureau, www.itsatrip.org.

Adobe & Roses Bed & Breakfast
(*North Valley*)
1011 Ortega NW
(505) 898-0654
www.virtualcities.com/ons/nm/q/nmq7701.htm

Adobe Garden at Los Ranchos Bed & Breakfast
(*North Valley*)
641 Chavez NW
(505) 345-1954
www.adobegarden.com

Adobe Nido Bed & Breakfast
(*North Valley*)
1124 Major Ave. NW
(505) 344-1310 or (866) 435-6436
www.adobenido.com

Bottger Mansion of Old Town
(*Old Town*)
110 San Felipe NW
(505) 243-3639 or (800) 758-3639
www.bottger.com

Brittania & W.E. Mauger Estate B&B
(*Downtown*)
701 Roma Ave NW
(505) 242-8755 or (800) 719-9189
www.maugerbb.com

Canyon Gods Guest House
(*Tres Pistolas Canyon*)
12 Monticello Dr. NW
(505) 292-7659
www.canyongods.com

Casa Del Granjero
(*North Valley*)
414 C de Baca Lane NW
(505) 897-4144 or (800) 701-4144
www.innewmexico.com

Casas de Suenos Old Town Country Inn
(*Old Town*)
310 Rio Grande SW
(505) 247-4560 or (800) 665-7002

Cinnamon Morning Bed & Breakfast
(*North Valley*)
2700 Rio Grande NW
(505) 345-3541 or (800) 214-9481
www.cinnamonmorning.com

Devonshire Adobe Inn
(*Westside*)
4801 All Saints Rd. NW
(505) 898-3366 or (800) 240-1149
www.devonshireadobeinn.com

Hacienda Antigua Inn
(*North Valley*)
6708 Tierra Dr. NW
(505) 345-5399 or (800) 201-2986
www.haciendaantigua.com

Hacienda de Colores
(*North Valley*)
1113 Montoya NW
(505) 247-0013 or (877) COLORES
www.haciendacolores.com

Los Poblanos Inn & La Quinta Cultural Center

(*North Valley*)
4803 Rio Grande Blvd. NW
(505) 344-9297 or (866) 344-9297
www.lospoblanos.com

Old Town Bed & Breakfast

(*Old Town*)
707 17th St. NW
(505) 764-9144 or (888) 900-9144
www.inn-new-mexico.com

Vista de Albuquerque

(*West Side*)
5336 Canada Vista Pl. NW
(505) 899-9301

B & Bs are also available in Corrales, Placitas, Bernalillo, the East Mountains and other areas of the state. Visit www.itsatrip.org for more listings.

Hotels: Downtown

Doubletree Hotel

201 Marquette NW
(505) 247-3344 or (888) 223-4113
www.doubletree.com

The Hotel Blue

717 Central NW
(505) 924-2400 or (877) 878-4868
www.thehotelblue.com

Hyatt Regency Albuquerque

330 Tijeras NW
(505) 842-1234 or (800) 233-1234
www.hyatt.com

La Posada de Albuquerque

Originally founded as a boutique hotel by fabled hotelier Conrad Hilton. Features a two-story arched lobby with a tiled fountain and hand-painted murals.
125 2nd St. NW
(505) 242-9090 or (800) 777-5732
www.laposada-abq.com

The Silver Moon Lodge

918 Central SW
(505) 243-1773 or (866) 425-8085
www.silver-moon-lodge.com

Hotels: Old Town

Best Western Rio Grande Inn

Decorated in New Mexico style with an on-site restaurant.
1015 Rio Grande Blvd. NW
(505) 843-9500 or (800) 959-4726
www.riograndeinn.com

Hotel Albuquerque at Old Town

Southwestern elegance with a lovely garden and wedding chapel.
800 Rio Grande Blvd. NW 87104
(505) 843-6300 or (877) 901-ROOM
www.hotelabq.com

Hotels: Mid-Town

AmeriSuites Midtown

2500 Menaul Blvd. NW
(505) 881-0544 or (800) 833-1516
www.amerisuites.com

Clubhouse Inn & Suites

1315 Menaul Blvd. NE
(505) 345-0010 or (866) 345-0010
www.clubhouseinn.com

Silver Moon Lodge downtown on Central Avenue. Photo © MarbleStreetStudio.com.

Hilton Albuquerque
1901 University NE
(505) 884-2500 or (800) 274-6835
www.hilton.com

MCM Elegante
2020 Menaul NE
(505) 884-2511 or (866) 650-4900
www.mcmelegante.com

Residence Inn by Marriott
3300 Prospect NE
(505) 881-2661 or (800) 331-3131
www.residenceinn.com/abqri

Hotels: Uptown

Albuquerque Marriott Hotel
2101 Louisiana NE
(505) 881-6800 or (800) 228-9290
www.marriotthotels.com/abqnm

Homewood Suites by Hilton Uptown
7101 Arvada NE
(505) 881-7300 or (800) 225-5466
www.homewoodsuites.com

Sheraton Albuquerque Uptown Hotel
2600 Louisiana NE
(505) 881-0000 or (800) 252-7772
www.sheratonuptown.com

Hotels: Fairgrounds Area

Best Western at Barcelona Suites
900 Louisiana NE
(505) 255-5566 or (877) 227-7848
www.newmexico-lodging.com

Nativo Lodge front entrance. Photo courtesy of the hotel

Hotels: Balloon Fiesta Park

Albuquerque Marriott Pyramid North
5151 San Francisco NW
(505) 821-3333 or (800) 262-2043
www.marriott.com

Courtyard by Marriott Journal Center
5151 Journal Center NE
(505) 823-1919 or (877) 905-4496
www.courtyard-abq.com

Hilton Garden Inn Albuquerque Journal Center
5320 San Antonio NE
(505) 314-0800 or (877) STAY-HGI
or (877) 782-9444
www.hiltongardeninn.com

Homewood Suites Journal Center
5400 San Antonio NE
(505) 998-4663 or (800) CALL HOME
www.homewoodsuites.com

**Nativo Lodge:
A New Mexico Heritage Hotel**
6000 Pan American Frwy. NE
(505) 798-4300 or (888) 628-4861
www.nativolodge.com

Hotels: Sunport (airport) area

**Best Western Inn Suites Hotel
& Suites Airport**
2400 Yale Blvd SE
(505) 242-7022 or (877) 771-7810
www.InnSuites.com

Fairfield Inn by Marriott
2300 Centre Ave. SE
(505) 247-1621 or (800) 228-2800
www.fairfieldinn.com/abqfa

Hampton Inn-Airport
2231 Yale SE
(505) 246-2255 or (800) 426-7866
www.hampton-inn.com/hi/albuquerque-airport

Santa Ana Pueblo's Hyatt Tamaya Resort & Spa. Photo courtesy the resort.

Wyndham Albuquerque Hotel
2910 Yale SE
(505) 843-7000 or (800) 227-1117
www.wyndham.com

RV Parks

Albuquerque Central KOA
12400 Skyline NW
(505) 296-2729 or (800) 562-7781
www.albuquerquekoa.com

American RV Park of Albuquerque
13500 Central SW
(505) 831-3545 or (800) 282-8885
www.americanrvpark.com

Enchanted Trails RV Park & Trading Post
14305 Central NW
(505) 831-6317 or (800) 326-6317
www.enchantedtrails.com

Palisades RV Park
9201 Central NW
(505) 831-5000 or (888) 922-9595
www.palisadespark.com

There are RV parks in Bernalillo, Isleta, Belen, Rio Rancho, Cedar Crest and other areas of the state. Visit www.itsatrip.org for details.

Resorts

Hyatt Tamaya Resort & Spa
Destination resort with meeting space, restaurants, golf courses, horseback riding, full-service spa, casino.
1300 Tuyuna Trail
Santa Ana Pueblo
(505) 867-1234 or (800) 55-HYATT
www.tamaya.hyatt.com

Sandia Resort & Casino
Destination resort with meeting space, restaurants, golf course and casino.
I-25 N and Tramway
Sandia Pueblo
(505) 796-7500 or (800) 526-9366
www.sandiacasino.com

Restaurants

New Mexican food, with its spicy hot flavors, is now a favorite well beyond the borders of the state, but that doesn't mean that dining out in Albuquerque is limited. The city is home to most of the major restaurant chains, but more importantly has a variety of locally-owned eateries offering a broad range of food types and styles.

Because **Old Town** is a magnet for visitors seeking the chance to shop for fun as well as fine items and to visit unique museums, it also offers dining choices for the hungry traveler. New Mexican style certainly, but afternoon tea, fondue and continental cuisine are all available within walking distance of the plaza.

Many **hotels** offer breakfast and/or late afternoon beverages and snacks as part of the room rate. Others have coffee shops or full-service restaurants on the premises, and still others are within walking distance of places to eat everything from "huevos rancheros" (New Mexico-style eggs) to a late evening snack.

As diverse as the menus are, so are the locations and experiences that go along with the dining. The Sandia Mountain foothills on the city's eastern edge offer restaurants at both the base and top of the Sandia Peak Tram (**Sandiago's** and **High Finance**) with outstanding views of the city and the Rio Grande Valley.

Adobe walls, shaded patios, and the smell of roasting chili are part of the appeal at **El Pinto** in the **North Valley** area. **Garduños**, with six locations around the city, serves New Mexico-style food with the question "Red or green?" meaning what kind of chile. And both give you the chance to buy salsa with their respective restaurant brands to take home.

One of the newest and most varied restaurant areas is just off I-25 **North at Jefferson**, where national chain brands mix with locally owned eateries. You can choose from fish, Chinese, Mediterranean, sandwiches and "American" food, all within walking distance of some hotels.

Along **Central Avenue**, the former Route 66, from the Old Town area on the west end to the Fairgrounds are choices from Thai to Brazilian to Italian. Sidewalk tables with umbrellas to shelter diners from the afternoon sun, or to allow them to enjoy the refreshing evening, are everywhere.

More upscale dining is also part of the Albuquerque mix, including many new trendy restaurants and the venerable **Rancher's Club**, probably the most upscale hotel restaurant in the area, located in the **Albuquerque Hilton Hotel**. One of the hot chefs in Albuquerque is Jennifer James,

The Pavilion and Gardens at Hotel Albuquerque in Old Town. Photo courtesy of the hotel.

whose innovative approach to food is evident in **Graze by Jennifer James**, which has generated lots of national publicity.

One of the most popular locations for hot spots is **downtown**, where a number of **clubs** have opened in the last few years. Several are on Central Avenue; others are within easy walking distance, but all generally appeal to a younger audience. For current information on entertainment in local clubs and area casinos, visit www.abqonline.com.

Downtown Albuquerque is best-known at night for its diverse hang-out hot-spots. Many of the clubs downtown double-up as small concert venues for local and nationally recognized bands. **The Launchpad**, a small and intimate venue, serves up heavy doses of punk, rock and alternative bands every night.

Downtown is not the only place to have fun. The **northeastern area** is home to several bars and clubs. One of the largest is **Graham Central Station**, which boasts four nightclubs under one roof: Bell Bottoms ('60's and '70's music), Denim & Diamonds (country-western feel), South Beach (today's hottest club music) and Alley Cats (karaoke).

If you like dance clubs, Albuquerque has much to offer. **OPM**, a nightclub downtown, plays techno house music encouraging clubbers to get up and dance!

There are also plenty of bars to choose from. Hotel, restaurant or just plain bars are located all over the city. **Downtown Distillery** has a relaxed ambience, two levels where patrons can mingle, unwind or play billiards with friends.

Albuquerque has been nationally recognized as a hot-spot for partying and nightlife by the famous comedian Dave Attell, who has visited the city twice for his nightlife show, "Insomniac with Dave Attell." Whether downtown or all around, clubbing and dancing or socializing at a bar, you can pick your choice of atmosphere for a fun night on the town.

New Mexico-style food is unique and delicious, and it's part of the fun of visiting here. So choose traditional or choose trendy—or a bit of both—and enjoy some of the following Albuquerque restaurants. Not all of them have a website, so visit the Albuquerque Convention & Visitors Bureau site at www.itsatrip.org for more information.

The following listings represent a partial selection of the large number of restaurants in the Albuquerque area. For additional places to eat, please consult the yellow pages or check on-line.

Graze by Jennifer James, located in Nob Hill. Photo © Dining by Albuquerque Originals.

American

66 Diner
(*University Area*)
1405 Central NE
(505) 247-1421
www.66diner.com

Gold Street Caffe
(*Downtown*)
218 Gold SW
(505) 765-1633

Graze by Jennifer James
(*Nob Hill area*)
3128 Central SE
(505) 268-4729
www.grazejj.com

Casa Vieja
(*Corrales*)
4541 Corrales Rd.
Corrales
(505) 898-7489

Santa Ana Café
Hyatt Regency Tamaya Resort
(*Santa Ana Pueblo*)
1300 Tuyuna Trail
(505) 867-1234
www.tamaya.hyatt.com

Season's Rotisserie & Grill
(*Old Town*)
2031 Mountain Rd. NW
(505) 766-5100
www.seasonsonthenet.com

Scalo Northern Italian Grill, Nob Hill. Photo © Marcia Keegan.

Asian

Bangkok Café
(*East Central area*)
5901 Central NE
(505) 255-5036

Japanese Kitchen
(*Coronado/Winrock area*)
Park Square, 6521 Americas Parkway
(505) 884-8937

Barbecue

The County Line of Albuquerque
(*Sandia foothills area*)
9600 Tramway NE
(505) 865-7477
www.countyline.com

Tea Room

The St. James Tearoom
(*Old Town area*)
901 Rio Grande NW Suite 130
(505) 242-3752
www.stjamestearoom.com

Continental/International

Ambrozia Café & Wine Bar
(*Old Town*)
108 Rio Grande NW
(505) 242-6560
www.ambroziacafe.com

Artichoke Café
(*Downtown*)
424 Central SE
(505) 243-0200
www.artichokecafe.com

Dining room of restaurant at Best Western Rio Grande Inn, Old Town. Photo courtesy of the hotel.

The Melting Pot–A Fondue Restaurant
(*Old Town*)
2011 Mountain Rd NW
(505) 843-6358
www.meltingpot.com

Prairie Star
Santa Ana Golf Club
(*Santa Ana Pueblo*)
288 Prairie Star Rd.
(505) 867-3327
www.santaanagolf.com

Tucanos Brazilian Grill
(Downtown)
110 Central SW
(505) 246-9900
www.tucanos.com

Italian

Scalo Northern Italian Grill
(*Nob Hill area*)
3500 Central SE
(505) 255-8781
www.scalonobhill.com

Vivace
(*Nob Hill area*)
3118 Central SE
(505) 268-5965

Mediterranean

Pars Cuisine
(*North I-25 corridor*)
4320 The 25 Way NE
(505) 345-5156
www.parscuisine.com

Yanni's Mediterranean Bar & Grill
(*Nob Hill area*)
3109 Central NE
(505) 268-9250

Steak/Seafood

High Finance Restaurant
(*Base of Tramway*)
40 Tramway Rd. NE
(505) 243-9742
www.highfinancerestaurant.com

High Noon Restaurant and Saloon
(*Old Town*)
425 San Felipe NW
(505) 765-1455 or (800) 731-1455

Rancher's Club of New Mexico
(*Midtown*)
1901 University NE (Hilton Hotel)
(505) 889-8071
www.ranchersclubofnm.com

New Mexican/Mexican/Native American
The New Mexican-style cooking found in many local restaurants in often influenced by family and tradition. Chile, however, is not an option. It is an essential ingredient in this flavorful and spicy style of food. Chili refers to the cooked dish. Chile is the spelling for the peppers and the seasoning.

The following is but a sample of restaurant choices offering New Mexican food. Be sure and check with the locals for more recommendations!

Casa de Ruiz—Church Street Café
(*Old Town*)
2111 Church St. NW
(505) 247-8522
www.churchstreetcafe.com

Durán Central Ave. (Pharmacy)
(*Old Town*)
1815 Central Ave. NW
(505) 247-4141

El Pinto Authentic New Mexico Restaurant
(*Far North 4th street*)
10500 4th St. NW
(505) 898-1771
www.elpinto.com

Garduños of Mexico
(*8 Albuquerque locations*)
(505) 298-5514 or (888) 666-5514
www.gardunosrestaurants.com

Pueblo Harvest Café
(*Indian Pueblo Cultural Center*)
2401 12th St. NW
(505) 843-7270
www.indianpueblo.org

Chile Ristras adorn the patios of many shops and houses in New Mexico.
Photo © MarbleStreetStudio.com.

Wineries

Another little-known fact about New Mexico is that there is a 400-year-old tradition of growing grapes and making wine. In the Albuquerque area, several wineries are open to the public and offer some award-winning wines. Check with New Mexico Wine Growers Association for information on wineries and events.
(866) 494-6366 or (866) 4-WINENM
www.nmwine.com
For those interested in vineyard/winery tours, contact the Vineyard Express.
(505) 292-3657 or (888) 501-2665
www.thevineyardexpress.net

Anderson Valley Vineyards
Tours and wine tasting.
4920 Rio Grande NW
(505) 344-7266
www.AVV-wines.com

Anasazi Fields Winery
Tours, wine tasting and retail.
26 Camino De Los Pueblitos
Placitas
(505) 867-3062
www.anasazifieldswinery.com

Casa Rondeña Winery
Wine tasting and retail.
733 Chavez NW
(505) 344-5911 or (800) 706-1699
www.casarondena.com

Gruet Winery
Tasting, tours and retail.
8400 Pan American Freeway NE
(505) 821-0055 or (888) 857-WINE
www.gruetwinery.com

St. Clair Winery & Bistro
Tours, tasting, retail and bistro with live jazz.
901 Rio Grande NW #B-100
(505) 243-9916 or (888) 870-9916
www.stclairwineyards.com/bistro.html

Microbreweries

Chama River Brewing Co.
(*1-25 Corridor*)
Award-winning, hand crafted ales and lagers; high quality steaks, seafood, pasta and sandwiches
4939 Pan American Freeway NE
(505) 342-1800
www.chamariverbrewery.com

Il Vicino Wood Oven Pizza & Brewery
A contemporary Italian Trattoria specializing in wood-oven pizza and in fine handcrafted ales. Two locations.
(*Nob Hill area*)
3403 Central N.E.
(505) 266-7855
(*Northeast Heights*)
11225 Montgomery NE
(505) 271-0882
www.ilvicino.com

Kelly's Brew Pub
(*Nob Hill area*)
Food, entertainment and over twenty in-house beers.
3222 Central SE
(505) 262-2739
www.kellysbrewpub.com

DAY TRIPS FROM ALBUQUERQUE

Albuquerque is surrounded by unique destinations no more than a few hours drive from the city.

Bosque del Apache Wildlife Refuge
Migratory waterfowl, including sandhill cranes; 377 identified species. Year-round birding, auto touring, hiking, visitor center. Open daily.
www.friendsofthebosque.org

16 miles south of Socorro via I-25, San Antonio exit, US 380 and NM 1 (505) 838-2121

Bandelier National Monument
12th-century ancestral Pueblo cliff dwelling ruins. Back country hiking and camping.
Admission: $10.00 per car
www.nps.gov/band or www.desertusa.com/ban

I-25 N to Santa Fe; NM 84 to Los Alamos; 14 mi S via NM 502/4 (505) 672-0343

Cerrillos
Charming town 27 miles south of Santa Fe. Came into being as a wild mining town. Contains many old Western storefronts and adobe buildings.
www.turquoisetrail.org/cerrillos.htm

I-40 E to Tijeras; north on NM 14

Corrales
Nestled between Albuquerque and Rio Rancho, the village of Corrales is rich with agriculture, history and art.
www.visitcorrales.com

NM 528 to Corrales Road

East Mountains
East of Albuquerque; rocky precipices of Sandia Mountain range. Includes Turquoise Trail, Sandia Crest Scenic Byway. See also Turquoise Trail, Sandia Peak.

Kasha-Katuwee Tent Rocks National Monument
2 miles of trails, hiking only.
Parking fee: $5.00 per car.
www.nm.blm.gov/recreation/albuquerque/kasha_katuwe.htm

Near Cochiti Lake, off NM 22. Information: BLM Albuquerque Office, (505) 761-8700

Museum of Fine Arts, Santa Fe. Photo © Marcia Keegan.

Downtown Cerrillos. Photo © Marcia Keegan.

West of Albuquerque, 25 miles SE of Grants off NM 33.
(888) ICE-CAVE

Ice Cave & Bandera Volcano
One of New Mexico's natural wonders.
800-ft. volcanic cone; hiking trail along rim; 17-mile-lava tube with ice cave.
www.icecaves.com

I-40 E to Tijeras; north on NM 14

Madrid
Boom/bust/boom Western town on Turquoise Trail. Celebrates its mining heritage at the Mine Shaft Museum/Tavern. Other area attractions: Eaves Movie Ranch, galleries, boutiques.
www.turquoisetrail.org/madrid.htm

I-40 east to Moriarty
(505) 379-4366

McCall's Pumpkin Patch
Seasonal: open late September to late October, when pumpkins are ripe. Hayrides, pumpkin picking, corn maze, pony rides, pig races.
Admission: $8.00 adults, $6.00 children
www.McCallPumpkinPatch.com

23 miles W of Magdalena on US 60

National Radio Astronomy Observatory—Very Large Array
World's largest radio telescope array. Self-guided tours 8:30 a.m. to dark. On Plains of San Augustin. Visitor Center. Turn off cell phones in area. Admission: free.
www.nrao.edu

Rio Rancho

One of New Mexico's fastest-growing communities, north of Albuquerque, west across the Rio Grande. Originally marketed as future homesites, community offers all visitor amenities.

http://ci.rio-rancho.nm.us/

Salinas Pueblo Mission National Monument

Once thriving American Indian trade communities of Tiwa- and Tompiro-speaking Puebloans inhabited this remote frontier area of central New Mexico. Early in the 17th century, Spanish Franciscans found the area ripe for missionary efforts. By the late 1670s, the Salinas district was depopulated of both Indians and Spaniards. What remains today are austere yet beautiful reminders of this earliest contact between Pueblo Indians and Spanish colonials. Ruins of four mission churches, at Quarai, Abó, and Gran Quivira and the partially excavated pueblo of Las Humanas. Located near Mountainair.

www.nps.gov/sapu

Abó: Ruins are 9 miles west on US 60 and one-half mile north on NM 513. (505) 847-2400.

Gran Quivira: Ruins are 26 miles south on NM 55. (505) 847-2770.

Quarai: Ruins are 8 miles north on NM 55 and 1 mile west. (505) 847-2290.

Santa Fe

Capital of New Mexico. Museums, galleries, restaurants, shopping. Includes historic Canyon Road and Museum Hill. Numerous celebrations and festivals. Santa Fe Ski Area.

www.santafe.org

60 miles north on I-25

Kasha-Katuwee Tent Rocks National Monument near Cochiti Pueblo. Photo © Marcia Keegan.

This row of frame houses in Madrid was once occupied by miners. Photo © Marcia Keegan.

Taos

135 miles north, I-25 to Santa Fe; exit on 599 north to by-pass Santa Fe; Hwy. 285 to Hwy. 68 to Taos.

Known for year-round recreation opportunities. Taos Ski Valley, river rafting on Rio Grande, Taos Pueblo. Numerous galleries, shops, restaurants.

www.taosvacationguide.com

Turquoise Trail

Exit 175 from I-40 East, 15 miles from Albuquerque on NM 14

National Scenic Byway between Albuquerque and Santa Fe. Through historic Golden, Cerrillos and Madrid. As a side trip, take 536 to summit of 10,680-ft. Sandia Crest and Sandia Peak Ski Area, restaurants at the top and bottom of Sandia Peak Tram.

www.turquoise trail.org

Wild Spirit Wolf Sanctuary

HC 61, Box 28, Ramah 87321 (505) 775-3304

Ramah, west of Grants and south of Gallup. Guided tours Tuesday–Sunday. Sanctuary dedicated to rescue and care for abused and abandoned captive-bred wolves and wolf-dogs.

www.wildspiritwolfsanctuary.org

Wildlife West Nature Park

122 acre park; wildlife includes whitetail deer, bobcats, cougars, coyotes, javelinas, raptors, mountain lions, wolves. Trails through constructed natural habitats; seasonal chuckwagon suppers with entertainment.

Hours: Summer 10 a.m.–6 p.m., winter noon–4 p.m.

Admission: Adults $5.00; seniors/students $4.00

www.wildlifewest.org

19 miles E of Albuquerque on I-40, Exit 187 at Edgewood. 3/4 miles W on N. Frontage Road. (505) 281-7655 or (877) 981-9453

Turquoise Trail, a scenic back way from I-25 at Tijeras up to Santa Fe. This road goes through Golden, Madrid and Cerrillos. Photo © Marcia Keegan.

NEW MEXICO'S PUEBLOS & RESERVATIONS

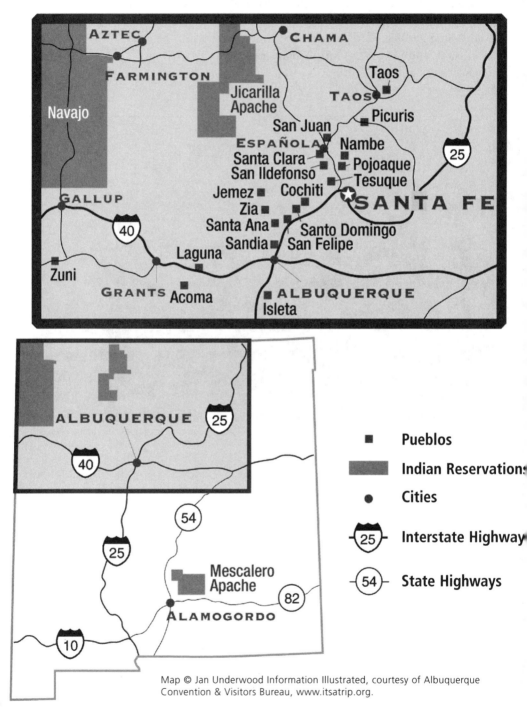

Legend:
- ■ Pueblos
- ▬ Indian Reservations
- ● Cities
- 25 Interstate Highway
- 54 State Highways

Map © Jan Underwood Information Illustrated, courtesy of Albuquerque Convention & Visitors Bureau, www.itsatrip.org.

INDIANS OF NEW MEXICO

Albuquerque, centrally located in New Mexico, offers access to a number of pueblos and reservations.

There are nineteen pueblos in New Mexico: Acoma, Cochiti, Isleta, Jemez, Laguna, Nambé, Picuris, Pojoaque, Sandia, San Felipe, San Ildefonso, San Juan, Santa Ana, Santa Clara, Santa Domingo, Taos, Tesuque, Zia and Zuni. Most are within an hour's drive of the city. There are also three reservations in the state: the Navajo, Jicarilla Apache and Mescalero Apache.

Special ceremonies and dances occur on a specific calendar at each pueblo and reservation. Drumbeats in the stillness of dawn, dance movements in cadence with the beat, piñon smoke scenting the air—all are part of the experience for a visitor.

Frequently, the works of talented artists and crafts people are on display, and sometimes food like the wonderful bread baked in the traditional "horno" oven can be purchased. Pueblos and reservations offer a window to another world with a living culture. When you visit, you are actually visiting someone's home.

Most of these areas welcome visitors. However, visitors are expected to observe appropriate cultural etiquette. Some pueblos have strict rules against photography, sketching and tape-recording. Visitors also are expected to show courtesy and respect the customs and traditions of the pueblo or reservation.

For a comprehensive guide to cultural etiquette, visit the website of the Albuquerque Convention & Visitors Bureau, (www.itsatrip.org/visitors/ americanindian) or the Indian Pueblo Cultural Center, (www.indianpueblo.org).

Indian Pueblo Cultural Center

There is no better way to become familiar with the nineteen Indian Pueblos of New Mexico than by visiting the Indian Pueblo Cultural Center in Albuquerque's near North Valley. Distinctive art is displayed along with separate exhibits about each pueblo. The main museum presents the development of pueblo culture.

Traditional Indian dances are performed every weekend at 11 a.m. and 2 p.m. Special events are also scheduled throughout the year, including American Indian Week in April. (The **Gathering of Nations**, the major Pow Wow of this celebration, takes place at The Pit, the University of New Mexico basketball arena in southeast Albuquerque.)

The center includes a small restaurant offering American Indian foods and a gift shop with fine pottery, paintings, sculpture, rugs, sand paintings, kachinas, traditional and contemporary jewelry, drums and

Eagle Dancers at IPCC. Spectators can view a variety of American Indian dances year round at the Indian Pueblo Cultural Center. Photo © Photo © Marcia Keegan, courtesy of the Indian Pueblo Cultural Center.

books. Their website, www.indianpueblo.org, offers an excellent introduction to all of the pueblos in the state.

2401 12th Street NW 87101

(505) 843-7270

www.indianpueblo.org

Another website for learning about the Indians in New Mexico comes from *New Mexico Magazine*, www.nmmagazine.com/NMGUIDE/nativeam.html. This page gives good information and contains links to pages for individual pueblos and tribes.

Albuquerque Area Pueblos

Closest to Albuquerque:

Isleta

Facilities include camping and fishing sites, an 18-hole golf course and a tribal operated gaming casino.
Photography: Limited to church only
Casino: Isleta Casino & Resort
Golf: Isleta Eagle Golf Course
Fishing: Isleta Lakes & Recreation Area
Feast Day: September 4
www.isletapueblo.com

13 miles south of Albuquerque on I-25, exit 215.

(505) 869-3111

Sandia

Facilities include Sandia Lakes Recreation Area, offering fishing, picnicking, nature trails and a bait and tackle shop. Bien Mur Market Center offers Indian arts and crafts. The tribe also operates a gaming casino and a hotel complex.
Bien Mur Market Center: 9 a.m.–5:30 p.m.
Photography: With permission, restricted
Casino: Sandia Resort & Casino
Golf: Sandia Golf Club
Fishing: Sandia Lakes Recreation Area
Feast Day: June 13
www.sandiapueblo.nsn.us

14 miles north of Albuquerque, exit 235.

(505) 867-3317

The entrance to Sandia Pueblo's casino, one of the largest in the state. Photo © Marcia Keegan.

Acoma is known as "Sky City" because of its strategic hilltop location. Photo © Marcia Keegan.

Take I-25 N to Bernalillo, exit 242, then 2 miles west.

(505) 867-3301

Santa Ana

8 miles northwest of Bernalillo. Tribal facilities include the Tamaya Cooperative, selling items like pottery and textiles; a garden center; restaurants; 45 holes of golf; and a gaming casino with a bowling alley. The pueblo is also home to the Hyatt Regency Tamaya Resort & Spa.

Photography: Prohibited
Casino: Santa Ana Star Casino
Golf: Santa Ana Golf Club, Twin Warriors Golf Club
Resort: Tamaya Resort & Spa (also Galleria Tamaya)
Feast Day: July 26
www.santaana.org

Within an Hour's Drive of Albuquerque

Take I-40 W to exit 108.

Sky City Cultural Center
(505) 859-2718 or
(800) 747-0181

Acoma

55 miles west of Albuquerque. Tours of pueblo itself by permission only; check at Cultural Center. Tour: $9.00 adults/$8.00 seniors; $6.00 ages 5–17; under age 5 is free.

Photography: $10.00 camera permit. Videotaping and digital photography are prohibited
Casino: Sky City Casino
Sky City Cultural Center
Fishing: Acoma Lake
Feast Day: September 2
www.nmmagazine.com/NMGUIDE/acoma.html

Cochiti

Between Albuquerque and Santa Fe
Photography: No photography or sketching allowed
Golf: Pueblo de Cochiti Golf Course
Fishing: Cochiti Lake Recreation Area
Feast Day: July 14
www.pueblodecochiti.org

Take I-25 N. Exit at NM 16 then go 14 miles.

(505) 465-2244

Jemez

55 miles northwest of Albuquerque
Photography: Permitted only at Jemez Red Rocks
Walatowa Visitor Center
Jemez Red Rocks Recreation Area
Jemez State Monument
Feast Day: November 12
www.jemezpueblo.org

Take I-25 N to Cuba exit. Continue 27 miles on US 550.

(505) 834-7235

Laguna

45 miles west of Albuquerque
Photography: Limited to certain areas, permission needed
Casinos: Route 66 Casino, Dancing Eagle Casino
& Travel Center
Feast Days: March 19 and September 19
www.nmmagazine.com/NMGUIDE/laguna.html

Take I-40 W 45 miles.

(505) 552-6654

The dramatic skyline of Laguna Pueblo is visible from I-40. Photo © Marcia Keegan.

Take I-25 N about 30 miles.

(505) 867-3381

San Felipe
30 miles northwest of Albuquerque. Visitors discouraged at pueblo itself.
Photography: Prohibited
Casino: San Felipe Casino Hollywood
San Felipe Travel Center
Speedway racetrack open seasonally
Feast Day: May 1
www.sanfelipecasino.com/pages/history.html

Take I-25 N about 35 miles.

(505) 465-2214

Santo Domingo
Half way between Albuquerque and Santa Fe.
Photography: Prohibited
Santo Domingo Arts & Crafts Market every Labor Day weekend
Feast Day: August 4
www.nmmagazine.com/NMGUIDE/domingo.html

Take I-25 N to US 550. Go about 25 miles.

(505) 867-3304

Zia
18 miles northwest of Bernalillo. Birthplace of the familiar ancient sun symbol, now used as symbol for New Mexico.
Photography: Prohibited
Fishing: Zia Lake
Feast Day: August 15
www.nmmagazine.com/NMGUIDE/zia.html

Northern Pueblos

Take I-25 N to Santa Fe; exit on 599 north to by-pass Santa Fe; Take US 84/285 N. Just after Pojoaque, turn right on NM 503.

(505) 455-2036

Nambé
23 miles north of Santa Fe
Fishing: Nambé Falls Recreation Area. $10.00 fishing fee
Photography: Fee, permits required
Feast Day: October 4
www.nmmagazine.com/NMGUIDE/nambe.html

Take I-25 N to Santa Fe; exit on 599 north to by-pass Santa Fe; Take US 84/285 N. to Española. Stay on 285.

(505) 852-4400

Ohkay Owingeh (San Juan)
5 miles north of Española
Photography: Fee
Fishing by permit at San Juan Lakes
Casino: Ohkay Casino and Resort
Headquarters of Eight Northern Indian Pueblos Council
Home of Eight Northern Indian Pueblos Arts & Crafts Show, held annually in July
Feast Day: June 24
www.nmmagazine.com/NMGUIDE/juan.html

Picuris

25 miles southwest of Taos
Entry fee: $3.00 per person
Photography: Camera, camcorder, sketching fee
Fishing: Pu-Na Lake
Museum: Picuris Pueblo Museum
Hotel Santa Fe in Santa Fe is owned by Picuris Pueblo
Feast Day: August 10
www.nmmagazine.com/NMGUIDE/picuris.html

Take I-25 N to Santa Fe; exit on 599 north to by-pass Santa Fe; Take US 84/285 N. to Española, then take 68 N. At Embudo turn onto NM 75.

(505) 587-2519

Pojoaque

15 miles north of Santa Fe
Casino: Cities of Gold Casino & Hotel
Info Center & Shop: Poeh Cultural Center
Golf: Towa Golf Resort
Feast Day: December 12
www.citiesofgold.com/PuebloMain.html

Take I-25 N to Santa Fe; exit on 599 north to by-pass Santa Fe; Take US 84/285 N. to Pojoaque.

(505) 455-2278

San Ildefonso

20 miles northwest of Santa Fe
Entry fee: $3.00 per car
Photography: Fee required for photography in village only
Fishing pond & picnic area
María Poveka Martínez Museum and San Ildefonso Pueblo Museum
Feast Day: January 23
www.nmmagazine.com/NMGUIDE/ildefonso.html

Take I-25 N to Santa Fe; exit on 599 north to by-pass Santa Fe; Take US 84/285 N. to Pojoaque, then turn on NM 502 towards Los Alamos for 7 miles.

(505) 455-2273

The Green Corn Dance at San Ildefonso Pueblo. Photo © Marcia Keegan.

Multi-storied Taos Pueblo still looks much like it did centuries ago. Photo © Marcia Keegan.

Take I-25 N to Santa Fe; exit on 599 north to by-pass Santa Fe; Take US 84/285 N. to Española. Get on NM 201 then go one mile SW on NM 30.

(505) 753-7326

Santa Clara

22 miles northwest of Santa Fe
Photography: Fee
Puye Cliff Dwellings and Santa Clara Canyon (hiking, camping and fishing by permit)
Casino: Big Rock Casino and Bowl
Golf: Black Mesa Golf Course
Feast Day: August 12
www.nmmagazine.com/NMGUIDE/clara.html

Take I-25 N to Santa Fe; exit on 599 north to by-pass Santa Fe; Take US 84/285 N. then Hwy68. Go straight through the town of Taos.

(505) 758-1028

Taos

North of Taos
Entry fee: $10.00 adults, $5.00 students
Photography: $5.00 fee per camera or video. (No photography on feast days.) Certain restrictions apply.
Casino: Taos Mountain Casino
Feast Day: September 30
www.taospueblo.com

Tesuque

10 miles north of Santa Fe
Photography: Prohibited
Casino: Camel Rock Casino
Tesuque Pueblo Flea Market, largest flea market in northern New Mexico
Feast Day: November 12
www.nmmagazine.com/NMGUIDE/tesuque.html

Take I-25 N to Santa Fe; exit on 599 north to by-pass Santa Fe; Take US 84/285 N. then Hwy68 10 miles and turn right at sign.

(505) 983-2667

Western Pueblos

Zuni

32 miles southwest of Gallup
Photography: Fee, but restricted and not allowed at any ceremonies
Hunting and fishing in the area
Inn at Halona Bed & Breakfast
No public feast day
www.ashiwi.net

Take I-40 W to NM 55 and follow signs.

(505) 782-7238

Procession of Zuni Pueblo women carrying clay pots called Ollas on their heads. They are known as Olla Women. Photo © Marcia Keegan.

Apache Mountain Spirit Dancer at the annual Gallup Inter-Tribal Indian Ceremonial, where tribes from all over the country gather for a parade, rodeo, ceremonial dances, and arts and crafts. Photo © Marcia Keegan.

Other Tribes

5 miles from Colorado border. From Albuquerque take US 550 and NM 537. Closest towns are Dulce and Chama.

(505) 759-3242

Jicarilla Apache Nation
Photography: Permission required in certain areas
Horse Lake Mesa Game Park
Little Beaver Roundup in July
Go-Jii-Yah Feast mid-September
Hunting and fishing in area
www.jicarillaonline.com

Mescalero Apache Reservation

Photography: Prohibited in some areas
Ski Area: Ski Apache
Casino: Inn of the Mountain Gods Resort & Casino
Hunting and fishing in area
www.innofthemountaingods.com/

Southeastern New Mexico; Take I-25 S to 380. closest town is Ruidoso.

(505) 464-4494

Navajo Nation

Gallup Inter-Tribal Indian Ceremonial
Navajo Nation Fair
Four Corners Navajo Tribal Park
Navajo Nation Museum and Library
Hubbell Trading Post National Historic Site
Navajo Nation Arts & Crafts Stores
Hunting and fishing in area
Capital: Window Rock, Arizona
www.navajo.org

27,000 square miles in Arizona, Utah, and northwestern New Mexico. Take I-40 W or US 550 NW.

(928) 871-6436

Navajo Indian hogan, or family dwelling, near Thoreau in western New Mexico.
Photo © Marcia Keegan.

CALENDAR OF EVENTS

Special events and celebrations in Albuquerque are a true reflection of the history and culture of the area—with a good dose of ambiance and recreation thrown in. Because the climate here is so moderate year-round, many activities are outdoors.

The following is not a comprehensive calendar, and information is subject to change. Check the Albuquerque Convention & Visitors Bureau website at www.itsatrip.org for the most current information. Dates given are approximate, since most change from year to year. This calendar does not include Indian feast days; refer to the American Indian section for dates.

Additionally, the local newspapers, the *Albuquerque Journal* and the *Albuquerque Tribune*, publish weekly sections focusing on activities/recreation/arts.

Ongoing events

Many venues offer various events throughout the year. Check their phone numbers and websites for what is happening at any particular time. See pages 225–231.

Annual Events

Rio Grande Arts & Crafts Festival–Spring Show

This juried fine-arts and crafts festival features more than 200 national artists and craftsmen, demonstrations, entertainment, food and fun.
www.riograndefestivals.com

Early March
EXPO New Mexico
(State Fairgrounds)
300 San Pedro NE,
Albuquerque 87108
(505) 292-7457

Fiery Foods & BBQ Show

Set the world on fire from Albuquerque, NM! This large gathering of people and products related to the fiery foods and barbecue industry draws attendees from around the world, including over 10,000 from the general public.
www.fiery-foods.com/ffshow

Early March
Sandia Resort &
Casino Events
Center, Tramway
exit off I-25
(505) 873-8680

Albuquerque Gem & Mineral Show

Over 35 dealers selling everything from amethyst cathedrals to Zebra rock—rocks and minerals inexpensive to moderately priced, gems (crystals, faceted, cabs, rough and set in jewelry), decorator items and jewelry, etc.), books and supplies, beads and lots more.
www.agmc.info

March
EXPO New Mexico
(State Fairgrounds)
300 San Pedro NE,
Albuquerque 87108
(505) 323-1520

Millions of visitors come to the Albuquerque International Balloon Fiesta® each year.
Photo © MarbleStreetStudio.com.

Indian tribes from all over North America perform at the Gathering of Nations PowWow held annually in Albuquerque. Photo © Marcia Keegan.

Late April
The Pit, UNM Arena, I-25 South, exit Cesar Chavez east.
(505) 836-2810

Gathering of Nations PowWow
Native American culture and pride, competition Indian dancing, over 3000 dancers, Indian traders market and the crowning of Miss Indian World.
www.gatheringofnations.com

Pride Weekend June
Expo New Mexico
(505) 873-8084

Annual Gay/Lesbian/Bisexual/Trans-gender Pride Pageant and Weekend
Pageant late April,
Sheraton Uptown Hotel
www.ABQpride.com

Memorial Day Weekend
Balloon Fiesta Park
Just west of I-25 N between Alameda and Tramway
(505) 899-3815

Albuquerque Wine Festival
Browse through handcrafted art, listen to upbeat music, and, best of all, taste all the great wines of New Mexico.
www.nmwine.com

New Mexico Arts & Crafts Fair

A gathering of over 220 of New Mexico's most talented artists and craftspeople, many of whom enjoy national and international reputations.

www.nmartsandcraftsfair.org

Late June
EXPO New Mexico
(State Fairgrounds)
300 San Pedro NE,
Albuquerque 87108
(505) 884-9043

New Mexico Wine Festival

Fine-wine-tasting event with juried art show, food, continuous live entertainment, children's activities and a New Mexico agricultural products showcase.

www.nmwine.com

Labor Day Weekend
noon–7 p.m.
Main St., Bernalillo
(866) 494-6366

New Mexico State Fair

One of the largest state fairs in the nation, with all traditional fair favorites—the midway, agricultural and arts exhibits, great food, PRCA rodeo, several concerts by national recording artists, and Indian and Spanish villages.

www.nmstatefair.com

Late September
EXPO New Mexico
(State Fairgrounds)
300 San Pedro NE
Albuquerque 87108
(505) 265-1791

Corrales Harvest Festival

Mercado *antiguo*, Food court, crafts, pet parade and entertainment

www.corrales-nm.org or www.visitcorrales.com/

Late September
Old San Ysidro
Church, Corrales
(505) 792-8912

Albuquerque International Balloon Fiesta

Albuquerque has a long and colorful history with the sport of ballooning. More than 100 years ago, a local bartender named "Professor" Van Tassell piloted a "gas bag" from the center of town up to nearly 14,000 feet and landed a few miles west of the city. From that beginning, hot-air ballooning has become synonymous with Albuquerque. The best-known event is the annual Albuquerque International Hot-Air Balloon Fiesta every October. It is known as the most photographed event in the world and attracts over 700 balloons, many more pilots and hundreds of thousands of spectators.

Popular events during Balloon Fiesta are the Mass Ascension, Balloon Glows and Special Shapes Rodeos. Mass Ascensions are held on all four weekend mornings and mid-week during Balloon Fiesta. Held just after dawn, the sight of several hundred balloons taking flight with the sunrise is stunning.

Balloon Glows are held in the evenings, with the launch field filled with balloons of every color, shape and size. As the propane burners are lit against the dark sky, they illuminate the balloons like giant colorful light bulbs. Perhaps the most

Early October
Balloon Fiesta Park
Just west of I-25 N
between Alameda
and Tramway.

Specific
information on
tickets, packaging
and events is
available at:
(505) 821-1000 or
(888)-422-7277

Balloons inflating in the early morning light before a mass ascension at the Albuquerque International Balloon Fiesta. Photo © MarbleStreetStudio.com.

popular balloons are the Special Shapes, everything from dinosaurs and dragons to motorcycles and Noah's Ark.

Special early morning round-trip motor coach transfers are available from several areas of the city, and parking is available on site for vehicles. Because the RV area is so popular, early reservations are recommended.

www.balloonfiesta.com or balloons@balloonfiesta.com

Mid October
North end of Balloon Fiesta Park. Just west of I-25 N between Alameda and Tramway
(505) 830-1077

Tender Loving Arts & Crafts Festival
More than 250 fine artists and craftsmen, entertainment, artists' demonstrations, food and fun. Second week of Balloon Fiesta—something to do after the day's ballooning event.
www.tenderlovingcrafts.com

Early November
EXPO New Mexico (State Fairgrounds) 300 San Pedro NE Albuquerque 87108
(505) 293-6133

Rio Grande Arts & Crafts Festival
This juried arts and crafts festival features more than 200 national artists and craftsmen, demonstrations, entertainment and food.
www.riograndefestivals.com

Early December
EXPO New Mexico (State Fairgrounds) 300 San Pedro NE Albuquerque 87108
(505) 292-7457

Weems International Artfest
New Mexico's biggest juried arts and crafts show typically draws over 40,000 people. Different local non-profit organizations are beneficiaries each year.
Admission: $4.00 adults, children free
www.weemsgallery.com/artfest.php

Christmas Under the Stars

December all month long

Enjoy the enchanting Bugg Family Christmas light display every evening in December. Located at Traditions! This shopping center carries Native American, Spanish, Mexican and Western arts, crafts, food and clothing, as well as several restaurants.
www.buynewmexico.com

December
1-25 north,
Budaghers Exit 257,
halfway between
Albuquerque and
Santa Fe
(505) 867-8600

River of Lights Holiday Light Festival

December all month long

Musical entertainment and spectacular light sculptures.
www.cabq.gov/biopark/garden

December
Rio Grande Botanic
Garden.
(505) 764-6200

Luminaria Tour

Christmas Eve, December 24

Annual motorcoach tour of selected areas of city decorated with hundreds of glowing luminarias.
www.cabq.gov, search for luminaria tour

Christmas Eve
Old Town Plaza
(505) 843-9200.

Christmas Celebrations at the Pueblos

December 24–28

Dances, sundown processions, luminarias and Midnight Mass at various Pueblos. Contact the individual Pueblos for information.
www.miaclab.org/communities

Christmas
Contact the
individual Pueblos.

Luminarias light up Historic Old Town during the December holidays.
Photo © MarbleStreetStudio.com.

INDEX